A New Star~~~
& Other ~~~~
from From~~~

In our continuing effort to publish the savviest, most up-to-date, and most appealing travel guides available, we've added some great new features.

Frommer's guides now include a new **star-rating system.** Every hotel, restaurant, and attraction is rated from 0 to 3 stars to help you set priorities and organize your time.

We've also added **seven brand-new features** that point you to the great deals, in-the-know advice, and unique experiences that separate travelers from tourists. Throughout the guide, look for:

Finds	Special finds—those places only insiders know about
Fun Fact	Fun facts—details that make travelers more informed and their trips more fun
Kids	Best bets for kids—advice for the whole family
Moments	Special moments—those experiences that memories are made of
Overrated	Places or experiences not worth your time or money
Tips	Insider tips—some great ways to save time and money
Value	Great values—where to get the best deals

Here's what critics say about Frommer's:

"Amazingly easy to use. Very portable, very complete."

—*Booklist*

"Detailed, accurate, and easy-to-read information for all price ranges."

—*Glamour Magazine*

"Hotel information is close to encyclopedic."

—*Des Moines Sunday Register*

"Frommer's Guides have a way of giving you a real feel for a place."

—*Knight Ridder Newspapers*

Frommer's®

PORTABLE

Amsterdam

2nd Edition

by George McDonald

WILEY

Wiley Publishing, Inc.

Published by:

WILEY PUBLISHING, INC.

909 Third Ave.
New York, NY 10022

ISBN 0-7645-6748-9
ISSN 1531-7595

Editor: John Vorwald
Production Editor: M. Faunette Johnston
Photo Editor: Richard Fox
Cartographer: Roberta Stockwell
Production by Wiley Indianapolis Composition Services

For information on our other products and services or to obtain technical
support, please contact our Customer Care Department within the U.S. at
800-762-2974, outside the U.S. at 317-572-3993 or fax 317-572-4002.

Wiley also publishes its books in a variety of electronic formats. Some content that appears in print may not be available in electronic formats.

Manufactured in the United States of America

5   4   3   2   1

Contents

List of Maps

*To Ken Wilkie, Amsterdammer by inclination and
enthusiast–editor, who first gave me the chance
to live and work "below sea level."*

ACKNOWLEDGMENTS

I'd like to thank Terri J. Kester, whose knowledge of Amsterdam's eating places is copious—and whose taste is pretty good, too. Also, Els Wamstecker, Press and Public Relations Officer from the always helpful Amsterdam Tourist Board.

ABOUT THE AUTHOR

George McDonald is a former deputy editor of and currently contributing writer for *Holland Herald*, the in-flight magazine for KLM Royal Dutch Airlines. He has written extensively about Amsterdam and the Netherlands for international magazines and travel books such as *Frommer's Belgium, Holland & Luxembourg, Frommer's Europe,* and *Frommer's Europe from $70 a Day.*

AN INVITATION TO THE READER

In researching this book, we discovered many wonderful places—hotels, restaurants, shops, and more. We're sure you'll find others. Please tell us about them, so we can share the information with your fellow travelers in upcoming editions. If you were disappointed with a recommendation, we'd love to know that, too. Please write to:

Frommer's Portable Amsterdam, 2nd Edition
Wiley Publishing, Inc. • 909 Third Ave. • New York, NY 10022

AN ADDITIONAL NOTE

Please be advised that travel information is subject to change at any time—and this is especially true of prices. We therefore suggest that you write or call ahead for confirmation when making your travel plans. The authors, editors, and publisher cannot be held responsible for the experiences of readers while traveling. Your safety is important to us, however, so we encourage you to stay alert and be aware of your surroundings. Keep a close eye on cameras, purses, and wallets, all favorite targets of thieves and pickpockets.

WHAT THE SYMBOLS MEAN

The following abbreviations are used for credit cards:

AE American Express	DISC Discover	V Visa
DC Diners Club	MC MasterCard	

FROMMERS.COM

Now that you have the guidebook to a great trip, visit our website at **www.frommers.com** for travel information on nearly 2,500 destinations. With features updated regularly, we give you instant access to the most current trip-planning information available. At Frommers.com, you'll also find the best prices on airfares, accommodations, and car rentals—and you can even book travel online through our travel booking partners. At Frommers.com, you'll also find the following:

- Online updates to our most popular guidebooks
- Vacation sweepstakes and contest giveaways
- Newsletter highlighting the hottest travel trends
- Online travel message boards with featured travel discussions

Planning Your Trip to Amsterdam

Amsterdam isn't hard to come to grips with even if you arrive there cold (in the preparedness sense). The local tourist organization, **VVV Amsterdam,** prides itself on being able to answer any conceivable travel question that any conceivable traveler might have, excepting only those that are illegal or of doubtful moral worth (this being Amsterdam both of these concepts have a lot of built-in elasticity). The city is foreign, of course, but not impossibly so, one reason being that so many Dutch speak English.

1 Visitor Information

TOURIST OFFICES

Before leaving for the Netherlands, you can obtain information on the country and its travel facilities by contacting the **Netherlands Board of Tourism (NBT),** which maintains offices in countries around the world. Their Internet address is **www.goholland.com**, and the e-mail address is **info@goholland.com**. In the **United States,** you can reach them at: 355 Lexington Ave., 21st Floor, New York, NY 10017 (© **212/370-7360;** fax 212/370-9507); c/o Northwest Airlines, 11101 Aviation Blvd., Suite 200, Los Angeles, CA 90045 (© **310/348-9339;** fax 310/348-9344); 225 N. Michigan Ave., Suite 1854, Chicago, IL 60601 (© **312/819-1636;** fax 312/819-1740).

For **Britain** and **Ireland,** NBT has a mailing address only: PO Box 30783, London WC2B 6DH (© **020/7539-7950;** fax 020/ 7539-7953; www.visitholland.com/uk; information@nbt.org.uk); in **Canada:** 25 Adelaide St. East, Suite 710, Toronto, ON M5C 1Y2 (© **416/363-1577;** fax 416/363-1470; info@goholland.com).

You can also contact the umbrella organization in the Netherlands for the country's many local VVV tourist information organizations (see Visitor Information under "Orientation," in chapter 2): **Netherlands Board of Tourism (NBT),** Vlietweg 15,

Amsterdam on the Web

The official site from the Netherlands Board of Tourism, **www.goholland.com**, is awkwardly designed (expanding your browser to its full size helps), but it does have useful advice. The most comprehensive site is VVV Amsterdam's **www.visitamsterdam.nl**. For a tighter focus on places to see and be seen, try **www.amsterdamhotspots.nl**. If you're interested in an American expat's experiences in the city, go to **www.homepage-amsterdam.com**. You'll love the clear images at **www.channels.nl**, one of the best virtual tours on the Net; you can direct your own tour and chat with others about Amsterdam.

Good eating out info is available from **www.dinner-in-amsterdam.nl** and **www.specialbite.nl**.

Postbus 458, 2260 MG Leidschendam (✆ **070/371-5705;** fax 070/ 320-1654; www.holland.com; info@nbt.nl).

2 Entry Requirements & Customs

DOCUMENTS

Citizens of the United States, Canada, Australia, and New Zealand need only a valid passport for a visit to the Netherlands for stays of less than 3 months. Citizens of the United Kingdom and Ireland, like all other citizens of the European Union (EU), need only an identity card—but as neither country has an official identity card it makes sense to carry the passport. If you are a citizen of another country, be sure to check the travel regulations before you leave.

If you are planning to stay longer than 3 months in the Netherlands, contact the **Bureau Vreemdelingenpolitie** (Foreigner Police Office) at Johan Huizingalaan 757 (✆ **020/559-6300**) in Amsterdam for further information.

No health and vaccination certificates are required, and drivers need only produce a valid driver's license from their home country.

Safeguard your passport in an inconspicuous, inaccessible place like a money belt and keep a copy of the critical pages with your passport number in a separate place. If you lose your passport, visit the nearest consulate of your native country as soon as possible for a replacement.

CUSTOMS
WHAT YOU CAN BRING INTO THE NETHERLANDS

Visitors 17 years and older arriving from countries that are not members of the European Union may bring in duty-free 200 cigarettes or 100 cigarillos or 50 cigars or 250 grams of tobacco, 1 liter of liquor or 2 liters of wine, and 50 milliliters of perfume. Import of most other goods is unlimited, so long as import duty is paid and does not exceed a value of 250€. Forbidden products include firearms, counterfeit goods, banned narcotic substances, and protected animals and plants and products made from them.

Duty-free shopping was abolished in all EU countries in 1999. Therefore, standard allowances do not apply to goods bought in another EU country and brought into the Netherlands.

There are no limitations on the amount of foreign currency you can bring into the country.

At your port of entry you enter either the EU Citizens or Non-EU Citizens section at Passport Control, and then one of two Customs clearance aisles, red or green, depending on whether or not you have "goods to declare."

If you're carrying valuables with you, take the receipts along. When you return home, these receipts will be proof that you owned such items before your trip to Amsterdam, and thus will protect you against any unwarranted duty charges. Also, keep receipts for current foreign purchases together and accessible to show Customs officials when returning home.

WHAT YOU CAN TAKE HOME

Returning **U.S. citizens** who have been away for at least 48 hours are allowed to bring back, once every 30 days, $400 worth of merchandise duty-free. You'll be charged a flat rate of 4% duty on the next $1,000 worth of purchases. Be sure to have your receipts handy. On mailed gifts, the duty-free limit is $100. You cannot bring fresh foodstuffs into the United States; tinned foods, however, are allowed. For more information, contact the **U.S. Customs Service,** 1300 Pennsylvania Ave. NW, Washington, DC 20229 (© **877/287-8867**) and request the free pamphlet *Know Before You Go.* It's also available on the Web at www.customs.gov. (Click on "Traveler Information," then "Know Before You Go.")

For a clear summary of **Canadian** rules, write for the booklet *I Declare,* issued by the **Canada Customs and Revenue Agency** (© **800/461-9999** in Canada, or 204/983-3500; www.ccra-adrc. gc.ca). Canada allows its citizens a C$750 exemption, and you're

Destination: Amsterdam— Red Alert Checklist

- Have you booked your tickets yet for classical music at the Concertgebouw and opera and dance at the Muziektheater (see "The Performing Arts," in chapter 7)?
- If you purchased traveler's checks, have you recorded the check numbers, and stored the documentation separately from the checks?
- Did you pack your camera and an extra set of camera batteries, and purchase enough film? Don't worry if you didn't because all of these items are easily available in Amsterdam.
- Do you have a safe, accessible place to store money?
- Did you bring your ID cards that could entitle you to discounts such as AAA and AARP cards, student IDs, and so on?
- Did you bring emergency drug prescriptions and extra glasses and/or contact lenses?
- Do you have your credit card PINs?
- If you have an E-ticket, do you have documentation?
- Do you have the address and phone number of your country's consulate in Amsterdam and/or its embassy in The Hague with you (see "Fast Facts: Amsterdam," in chapter 2)?
- Did you pack that umbrella? You *might not* need it, but you likely will.

allowed to bring back duty-free 1 carton of cigarettes, 1 can of tobacco, 40 imperial ounces of liquor, and 50 cigars. In addition, you're allowed to mail gifts to Canada valued at less than C$60 a day, provided they're unsolicited and don't contain alcohol or tobacco (write on the package "Unsolicited gift, under $60 value"). All valuables should be declared on the Y-38 form before departure from Canada, including serial numbers of valuables you already own, such as expensive foreign cameras. *Note:* The $750 exemption can only be used once a year and only after an absence of 7 days.

Citizens of the U.K. who are returning from a European Union (EU) country will go through a separate Customs Exit (called the "Blue Exit") especially for EU travelers. In essence, there is no limit on what you can bring back from an EU country, as long as the items are for personal use (this includes gifts), and you have already paid the necessary duty and tax. However, Customs law sets out guidance levels. If you bring in more than these levels, you may be asked to prove that the goods are for your own use. Guidance levels on goods bought in the EU for your own use are 800 cigarettes, 200 cigars, 1kg smoking tobacco, 10 liters of spirits, 90 liters of wine (of this not more than 60l can be sparkling wine), and 110 liters of beer. For more information, contact **HM Customs & Excise,** Passenger Enquiry Point, 2nd Floor Wayfarer House, Great South West Road, Feltham, Middlesex, TW14 8NP (© **0181/910-3744;** from outside the U.K. 44/181-910-3744), or consult their website at www.passport.gov.uk.

The duty-free allowance in **Australia** is A$400 or, for those under 18, A$200. Upon returning to Australia, citizens can bring in 250 cigarettes or 250 grams of loose tobacco and 1,125 milliliters of alcohol. If you're returning with valuable goods you already own, such as foreign-made cameras, you should file form B263. A helpful brochure, available from Australian consulates or Customs offices, is *Know Before You Go.* For more information, contact **Australian Customs Services,** GPO Box 8, Sydney NSW 2001 (© **02/6275-6666** in Australia; 202/797-3189 in the U.S.), or go to **www.customs.gov.au.**

The duty-free allowance for **New Zealand** is NZ$700. Citizens over 17 can bring in 200 cigarettes, or 50 cigars, or 250 grams of tobacco (or a mixture of all 3 if their combined weight doesn't exceed 250g); plus 4.5 liters of wine and beer, or 1.125 liters of liquor. New Zealand currency does not carry import or export restrictions. Fill out a certificate of export, listing the valuables you are taking out of the country; that way, you can bring them back without paying duty. Most questions are answered in a free pamphlet available at New Zealand consulates and Customs offices: *New Zealand Customs Guide for Travellers, Notice no. 4.* For more information, contact **New Zealand Customs,** 50 Anzac Ave., P.O. Box 29, Auckland (© **09/359-6655**).

3 Money

CURRENCY

The **euro** (€) is the currency in the Netherlands. There are 100 euro cents to each euro. Eight euro **coins** are in circulation: .01€, .02€, .05€, .10€, .20€, .50€, 1€, and 2€. The seven euro **banknotes** are: 5€, 10€, 20€, 50€, 100€, 200€, and 500€. The price conversions in this book are based on an exchange rate of 1€ = US$1. Bear in mind that exchange rates fluctuate daily.

Note: At this writing, the dollar/euro rate was close enough to parity to make the simple mental math of US$1 = 1€ worthwhile for a comparison of prices between dollars and euros. But the rate was changing fast (to the dollar's disadvantage) and the further it moves away from parity the more significant will be any inaccuracy where large amounts are concerned. The dollar/euro rate is sure to fluctuate, but so long as it remains close to 1 for 1, it makes calculation simple for American visitors.

The euro is based on the decimal system, but the Netherlands uses the continental numbering system in which a comma replaces the decimal point. Consequently, you will not see prices written in the familiar format of 1.95, 3.50, 5.00, and so on, but as 1,95; 3,50; 5,00; and so on. The continental numbering system also places a point where we would place a comma, so that bigger numbers will be seen as 1.250,55; 2.327,95; instead of as 1,250.55; 2,327.95; and so on. Just remember to reverse the system you're used to: comma in place of point; point in place of comma.

It's a good idea to exchange at least some money—just enough to cover airport incidentals and transportation to your hotel—before you leave home, so you can avoid the less-favorable rates you'll get at airport currency exchange desks. Check with your local American Express or Thomas Cook office or your bank. American Express cardholders can order foreign currency over the phone at © **800/ 807-6233.**

For details on **currency exchange,** see "Fast Facts: Amsterdam," in chapter 2.

ATMS

ATMs (automated teller machines), which you find all over the city, are linked to a network that most likely includes your bank at home. **Cirrus** (© **800/424-7787;** www.mastercard.com) and **PLUS** (© **800/843-7587;** www.visa.com) are the two most popular networks in the United States; call or check online for ATM locations at your destination. Be sure you know your four-digit PIN before you leave home and be sure to find out your daily withdrawal limit before you depart. You can also get cash advances on your credit card at an ATM. Keep in mind that credit card companies try to protect themselves from theft by limiting the funds someone can withdraw away from home. It's therefore best to call your credit card company before you leave and let them know where you're going and how much you plan to spend. You'll get the best exchange rate if you withdraw money from an ATM, but keep in mind that many banks impose a fee every time a card is used at an ATM in a different city or bank. On top of this, the bank from which you withdraw cash may charge its own fee.

You can withdraw euros from bank automated teller machines (ATMs) at many locations in the city (see "Fast Facts: Amsterdam," in chapter 2, for more details). You find ATMs at Schiphol Airport, Centraal Station and other main train stations, and throughout the city.

TRAVELER'S CHECKS

Traveler's checks are something of an anachronism from the days before the ATM made cash accessible at any time. Traveler's checks used to be the only sound alternative to traveling with dangerously large amounts of cash. They were as reliable as currency, but, unlike cash, could be replaced if lost or stolen.

These days, traveler's checks seem less necessary because most cities have 24-hour ATMs that allow you to withdraw small amounts of cash as needed. However, you're likely to be charged an ATM withdrawal fee if the bank is not your own, so if you're withdrawing money every day, you might be better off with traveler's checks—provided that you don't mind showing identification every time you want to cash one.

You can get traveler's checks at almost any bank. **American Express** offers denominations of $20, $50, $100, $500, and (for cardholders only) $1,000. You'll pay a service charge ranging from 1% to 4%. You can also get American Express traveler's checks over the phone by calling © **800/221-7282;** Amex gold and platinum cardholders who use this number are exempt from the 1% fee. AAA members can obtain checks without a fee at most AAA offices.

Visa offers traveler's checks at Citibank locations nationwide, as well as at several other banks. The service charge ranges between 1.5% and 2%; checks come in denominations of $20, $50, $100, $500, and $1,000. Call © **800/732-1322** for information. **MasterCard** also offers traveler's checks. Call © **800/223-9920** for a location near you.

If you choose to carry traveler's checks, be sure to keep a record of their serial numbers separate from your checks. You'll get a refund faster if you know the numbers.

CREDIT CARDS

Credit cards are invaluable when traveling. They are a safe way to carry money and provide a convenient record of all your expenses. You can also withdraw cash advances from your credit cards at any bank (though you'll start paying hefty interest on the advance the moment you receive the cash.) At most banks, you don't even need to go to a teller; you can get a cash advance at the ATM if you know your PIN. If you've forgotten yours, or didn't even know you had one, call the number on the back of your credit card and ask the bank to send it to you. It usually takes 5 to 7 business days, though some banks will provide the number over the phone if you tell them your mother's maiden name or pass some other security clearance. Keep in mind, though, that your credit card company will likely charge a commission (1% or 2%) on every foreign purchase you make.

Visa and **MasterCard** (also known as **EuroCard** in Europe) are the most widely used cards in the Netherlands. **American Express** is often accepted, mostly in the middle- and upper-bracket category. **Diners Club** is not as commonly accepted as American Express. Credit cards are not so commonly accepted in Holland as in the United States and Britain. Many restaurants and shops, and some hotels, don't accept them at all, and others add a 5% surcharge for card payment. You can use these cards to withdraw cash from many ATMs (see above).

Should your credit card be lost or stolen while you're in Holland, contact: **American Express** (© 020/504-8666); **Diners Club** (© 020/654-5500); **MasterCard** (© 030/283-5555); **Visa** (© 0800/022-4176).

4 When to Go

THE WEATHER

In Amsterdam, if you don't like the weather wait for a minute. The summertime temperature doesn't often rise above 75°F (24°C), making for a pleasant, balmy, urban climate. July and August are the best months for in-line skating in the Vondelpark, soaking up some rays on cafe terraces, eating at an outside restaurant terrace in the evening, and going topless on the beach at Zandvoort. September usually has a few weeks of fine late-summer weather; and there are even sunny spells in winter, when brilliant, crisp weather alternates with clouded skies.

Although the temperature rarely dips below freezing in winter, remember that Amsterdam and much of Holland is below sea level, making fog, mist, and dampness your too-frequent companions. This damp chill often seems to cut through to your very bones, so you'll want to layer yourself in Gore-Tex or something similar in the colder months. There are, however, plenty of bright but cold days in winter, and if the temperature falls far enough, canals, rivers, and lakes freeze to become sparkling highways for skaters through the city and surrounding countryside. Throughout the year, you can also expect some rain. The average annual rainfall is 25 inches. Most of it falls November through January, though substantial showers can occur year-round.

Some pointers on being prepared for Amsterdam's often unpredictable weather: First, invest in a fold-up umbrella and hope you never have to use it; likewise, carry a raincoat (with a wool liner for winter). Second, pack a sweater or two (even in July) and be prepared to layer your clothing at any time of year. Don't worry: You're allowed to leave some space for T-shirts, skimpy tops, and sneakers.

Amsterdam's Average Monthly Temperature & Days of Rain

	Jan	Feb	Mar	Apr	May	June	July	Aug	Sept	Oct	Nov	Dec
Temp. (°F)	36	36	41	46	54	59	62	62	58	51	44	38
Temp. (°C)	2	2	5	8	12	15	17	17	14	11	7	3
Days of rain	21	17	19	20	19	17	20	20	19	20	22	23

THE BEST TIMES TO GO

High season is the spring tulip season (early Apr to mid-May) and the school vacations in July and August. The city is very busy at both times, which means that hotel rooms are hard to find and bargains don't exist at all (but who wants to tiptoe through the tulips in Nov, or sit on a sidewalk cafe terrace in a snowstorm?). If you're planning to travel at these times, you should book several months in advance. Summer is also the best time for cycling, which is an essential Dutch experience; try a canal bike if you're squeamish about going on the roads.

In winter, room rates are generally cheaper, and cafes and restaurants are less crowded and more genuine in feel. You won't find such a big line to get into the Anne Frank House (though you'll still find a line); you'll be able to stand longer in front of Rembrandt's *The Night Watch* and your favorite van Gogh; and you might get a chance to go skating on the canals. You also get a better view of those canals, because the trees that border them shed their screen of leaves in the winter; and as an added bonus, the lights from all those canalside windows, whose curtains are never closed, glow with Japanese-lantern charm on the inky surface.

There's no worst of times to visit Amsterdam: It's a year-round stimulation of the brain's pleasure center.

HOLIDAYS

A Dutch holiday can add a festive note to your trip, particularly if it involves a parade or special observance somewhere in the country. But expect banks, shops, and most museums to be closed, and public transportation to operate on Sunday schedules for the following holidays: **New Year's Day** (Jan 1); **Good Friday, Easter Sunday, Easter Monday; Ascension Day** (Thurs, 40 days after Easter); **Queen's Day** (Queen Beatrix's official birthday, Apr 30); **Pentecost Sunday** (7th Sun after Easter) and **Pentecost Monday;** and **Christmas Day** (Dec 25) and **December 26.**

In addition, there are two World War II "Remembrance Days," neither of which is an official holiday, though some establishments close: May 4 honors all those who died in the war; May 5 celebrates the Liberation.

AMSTERDAM CALENDAR OF EVENTS

One of the biggest and most eagerly awaited winter events in Holland is the **Elfstedentocht (Eleven Cities Race),** in which skaters compete over a 201km (125-mile) course through the Friesland province north of Amsterdam. The first race was run in 1909, and it has been run only 13 times since. Perhaps the weather and ice conditions will allow the race to be held when you are visiting. If so, it's well worth going out of your way to see—and even to take part in. Contact **Provincial VVV Friesland** ((C) **0900/202-4060**).

The following listing includes events outside Amsterdam, but relatively close by.

January

New Year, throughout the center, but mostly at the Dam and Nieuwmarkt. This celebration is wild, and not always so wonderful. Many of Amsterdam's youthful spirits celebrate the New Year with firecrackers, which they cheerfully—you could even say drunkenly—throw at the feet of passersby. This keeps hospital emergency departments busy. January 1.

February

Carnival. Amsterdammers' chance to show that they can party just as wildly as their southern compatriots at *their* carnivals in Maastricht and Den Bosch. An objective observer (one who's still sober) would have to report that the Amsterdammers fail miserably, mainly because the southerners are the true Dutch experts on the art of carnival. Contact **VVV Amsterdam** (© **0900/ 400-4040**). Early February.

March

HISWA, RAI. The name might look like some strange hiero-glyphic, but this refers to the annual Amsterdam Boat Show at the RAI Convention Center. Holland is big on boats, and here you'll see just how big. Contact **RAI** (© **020/549-1212**). February 25 to March 2, 2003; similar dates in 2004.

Stille Omgang. This silent procession along Kalverstraat is walked by Catholics every year to celebrate the "Miracle of the Host," which occurred in 1345. The procession begins at the Royal Palace on the Dam and goes from midnight to 2:30am. Contact the **Gezelschap voor de Stille Omgang** (© **020/524-5415**). Sunday closest to March 15.

Opening of Keukenhof Flower Gardens, Lisse. The greatest flower show on earth blooms with a spectacular display of tulips and narcissi, daffodils and hyacinths, bluebells, crocuses, lilies, amaryllis, and many other flowers at this 70-acre garden in the heart of the bulb country. There's said to be nearly 8 million flow-ers, but who's counting? Contact **Keukenhof Gardens** (© **025/ 246-5555**). Late March to mid-May.

April

National Museum Weekend. A weekend during which most museums in Amsterdam and 440 other museums throughout the Netherlands offer free and reduced admission and have special exhibitions. Contact Stichting Museumjaarkaart (© **0900/404-0910**). April 12 and April 13, 2003; similar dates in 2004.

Koninginnedag (Queen's Day). This nationwide holiday for the House of Orange is vigorously celebrated in Amsterdam, with the city center so jam-packed with people that it's virtually impossible to move. A street market all over the city features masses of stalls, run by everyone from individual kids selling old toys to profes-sional market folk in town to make a killing. Orange ribbons, orange hair, and orange-painted faces are everywhere, as are Dutch flags. Street music and theater combine with probably too much drinking, but Koninginnedag remains a good-natured if boister-ous affair. *Tip:* Wear something orange, even if it's only orange suspenders or an orange ribbon in your hair. Contact **VVV Amsterdam** (© **0900/400-4040**). Gay and lesbian celebrations center on the city's main gay areas and the Homomonument (see "Other Monuments & Sights," in chapter 5). There are stage performances, from belly-dancing to drag, stalls publicizing various gay and lesbian organizations, and food and drink. April 30.

May

Bevrijdingsdag (Liberation Day), throughout the city. A slightly less frenetic version of Koninginnedag (see "April," above), recalling the country's liberation from Nazi occupation at the end of World War II. Canadian troops made it into the city first, so Canadian flags are popular accessories. More street markets, music, and theater. Contact **VVV Amsterdam** (© **0900/ 400-4040**). Gay and lesbian participation includes stage performances, from belly-dancing to drag, stalls publicizing various gay and lesbian organizations, and food and drink. May 5.

Oosterpark Festival. A multicultural festival of song and dance held at the Oosterpark in multiracial district Amsterdam Oost (East). Contact VVV Amsterdam (© **0900/400-4040**). First week of May.

Drum Rhythm Festival, Westergasfabriek. Feel the rhythm in your soul at this annual festival that attracts some good acts. Contact **Westergasfabriek** (© **020/581-0425**). Mid-May.

Floating Amsterdam transforms the lower reaches of the Amstel River into an outdoor theater. Performances are held near the Muziektheater. Contact VVV Amsterdam (© **0900/400-4040**) or Amsterdam Uit Buro (© 0900/019-1040). Last 2 weeks in May.

Open Ateliers, the Jordaan. Could be subtitled "Artists Working in Garrets," as around 50 Jordaan artists throw open the doors of their studios to an awestruck public. This is a biennial event. Contact **Open Ateliers Jordaan** (© **020/638-1885**). End of May, 2003.

June

Echo Grachtenloop (Echo Canal Run). You can either watch or join in as thousands of footloose people run along the city-center canals. The routes are 5km, 10km, and 18km (3, 6, and 11 miles). Contact De Echo (© **020/585-9222**). First Sunday in June.

Amsterdam Roots Festival. Various venues. This festival features music and dance from all over the world. Workshops, films, and exhibits are also offered. Contact **Stichting Melkweg** (© **020/ 624-1777**). Early to mid-June.

Open Garden Days, Herengracht, Keizersgracht, and Prinsengracht. If you wonder what the gardens behind the gables of all those fancy canalside houses look like, this is your chance to find out. A number of the best are open to the public for a few days each June. Contact **Stichting De Amsterdamse Grachtentuin** (© **020/422-2379**). Mid-June.

Vondelpark Open-Air Theater. Everything goes here: theater, all kinds of music (including full-scale concerts by the famed Concertgebouw Orchestra) and dance, even operetta. Contact **Vondelpark Open-Air Theater** (© **020/673-1499**). June to end of August.

Over Het IJ Festival. Opposite Centraal Station, on the other side of the IJ channel. Avant-garde theater, music, and dance performed beside the water on an old wharf. Contact **Over Het IJ Festival** (© **020/673-1499**). End of June to end of July.

July

Arts Adventure, venues throughout the city. An extension of the cultural program through the previously dormant summer months—when most tourists visit the city. It includes more off-beat and informal events across the full range of the arts than would be the case with the main (Sept-June) cultural program of opera, ballet, and classical music. Contact VVV Amsterdam (© **0900/400-4040**) or Amsterdam Uit Buro (© **0900/019-1040**). July and August.

August

Gay Pride Festival. This is a big event in Europe's most gay-friendly city. A crowd of 150,000 people turns out to watch the highlight Boat Parade's display of 100 or so outrageously decorated boats cruising on the canals. In addition, there are street discos and open-air theater performances, a sports program, and a film festival. (The entire festival's future is in the balance, and subject to the City Council not revoking its permission on "public order" grounds.) Contact **Gay Business Amsterdam** (©/fax **020/620-8807**). Assuming the event goes ahead, dates are July 31 to August 3, 2003, with the Boat Parade August 2; and August 5 to August 8, 2004, with the Boat Parade August 7.

Prinsengracht Concert, Prinsengracht Canal. Classical music floats up from a boat moored outside the Pulitzer Hotel on an evening in August. Contact Hotel Pulitzer Amsterdam (© **020/523-5235**). Third week in August.

Uitmarkt, Dam and other venues. Amsterdam previews the soon-to-open cultural season with this great open market of information and free performances at impromptu outdoor venues and theaters and concert halls. Both professional and amateur groups take part in the shows, which run the gamut of music, opera, dance, theater, and cabaret. Contact **Amsterdam Uitmarkt** (© **020/626-2656**). Last weekend in August.

September

Bloemencorso, Aalsmeer to Amsterdam. Every year for nearly half a century, Amsterdam has been the final destination for the Flower Parade that originates in Aalsmeer. The parade features a large number of floats that carry a variety of in-season flowers (so don't expect to see tulips). The parade follows an established route and ends at the Dam. Contact **Stichting Bloemencorso** (② 029/793-9393). First Saturday in September

Concert and Theater Season is in full swing at venues throughout the city, such as the Concertgebouw, Muziektheater, and Stadsschouwburg, but also at lots of smaller places. Contact VVV Amsterdam (② **0900/400-4040**) or Amsterdam Uit Buro (② 0900/019-1040). September to May.

Jordaan Festival. This loosely organized festival in the trendy Jordaan neighborhood features food, games, fun, and lots of drinking and music in the street and in many cafes in the area. Contact **Stichting Jordaan Festival** (② **020/624-6908**). Early September.

November

Leather Pride is a growing happening of parties and other events for gays and lesbians from around the world. Contact **Leather Pride Nederland** (② and fax **020/422-3737**). First weekend of November.

Crossing Border Festival, Amsterdam. Literature, pop music, and cinema are combined in this international festival. Contact **VVV Amsterdam** (② **0900/400-4040**). Mid-November.

Sinterklaas Arrives. Holland's equivalent of Santa Claus (St. Nicholas) launches the Christmas season when he arrives in the city by boat at the Centraal Station pier. Accompanied by black-painted assistants, called *Zwarte Piet* (Black Peter), who hand out sweets to kids along the way, he goes in stately procession through Amsterdam before being given the keys to the city by the mayor at the Dam. Contact **VVV Amsterdam** (② **0900/400-4040**). Third Saturday of November.

Spiegelkwartier Open House, Spiegel Quarter. Amsterdam's famous art and antiques quarter throws open its doors to all for 2 days—of course, you won't be locked out at other times either. Late November or early December.

December

Sinterklaas, throughout Holland. Saint Nicholas's Eve is the traditional day in Holland for exchanging Christmas gifts. Join some Dutch friends or a Dutch family, if possible. December 5.

5 Tips for Travelers with Special Needs

TRAVELERS WITH DISABILITIES

Most disabilities shouldn't stop anyone from traveling. There are more options and resources out there than ever before.

The old center of Amsterdam—filled with narrow cobbled streets, steep humpback bridges, zillions of little barrier pillars called *Amsterdammetjes,* and bicycles parked all over the place—can be hard going. But many hotels and restaurants provide easy access for people with disabilities, and some display the international wheelchair symbol in their brochures and advertising. It's always a good idea to call ahead to find out just what the situation is before you book; in particular, bear in mind that many older hotels have no elevator and have steep, narrow stairways. Many, but not all, museums and other sights are wheelchair accessible, wholly or partly, and some have adapted toilets. Always call ahead to check on accessibility at sights you wish to visit.

The Netherlands Board of Tourism issues a *Holland for the Handicapped* brochure. Schiphol Airport has a service to help travelers with disabilities through the airport. Not all trams in Amsterdam are easily accessible for wheelchairs, but the new trams being introduced on some routes have low central doors that are accessible. The Metro system is fully accessible, but that's not as good as it sounds because few Metro stations are near places where visitors want to go. Taxis are also difficult, but new mini-van taxis are an improvement. Or, call ahead to book with **Boonstra Taxis** (✆ **020/613-4134**), which has wheelchair-accessible cabs. There's comprehensive assistance for travelers on **Netherlands Railways** (✆ **030/235-5555**) trains and in stations. If you give them a day's notice of your journey by visiting a station or calling ahead they can arrange for assistance along the way.

AGENCIES/OPERATORS

- **Flying Wheels Travel** (✆ **800/535-6790;** www.flyingwheels travel.com) offers escorted tours and cruises that emphasize sports and private tours in minivans with lifts.
- **Access Adventures** (✆ **716/889-9096**), a Rochester, New York-based agency, offers customized itineraries for a variety of travelers with disabilities.
- **Accessible Journeys** (✆ **800/TINGLES** or 610/521-0339; www.disabilitytravel.com) caters specifically to slow walkers and wheelchair travelers and their families and friends.

ORGANIZATIONS

- **The Moss Rehab Hospital** (© 215/456-9603; www.moss resourcenet.org) provides friendly, helpful phone assistance through its **Travel Information Service.**

- **The Society for Accessible Travel and Hospitality** (© 212/447-7284; fax 212-725-8253; www.sath.org) offers a wealth of travel resources for all types of disabilities and informed rec- ommendations on destinations, access guides, travel agents, tour operators, vehicle rentals, and companion services. Annual membership costs $45 for adults; $30 for seniors and students.

- **The American Foundation for the Blind** (© 800/232-5463; www.afb.org) provides information on traveling with Seeing Eye dogs.

- **The Royal Association for Disability and Rehabilitation (RADAR),** Unit 12, City Forum, 250 City Rd., London EC1V 8AF (© 020/7250-3222), publishes three holiday "fact packs" for £2 each or £5 for all three. The first one provides general information, including planning and booking a holi- day, insurance, and finances; the second outlines transporta- tion available when going abroad and equipment for rent; the third covers specialized accommodations.

PUBLICATIONS

- **Mobility International USA** (© 541/343-1284; www.miusa. org) publishes *A World of Options,* a 658-page book of resources, covering everything from biking trips to scuba out- fitters, and a biannual newsletter, *Over the Rainbow.* Annual membership is $35.

- **Twin Peaks Press** (© 360/694-2462) publishes travel-related books for travelers with special needs.

- *Open World for Disability and Mature Travel* magazine, published by the Society for Accessible Travel and Hospitality (see above), is full of good resources and information. A year's subscription is $13 ($21 outside the U.S.).

GAY & LESBIAN TRAVELERS

In Amsterdam, you can get information, or just meet people, by vis- iting **COC,** Rozenstraat 14 (© **020/626-3087;** www.cocamsterdam. nl), the Amsterdam branch of the Dutch lesbian and gay organiza- tion. On the premises there is a daytime cafe serving coffee and quiches, a meeting space for special interest groups, weekend discos (mainly men on Fri, women on Sat), and a special ethnic evening called Strange Fruit on Sundays. The **Gay and Lesbian Switchboard** (© 020/623-6565; www.switchboard.nl), open daily from 10am to 10pm, can provide you with all kinds of information and advice.

You shouldn't have much trouble finding information about gay and lesbian bars and clubs because they are well publicized. Also see "Gay & Lesbian Bars" under "The Bar Scene," in chapter 7. The free biweekly listings magazine *Shark,* amusingly subtitled "Underwater Amsterdam," is a great source of cultural information, in particular for the off-beat and alternative scenes, and comes with a centerfold pullout, titled *Queer Fish,* which has excellent lesbian and gay listings. *Gay News Amsterdam* and *Gay & Night,* competing bilingual monthly magazines in both Dutch and English, are available free in gay establishments around the city but lack extensive listings information.

The International Gay & Lesbian Travel Association (IGLTA) (© 800/448-8550 or 954/776-2626; fax 954/776-3303; www.iglta.org) links travelers up with gay-friendly hoteliers, tour operators, and airline and cruise-line representatives. It offers monthly newsletters, marketing mailings, and a membership directory that's updated once a year. Membership is $200 yearly, plus a $100 administration fee for new members.

PUBLICATIONS

- *Frommer's Gay & Lesbian Europe* is an excellent travel resource.
- *Out and About* (© 800/929-2268 or 415/644-8044; www.outandabout.com) offers guidebooks and a newsletter 10 times a year packed with solid information on the global gay and lesbian scene.
- *Spartacus International Gay Guide* and *Odysseus* are good, annual English-language guidebook focused on gay men, with some information for lesbians. You can get them from most gay and lesbian bookstores, or order them from Giovanni's Room bookstore, 1145 Pine St., Philadelphia, PA 19107 (© 215/923-2960; www.giovannisroom.com).
- *Gay Travel A to Z: The World of Gay & Lesbian Travel Options at Your Fingertips* by Marianne Ferrari (Ferrari Publications) is a very good gay and lesbian guidebook series.

SENIOR TRAVEL

Mention the fact that you're a senior when you first make your travel reservations. All major airlines and many hotels offer discounts for seniors. Major airlines also offer coupons for domestic travel for seniors over sixty. Typically, a book of four coupons costs less than $700, which means you can fly anywhere in the continental U.S. for under $350 round-trip. In most cities, people over the age of 60 qualify for reduced admission to theaters, museums, and other attractions, as well as discounted fares on public transportation.

Sightseeing attractions and entertainments in the Netherlands often offer senior discounts, but some of these places offer these reductions only to Dutch citizens, on production of an appropriate ID. Be sure to ask when you buy your ticket.

In Amsterdam, the **VVV tourist offices** can furnish addresses and telephone numbers for church and social organizations whose activities are slanted toward the upper age brackets. They can also advise you of municipal social agencies for help with specific problems.

PUBLICATIONS

- *The Book of Deals* is a collection of more than 1,000 senior discounts on airlines, lodging, tours, and attractions around the country; it's available for $9.95 by calling © **800/460-6676**.
- *101 Tips for the Mature Traveler* is available from Grand Circle Travel (© **800/221-2610** or 617/350-7500; fax 617/346-6700).
- *The 50+ Traveler's Guidebook* (St. Martin's Press).
- *Unbelievably Good Deals and Great Adventures That You Absolutely Can't Get Unless You're Over 50* (Contemporary Publishing Co.).

6 Getting There

BY PLANE

FROM THE U.S.   Partner airlines **KLM Royal Dutch Airlines** (© **800/374-7747**; www.klm.com) and **Northwest Airlines** (© **800/447-4747**; www.nwa.com), together offer direct flights and easy connections from most U.S. cities to Amsterdam's Schiphol Airport. These include service twice daily from New York; daily from Chicago, Los Angeles, and Houston; and two to six times a week from Atlanta, Baltimore, Boston, Detroit, Memphis, Minneapolis/St. Paul, San Francisco, Orlando, and Washington, D.C.

Other airlines fly direct from the United States to Amsterdam. **United Airlines** (© **800/241-6522**; www.ual.com) flies nonstop from Washington Dulles. **Delta Airlines** (© **800/241-4141**; www. delta-air.com) has daily nonstop service from Atlanta and New York.

Martinair (℡ 800/627-8462; www.martinairusa.com) has nonstop flights year-round from Miami, Orlando, Tampa, and Denver, and from May to September from Newark, Los Angeles, and Oakland.

FROM CANADA KLM/Northwest (℡ 800/361-5073; www.klm.com; www.nwa.com) has daily nonstop flights from Toronto, and several flights a week from Calgary, Montreal, Ottawa, Winnipeg, and Vancouver.

Air Canada (℡ 800/555-1212; www.aircanada.ca) flies daily from Toronto to Amsterdam.

FROM THE U.K. London and many smaller British cities have daily flights by **British Airways** (℡ 0845/773-3377; www.british-airways.com), **KLM UK** (℡ 0870/507-4074; www.klmuk.com), and **British Midland** (℡ 0870/607-0555; www.britishmidland.co.uk).

Easy Jet, from London (Gatwick and Luton), Liverpool, Edinburgh, Glasgow, and Belfast to Amsterdam: UK (℡ 0870/600-0000); Holland (℡ 023/568-4880; www.easyjet.com).

FROM IRELAND Aer Lingus (℡ 01/886-8888; www.aerlingus.ie) flies daily from Dublin.

FROM AUSTRALIA KLM (℡ 1300/303-747; www.klm.com) flies from Sydney to Amsterdam 3 days a week. **Qantas** (℡ 800/227-4500; www.qantas.com.au) flies twice a week.

FROM NEW ZEALAND KLM (℡ 09/309-1782; www.klm.com) flies from Auckland to Amsterdam.

BY BOAT

DFDS Seaways (U.K.: ℡ 08705/000-333; www.dfdsseaways.co.uk. Netherlands: ℡ 025/553-4546; www.dfdsseaways.nl), has daily car-ferry service from Newcastle in northeast England to IJmuiden on the North Sea coast west of Amsterdam; the overnight journey time is 14 hours. At press time, the fare for a foot passenger, one-way, was £51. From IJmuiden, you can either go by train to Amsterdam Centraal Station, or by jetfoil with Fast Flying Ferries to a pier behind Centraal Station.

P&O North Sea Ferries (℡ 01482/377-177 in the U.K.; ℡ 018/125-5555 in the Netherlands; www.ponsf.com), has daily car-ferry service between Hull in northeast England and Rotterdam Europoort; the overnight journey time is 14 hours. At press time, the fare for a foot passenger, one-way, was £53. Ferry company buses shuttle between the Rotterdam Europoort terminal and Rotterdam

Centraal Station, from which, there are frequent trains to Amsterdam.

Stena Line (U.K.: ✆ **01233/647-047.** Netherlands: ✆ **017/438-9333;** www.stenaline.com) has a daily overnight freight-ferry service that carries some private vehicles (no passengers without vehicles) between Harwich in southeast England and Hoek van Holland (Hook of Holland) near Rotterdam; journey time is 8 hours, 30 minutes. At press time, the fare for a foot passenger, one-way, was £24.

BY TRAIN

Rail service to Amsterdam from other cities in the Netherlands and elsewhere in Europe is frequent and fast. International and Inter-City express trains arrive at Centraal Station from Brussels and Paris, and from several German cities and from more distant locations in Eastern Europe, Spain, Austria, Switzerland, and Italy. There's also the Amsterdam/Brussels Inter-City train, and connections can be made in Brussels to the North Express, the Oostende-Vienna Express, the Oostende-Moscow Express, and the Trans-Europe Express. **Nederlandse Spoorwegen** (Netherlands Railways; www.ns.nl) trains arrive in Amsterdam from towns and cities all over Holland. Schedule and fare information on travel in Holland is available by calling ✆ **0900/9292,** and for international trains, call ✆ **0900/9296.**

The distinctive burgundy-colored **Thalys** (www.thalys.com) high-speed train, with a top speed of 300kmph (186 mph), connecting Paris, Brussels, Amsterdam, and (via Brussels) Cologne, has cut travel times from Amsterdam to Paris to 4¼ hours, and to Brussels to 2¼ hours—figures that will be reduced to closer to 3¼ hours and 1¾ hours respectively when the high-speed rail lines in Holland are operational. For Thalys information and reservations in France, call ✆ **08/3635-3536;** in Belgium, ✆ **0800/95-777;** in Germany, ✆ **0221/19419;** and in Holland, ✆ **0900/9296.** Tickets are also available from main train stations and travel agents. One-way weekday first-class (Comfort 1) fares from Paris to Amsterdam in late 2000 were about $120; tourist class (Comfort 2) one-way tickets were about $80; on weekends the respective one-way fares were $75 and $68. Four Thalys trains run between Paris and Amsterdam every day via Brussels.

Britain is connected to the Continent via the Channel Tunnel. On the **Eurostar** (www.eurostar.com) high-speed train (top speed 258kmph/160 mph), the travel time between London Waterloo

Station and Brussels Midi Station (the closest connecting point for Amsterdam) is 3¼ hours. On weekends, the respective one-way fares are £140 and £100. Departures from London to Brussels are approximately every 2 hours at peak times. For Eurostar reservations, call ℭ **0345/303-030** in Britain, and ℭ **020/423-4444** in Holland.

The **Eurailpass** allows unlimited first-class travel throughout the rail systems of many European countries, including the Netherlands, at a cost of $554 for 15 days, $718 for 21 days, $890 for 1 month, $1,260 for 2 months, and $1,588 for 3 months. The **Eurail Youth Pass** allows unlimited second-class travel to those under 26 years of age at a cost of $388 for 15 days, $499 for 21 days, $623 for 1 month, $882 for 2 months, and $1,089 for 3 months. Other deals are available as well. Both the Eurailpass and the Eurail Youth Pass should be purchased before leaving the United States (they're more expensive if you buy in Europe) and are available through **Rail Europe** (ℭ **800/438-7245;** www.raileurope. com), and through travel agents.

BY BUS

Eurolines (www.eurolines.com) coach service operates between London Victoria Bus Station and Amsterdam Amstel Station (via ferry), with four departures daily in the summer. Travel time is just over 12 hours. For reservations, contact Eurolines (ℭ **0990/808-080** in Britain or 020/560-8788 in Holland).

BY CAR

Holland is crisscrossed by a network of major international highways. European expressways E19, E35, E231, and E22 converge on Amsterdam from France and Belgium to the south and from Germany to the north and east. These roads also have Dutch designations; as you approach the city they are, respectively: A4, A2, A1, and A7. Amsterdam's ring road is A10. Distances between destinations are relatively short, traffic is invariably heavy but road conditions are otherwise excellent, service stations are plentiful, and highways are plainly signposted.

If you want to drive from Britain to Amsterdam, you can use the fast and efficient **Le Shuttle** auto transporter through the Channel Tunnel from Folkestone to Calais (a 35-min. trip), and drive up from there. Le Shuttle has departures every 15 minutes at peak times, every 30 minutes at times of average demand, and every hour at night. Fares range from £120 to £190 ($190-$290) per car, depending on the day, time, and other variables. The cheapest transits are usually midweek between 2 and 5am. For information, call © 0990/353-535 for Le Shuttle reservations in Britain, © 03/21-00-61-00 in France, © 020/504-0540 in Holland. Reserving in advance makes sense at the busiest times, but the system is so fast, frequent, and simple that you may prefer to retain travel flexibility by just showing up, buying your ticket, waiting in line for a short while, and then driving aboard.

2

Getting to Know Amsterdam

Amsterdam Center is small enough that its residents think of it as a village, but it can be one confusing village until you get the hang of it. It's easy to think you are headed in one direction along the canal ring, only to discover that you are going completely the other way. Those concentric rings of major canals are the city's defining characteristic, along with several important squares that act as focal points.

This chapter explains how the city is laid out, introduces you to its neighborhoods, tells you how to get around, and squeezes in a bunch of other useful stuff besides.

1 Orientation

ARRIVING
BY PLANE

After you deplane, moving walkways take you to the Arrivals Hall, where you pass through Passport Control, Customs, and Baggage Reclaim. Facilities like free luggage carts, currency exchange, ATMs, restaurants, bars, shops, baby-rooms, restrooms, and showers are available. Beyond these, Schiphol Plaza combines train station access, the Airport Hotel, a shopping mall (sporting that most essential Dutch service—a flower store), bars and restaurants, restrooms, baggage lockers, airport and tourist information desks, car-rental and hotel reservation desks, check-in for scheduled domestic flights (also available are charter and air-taxi aircraft, including helicopters), and more, all in a single location. Bus, shuttle, and taxi stops are just outside.

For tourist information and to make hotel reservations, go to the **Holland Tourist Information (HTi)** desk in Schiphol Plaza (© **0900/400-4040**), open daily from 7am to 10pm.

The airport has multistory **parking garages** within walking distance of Schiphol Plaza and a network of short- and long-term parking lots linked by frequent shuttle to the passenger terminal.

GETTING TO AMSTERDAM The Dutch Railways' Schiphollijn (Schiphol Line) **trains** for Amsterdam's Centraal Station (with stops at De Lelylaan and De Vlugtlaan stations in west Amsterdam) depart from Schiphol Station, downstairs from Schiphol Plaza. Frequency ranges from four trains an hour at peak times to one an hour at night. The fare is 2.95€ one-way; the trip takes around 20 minutes.

An alternative route serves both Amsterdam Zuid/World Trade Center station and RAI station (beside the big RAI Convention center). Be sure to check which one is best for your hotel (including any tram or bus interchange). If you're staying at a hotel near Leidseplein, Rembrandtplein, in the Museum Quarter, or in Amsterdam South, this route may be a better bet for you than Centraal Station. The fare is 2.95€ one-way; the trip takes around 15 minutes. From Amsterdam Zuid/World Trade Center, take tram no. 5 for Leidseplein and the Museum Quarter; from RAI, take tram no. 4 for Rembrandtplein.

The **KLM Hotel Bus** shuttles between the airport and Amsterdam, serving 16 top hotels directly and many more that are close to these stops. The fare is 8€ one-way, 14€ round-trip. No reservations are needed and buses depart from in front of Schiphol Plaza every 20 minutes from 7am to 6pm and every 30 minutes from 6 to 9:30pm. Check at the KLM Hotel Desk for information. If you're not staying at one of the above hotels, the clerks can tell you which shuttle stop is closest to your chosen lodgings. In addition, many individual hotels near the airport and in town have their own shuttle service.

Bus no. 197 departs every half-hour from in front of Schiphol Plaza for Amsterdam's downtown Marnixstraat bus station. The fare is 3.40€. This bus is a lot slower than both the train and the KLM Hotel Bus.

Taxis are expensive, but they're the preferred choice if your luggage is burdensome or if there are two or more people to share the cost. You find taxi stands at both ends of the sidewalk in front of Schiphol Plaza. Taxis from the airport are all metered. Expect to pay around 38€ to the Center. Remember, a service charge is already included in the fare.

BY TRAIN

Traveling by train in the Netherlands is convenient, with frequent service to many places around the country and modern, clean trains that run on time. Whether you arrive by Thalys high-speed train from Brussels or Paris, by ordinary international train, or by Netherlands Railways train from elsewhere in Holland, you'll likely find yourself deposited at Amsterdam's Centraal Station, built over 100 years ago on an artificial island in the IJ channel. The building, an ornate architectural wonder on its own, is the focus of much activity. It's at the hub of the city's concentric rings of canals and connecting main streets, and is the originating point for most of the city's trams, Metro trains, and buses.

For information on trains (and other public transportation) in Holland, call ℂ **0900/9292;** for international trains, call ℂ **0900/ 9296.**

An array of tram stops are on either side of the main station exit— virtually all of Amsterdam's hotels are within a 15-minute tram ride from Centraal Station. The Metro station is downstairs, just outside the main exit. City bus stops are to the left of the main exit, and the taxi stands are to the right. (You'll find details on public transportation within the city under "Getting Around," later in this chapter.) At the public transportation tickets and information office on Stationsplein, you can buy a *strippenkaart* or *dagkaart* for trams, Metros, and buses (see "Getting Around," later in this chapter).

BY BUS

International coaches—in particular those of **Eurolines** (ℂ **020/ 560-8788;** www.eurolines.com)—arrive at the bus terminal opposite Amstel train station in the south of the city. From here you can go by train and Metro train to Centraal Station, and by tram no. 12 to the Museumplein area and to connecting points for trams to the Center.

BY CAR

European expressways E19, E35, E231, and E22 converge on Amsterdam from France and Belgium to the south and from Germany to the north and east. As you approach the city, you'll also notice that these roads also have Dutch national numbers, respectively A4, A2, A1, and A7. Amsterdam's ring road is designated A10.

In many European cities, the best advice is to drive to the city, park your car, and never touch it again till you leave. In Amsterdam, even better advice is not to bring it into the city in the first place (for a sufficiency of reasons why not, see the "By Car" section under "Getting Around," later in this chapter).

VISITOR INFORMATION

Few countries have a more organized approach to tourism or are more meticulous in their attention to detailed travel information than the Netherlands. Every province and municipality has its own tourist organization and even small towns and villages have efficient information offices with multilingual attendants on duty. These amazing tourist offices all have the tongue-twisting name **Vereniging voor Vreemdelingenverkeer (Association for Foreigner Travel).** Even the Dutch don't much like saying that every time so they call it simply the **VVV** (pronounced *vay-vay-vay*). All tourist information offices in the Netherlands, from big city and province-wide offices down to the tiniest village booth, are called VVV Whatever—VVV Amsterdam, VVV Delft, VVV Haarlem, VVV Leiden, and so on, and the blue-and-white, triangular VVV logo is a common sight around the country. VVV offices can book accommodations for you, help with travel arrangements, tell you what's on where, and . . . well, if there's anything they can't do, I have yet to discover it. To find the offices anywhere in the country, look for a blue-and-white roadside sign bearing the letters VVV.

Amsterdam's excellent but often overloaded tourist information organization, **VVV Amsterdam** (✆ **0900/400-4040;** fax 020/625-2869; www.visitamsterdam.nl), has an office inside Centraal Station, on platform 2, another just outside the station at Stationsplein 10, and a booth at Leidseplein 1 (tram: 1, 2, 5, 6, 7, 10), on the corner of Leidsestraat. All three locations are invariably extremely busy—don't visit a VVV office to purchase tickets for public transportation, unless you're also going there for something else that only the VVV can supply. Handle the VVV phone number with caution, as it costs a steep .55€ a minute, which is tolerable if you get an instant response and not so good if you have to hold. VVV Amsterdam's correspondence address is Postbus 3901, 1001 AS Amsterdam. The VVV can help you with almost any question about the city and it also reserves hotel rooms, books tours, sells special reduced-rate passes for attractions and public transportation, provides brochures and maps, and more. The offices are open daily from 9am to 5pm in the low season; the evening open hours gradually increase and then decrease back to the baseline time on a somewhat unpredictable schedule as the high season proceeds.

Be sure to pick up a copy of the VVV's *Day by Day/What's On in Amsterdam,* for 2€. This monthly magazine is full of details about the month's art exhibits, concerts, and theater performances,

Your Passport to Amsterdam

A sound way to get the most out of your trip is to avail yourself of the **Amsterdam Pass.** The credit card-size pass is valid for 1 day for 26€, 2 days for 36€, and 3 days for 46€. It allows free travel on public transportation; free admission to more than 20 museums and attractions, including to the Rijksmuseum or the Van Gogh Museum (not both), and Stedelijk Museum, and discounted admission to more museums and attractions; a free canal boat cruise; discounted excursions, including reduced rates on the Museum Boat and the Canal Bus; and discounts in selected restaurants and stores. Total possible savings on the pass are in the region of 100€.

and lists restaurants, bars, dance clubs, and more. Or purchase a copy of the yellow **Visitors Guide,** like a miniature Yellow Pages, which has a wealth of addresses and phone numbers. The **Amsterdam Uit Buro (AUB) Ticketshop,** Leidseplein 26 (© **0900/0191;** www.aub.nl; tram: 1, 2, 5, 6, 7, 10), can give you information regarding cultural events and books tickets for almost every venue in town. The office is open Monday through Wednesday and Saturday from 10am to 6pm, Thursday from 10am to 9pm, and Sunday from noon to 6pm. Using their service instead of chasing down tickets on your own can save you precious hours. You can purchase tickets with a credit card by phone daily from 9am to 9pm, and online at any time. AUB publishes the free monthly magazine *Uitkrant* (it's in Dutch, but it isn't difficult to understand the listings information).

CITY LAYOUT

Amsterdammers will tell you it's easy to find your way around their city. However, when each resident offers you a different pet theory of how best to maintain your sense of direction, you begin to sense that the city's layout can be confusing. Some of the natives' theories actually do work. If you try to "think in circles," "follow the canals" (the one I use most), or "watch the way the trams go," you might be able to spend fewer minutes a day consulting a map or trying to figure out where you are and which way to walk to find the Rijksmuseum, a restaurant, or your hotel.

STREET MAPS   A map is essential. The maps in this book will help you understand Amsterdam's basic pattern of waterways and the relationships between the major squares or landmarks and the major connecting thoroughfares. Once you get the hang of the necklace pattern of the four major canals and become familiar with the names (or series of names) of each of the five principal roads that go through into the Center, all you need do as you walk along is keep track of whether you're walking toward or away from the Dam, the heart of the city, or simply circling around it.

The most detailed and helpful maps of Amsterdam are those published by Suurland-Falkplan. Their handy **Amsterdam Tourist Map,** small and easy to unfold, is available from news vendors for 2.50€. It shows every street and canal; gives tram routes and tram stops; pinpoints churches and many museums; locates address numbers; and identifies one-way streets, bridges, and canals. For more detailed coverage of the entire city and its suburbs, including a street name index, buy Suurland-Falkplan's **Stadsplattegrond Amsterdam** for 6€. The VVV tourist information offices have several other maps available, including the small but detailed **VVV Amsterdam** map, which costs 2€.

Now, all you need to know is that, in Dutch, *straat* means "street," *gracht* means "canal," *plein* means "square," and *laan* means "avenue," all of which are used as suffixes attached directly to the name of the thoroughfare (for example, Princes' Canal becomes Prinsengracht).

NEIGHBORHOODS IN BRIEF

From the standpoint of tourism and for the purposes of locating the hotels and restaurants reviewed in this book, I've divided the city of Amsterdam into six major neighborhoods.

The Old Center   This core area around the Dam and Centraal Station, and through the neighborhood known as De Wallen (The Walls), which contains the Red Light District, is the oldest part of the city. It includes the main downtown shopping areas and attractions such as the Royal Palace, the Amsterdam Historical Museum, Madame Tussaud's, and many of the canal-boat piers.

The Canal Belt   The semicircular, multistrand "necklace" of waterways called the *Grachtengordel* in Dutch was built around the old Center during the city's 17th-century Golden Age. Its vista of elegant, gabled mansions fronting long, tree-lined canals forms the image that's most often associated Amsterdam. It includes many hotels, both large and small, restaurants, sightseeing attractions such as the Anne Frankhuis and the canal house museums, and antiques shops

Around Leidseplein The city's most happening nightlife square and its immediate surroundings, cover such a small area that it could perhaps have been included under "The Canal Belt." But so distinctive is it that it demands to be picked out and highlighted on its own. In addition to performance venues, movie theaters, bars, and cafes, there are plenty of good hotels and restaurants in this oftentimes frenetically busy area.

Around Rembrandtplein Like Leidseplein, but on a somewhat reduced scale, this square is the focus for a swatch of hotels, restaurants, cafes, and nightlife venues that's lively enough to justify picking it out from its surroundings.

The Jordaan This nest of small streets and canals lies west of the Center, beyond the major canals. Once a working-class neighborhood, it's become fashionable, like New York City's SoHo, with a growing number of upscale boutiques and restaurants. Still, its "indigenous" residents are alive and well and show no sign of succumbing to the gentrification going on around them.

Museumplein & Vondelpark Gracious and residential, this area surrounds the three major museums on Museumplein—the Rijksmuseum, the Van Gogh Museum, and the Stedelijk Museum—and hosts the Concertgebouw concert hall, many restaurants, Amsterdam's most elegant shopping streets (Pieter Cornelisz Hooftstraat and Van Baerlestraat), and its best-known park. The U.S. Consulate is here, too.

Amsterdam East A residential zone on the far bank of the Amstel River that's the location of sightseeing attractions like the Maritime and Tropical museums, and also of Artis, the local zoo. It's an area of Amsterdam that's rich in ethnic minority groups. The segment along the Amstel contains great views, a status-symbol hotel and restaurant, and a top performance venue.

Amsterdam South This prestigious modern residential area is the site of a number of hotels, particularly along Apollolaan, a broad avenue the locals call the Gold Coast for its rows of expensive houses.

Amsterdam West The district west of the Singelgracht canal covers a lot of ground but doesn't have much to recommend it in the way of sights and delights.

Amsterdam Neighborhoods

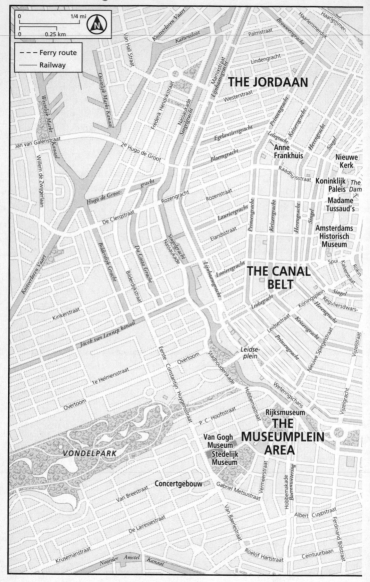

Amsterdam North   On the north bank of the IJ channel, this district has been little more than a dormitory suburb up until now, but there are some signs that this is beginning to change and that dining and entertainment possibilities are opening up.

2 Getting Around

When you look at a map of Amsterdam, you may think the city is too large to explore on foot. This isn't true: It's possible to see almost every important sight on a 4-hour walk. Be sure to wear good walking shoes, as those charming cobbles get under your soles and on your nerves after a time, so leave your thin-soled shoes or boots at home.

If you're going around on foot, remember that cars have the right of way when turning. Don't step in front of one thinking it's going to stop for you. And be aware that many motorists consider road signs and red lights to be no more than interesting and occasionally useful suggestions. When crossing a street, watch out for trams, buses, and bikes, too. Look both ways before walking across a dedicated bike lane—some bikers get unreasonably irritated if you force them to crash into you.

Kids are irresistibly attracted to water, so watch out for them anywhere near the vast expanse of water in this city of 160 canals. Protective fencing rarely exists and the low metal railings that are supposed to keep cars from rolling into the water are ideally positioned for small feet to stumble over.

BY PUBLIC TRANSPORTATION

The central information and ticket sales point for Amsterdam's **Gemeente Vervoerbedrijf (GVB/Municipal Transportation Company)** is **GVB Tickets & Info,** Stationsplein (© **0900/9292;** www.gvb.nl), in front of Centraal Station, open Monday through Friday from 7am to 9pm, Saturday and Sunday from 8am to 9pm. You can buy some tickets here for less money than if you bought them from tram drivers and conductors and bus drivers.

Most tram and bus shelters and all Metro stations have maps that show the entire urban transit network. All stops have signs that list the main stops yet to be made by the trams or buses that can be boarded at that location. Detailed maps of the network are available from the GVB Tickets & Info office for .70€.

Daytime hours of operation for public transportation are from 6am (trams start at 7:30am on Sun) to around 12:30am. Night buses operate a limited service thereafter, with buses usually on an hourly schedule.

TICKETS & FARES   There are 11 fare zones in greater Amsterdam, but you likely won't travel often beyond the Center zone 5700 (Centrum). Make sure your ticket is validated for the number of zones you plan to travel through and for the duration of the ride (see below for how to validate).

Children ages 3 and under travel free; children ages 4 to 11 ride on reduced-rate tickets.

You can purchase tickets from VVV Amsterdam tourist information offices, the GVB Tickets & Info office (see above), tram drivers or conductors (on some trams there's an onboard ticket automat instead), bus drivers, train and Metro station ticket booths, and automats at train and Metro stations. Not every kind of ticket is available from each of these sources, and some tickets can be purchased also from post offices and some newsstands.

Several types of tickets are valid on trams, buses, and the Metro. The most popular type is a **strippenkaart (strip card),** for which the fare system is based on canceling one more of the ticket's strips than the number of zones you travel through—two strips for one zone, three strips for two zones, and so on. A strip card is good for any number of transfers on trams, buses, and Metro trains within 1 hour of the time stamped on it (this goes up in steps to a maximum 3½ hr. as the number of validated zones increases). More than one person can use a strip card, so long as it is stamped for each passenger. On buses, the driver stamps your card. An eight-strip card is 5.60€, a 15-strip card 5.90€, and a 45-strip card 17.40€.

An *enkeltje* **(single ticket)** is 1.40€ for one zone and 2.10€ for two zones; a *retourtje* **(return ticket),** valid twice on the same day, is 4.30€. A *dagkaart* **(day card),** which is valid also at night, is 5.20€. Also available are multiple-day cards valid from 2 to 9 days, for 8.30€ to 25€.

Note: You need to use public transportation a lot to make the day and multiday cards worthwhile. Should you plan to walk most of the time and take trams only around the Center, you're probably better off with a strip card.

If you are staying in town for a week or more, you might want to consider one of seven different *sterrabonnement* **(star subscription)** cards. These run from 8.90€ for a single-zone card for a week, to 175€ for a multiple-zone card for a month (and ten times the appropriate monthly rate for a year). It's best to ask about these—and other special tickets such as those for night buses, multiple trips, and groups of ten or more people—at the GVB Tickets & Info office (see above).

Validation: On trams, be sure to stamp your ticket in the yellow machines in the front, middle, and rear of the vehicle, or visit the conductor at the rear. To use the machine with a strip card, fold your card at the line and punch it in. Don't punch in each individual strip but count down the number of strips you need and punch in the last one; if you need more than one strip card to cover the required number, stamp the last strip on the old card and the last strip required on a new one. At Metro stations use the machines at platform entrances and on the platforms (you must have a valid ticket to be allowed on the Metro platforms). Make sure the machine actually did stamp your ticket, and with the correct date.

Most Amsterdam trams either have a conductor or operate on the honor system, but teams of roving inspectors do their best to keep everyone honest. The fine for riding without a ticket or not having one properly stamped is 30€, plus 2.10€ for a ticket, payable on the spot.

BY TRAM & BUS   Half the fun of Amsterdam is walking along the canals. The other half is riding the smooth new blue-and-light-gray trams (and some surviving clackety old yellow ones) that roll through most major streets. There are 17 tram routes, 10 of which (1, 2, 4, 5, 9, 13, 16, 17, 24, and 25) begin and end at Centraal Station, so you know you can always get back to that central point if you get lost and have to start over again. The other tram routes are 3, 6, 7, 10, 12, and 14. To board a tram, push the *deur open* (door open) button on the outside of the car beside the door; you board trams that have conductors at the rear and the doors open automatically. Getting off, you also have to push a *deur open* button. Tram doors close automatically and they do it quite quickly, so don't hang around but do tread on the bottom step to prevent the door from closing.

An extensive bus network complements the trams. Many bus routes begin and end at Centraal Station. A minibus service, *De Opstapper,* is helping to solve one of Amsterdam's toughest public transportation problems: how to get access to the long and narrow canalside streets in the city center. White *Opstapper* (literally "step aboarder") minibuses go in both directions along Prinsengracht, between Centraal Station, the Amstel River, and Waterlooplein. A bus departs every 10 minutes from each terminus, Monday through Saturday from 7:30am to 6:30pm. There are no regular stops; just hold out your hand and the driver will stop, and then tell the driver when you want to get out again. You can use any valid public transportation ticket; with a *strippenkaart*, the full one-zone trip—which makes a great mini-sightseeing tour—requires two strips.

BY METRO It can't compare to the labyrinthine systems of Paris, London, and New York, but Amsterdam does have its own Metro, with four lines—50, 51, 53, and 54—that run partly overground and bring people in from the suburbs. You may want to take them simply as a sightseeing excursion, though to be frank, few of the sights on the lines are worth going out of your way for. On these lines you validate your strip card on the platform before boarding. Due to open in 2004 (but almost sure to be delayed), the Noord/Zuid (North/South) Metro line will have greater utility for tourists, bisecting as it will the city from north to south, from Buikslotermeerplein in Amsterdam Noord, under the IJ to Centraal Station, Rokin, Ceintuurbaan, and Station Zuid/World Trade Center.

BY TRAIN The railway network is not as useful within Amsterdam as the tram, bus, and Metro network. In addition to Centraal Station, which is the public transportation hub, there are seven stations in the city: Zuid/World Trade Center, RAI, and Amstel in the south; Lelylaan, De Vlugtlaan, and Sloterdijk in the west; and Muiderpoort in the east. Because the transportation network is tightly integrated, all train stations are also served by two or more of the other modes. The excellent Dutch railway network comes into its own for longer distances. It's by far the best way to get to Schiphol Airport, Haarlem, Amsterdam's North Sea coast resort Zandvoort, Hoorn on the IJsselmeer shore, and all other points in Holland.

BY TAXI It used to be that you couldn't simply hail a cab from the street in Amsterdam, but nowadays they often stop if you do. Otherwise, call **Taxi Centrale** (✆ **0900/677-7777**) or find one of the taxi stands sprinkled around the city, generally near the luxury hotels or at major squares such as the Dam, Centraal Station, Spui, Rembrandtplein, Westermarkt, and Leidseplein. Taxis have rooftop signs and blue license tags, and are metered. Fares—which include the tip—begin at 2.20€ when the meter starts and run up at the rate of 1.80€ a kilometer, or 1.10€ a mile. Make sure the meter starts out at the correct rate, bearing in mind that the tariffs listed above are likely to increase somewhat during the lifetime of this book.

ON THE WATER

With all the water Amsterdam has, it makes sense to use it for transportation. Although the options for canal transport are limited (with the exception of cruises and excursions), they do exist, and as an additional benefit they offer a unique and attractive view of the city. Given the ongoing redevelopment work in the old harbor areas, where new residential projects are sprouting like tulips in springtime, it seems likely that water transportation will be increasingly important in the future. See also "Canal Tour-Boats," "Water Bikes," and "Powerboats," under "Organized Tours," in chapter 5.

BY FERRY   IJ ferries connect the Center with Amsterdam Noord (North), across the IJ channel. The short crossings are free, which makes them ideal minicruises for the cash-strapped, and they provide a good view of the harbor. Ferries depart from piers behind Centraal Station along De Ruyterkade. One route goes every 10 to 15 minutes between Pier 7 and Buiksloterweg on the north shore. A second route, employing new ferries introduced in 2002, goes every 20 to 30 minutes from Pier 8 to IJplein, a more easterly point on the north shore. Both services operate round the clock.

BY WATER BUS   Two different companies operate water buses that bring you to, or close to, many of the city's top museums, other attractions, sights, and shopping and entertainment districts. **Canal Bus** (© 020/623-9886) has three routes—Green Line, Red Line, and Blue Line—with a total of 11 stops that include: Centraal Station, Westermarkt, Leidseplein, Rijksmuseum (with an extension to the RAI Convention Center when big shows are on there), Waterlooplein, and East Amsterdam. Hours of operation are daily from 10am to 5pm, with two buses an hour at peak times. A daypass, valid until noon next day and including a discount on museum admissions, is 14€ for adults, 10€ for children under 14 (children young enough to sit on an adult's lap go free). The **All Amsterdam Transport Pass,** valid on the Canal Bus, trams, buses and the Metro, is 17€ a day, and is available from GVB Tickets & Info, VVV tourist information offices, and the Canal Bus company. It's a good value if you make extensive use of its unlimited travel facility on both the Canal Bus and GVB public transportation.

The **Museumboot (Museum Boat)** (© 020/530-1090)—*boot* is pronounced just like boat—operates a circular scheduled service every 30 minutes in summer and every 45 minutes in winter from 9:30am to 5pm, from Prins Hendrikkade, in front of Centraal Station to Westermarkt, Leidseplein, Museum Quarter, Herengracht, Waterlooplein, and the Eastern Dock. A day ticket is 14€ for adults, 9€ for children 4 to 12, and free for children under 4, and entitles you to discounts of up to 50% on admission to some museums and attractions. Or, from 1pm, you can purchase a "stop-ticket" from the boatman at any of the seven stops.

BY WATER TAXI   Since you're in the city of canals, you might like to splurge on a water taxi. These launches do more or less the same thing as landlubber taxis, except that they do it on the canals and the Amstel River, and in the harbor. You can move faster than on land and you get your very own canal cruise. To order one, call **Watertaxi** (© 020/535-6363), or pick one up from the dock outside Centraal Station, close to the VVV office. For up to eight people the fare is 70€ for 30 minutes and 50€ for each subsequent half-hour.

BY BIKE

Instead of renting a car, follow the Dutch example and ride a bike (*fiets*). Sunday, when the city is quiet, is a particularly good day to pedal through the park and to practice riding on cobblestones and dodging trams before venturing forth into the fray of an Amsterdam rush hour. There are 600,000 bikes in the city, so you'll have plenty of company. Bike-rental rates are around 7€ a day or 30€ a week; a deposit is required.

Going by bike is mostly safe—or at any rate not as suicidal as it looks—thanks to a vast network of dedicated bike lanes. Bikes even have their own traffic lights. Amsterdam's battle-scarred bike-borne veterans of the traffic wars make it almost a point of principle to ignore every safety rule ever written and though they mostly live to tell the tale, don't think the same will necessarily apply for you (see "Biking in Amsterdam," below).

MacBike rents a range of bikes, including tandems and six-speed touring bikes. Outlets are at Mr. Visserplein 2 (© **020/620-0985;** tram: 9, 14); Marnixstraat 220 (© **020/626-6964;** tram: 10, 13, 14, 17); and 's-Gravesandestraat 49 (© **020/693-2104;** tram: 7, 10). **Bike City,** Bloemgracht 70 (© **020/626-3721;** tram: 13, 14, 17), near the Anne Frankhuis, rents bikes, provides maps and suggested

Biking in Amsterdam

It takes a while to get used to moving smoothly and safely through the whirl of trams, cars, buses, trucks, fellow bikers, and pedestrians, particularly if you're on a typically ancient and much-battered *stadfiets* (city bike), also known as an *omafiets* (grandmother bike)—the only kind that makes economic sense here, since anything fancier will attract a crowd of people wanting to steal it. It's better to develop your street smarts slowly. I know this sounds like wimpish advice—you might have mountain-biked from one end of the Rockies to another for all I know—but remember that not everyone on the *straat* is as sensible as you are.

The first rule of biking in Amsterdam: Don't argue with trams—they bite back, hard. The second rule: Cross tram lines perpendicularly so your wheels don't get caught in the grooves, which could pitch you out of the saddle. And the third rule: Don't crash into civilians (pedestrians). That's about it. Like everyone else, you'll likely end up making up the rest of the rules as you go along.

routes both inside and outside the city, and will even store and maintain your own bike. **Damstraat Rent-a-Bike,** Damstraat 22-24 (© **020/625-5029;** tram: 4, 9, 14, 16, 24, 25), has a central location near the Dam. Feminists both male and female might want to give their business to **Zijwind Fietsen,** a women's cooperative, at Ferdinand Bolstraat 168 (© **020/673-7026;** tram 25), though it's a bit out from the Center.

Warning: Always lock both your bike frame and one of the wheels to something solid and fixed, because theft is common.

BY CAR

To drive in the Netherlands, you need only a valid passport, your driver's license, and, if you're bringing your own car, a valid registration and green card proving international insurance.

Don't rent a car to get around Amsterdam. You will regret both the expense and the hassle. The city is a jumble of one-way streets, narrow bridges, and no-parking zones. In addition, it's not uncommon to hear that an automobile, apparently left parked with the hand brake carelessly disengaged, has rolled through a flimsy foot-high railing and into a canal. Should you choose to park, you need either to feed the parking meter or to have a parking permit prominently displayed in your car. Your hotel can sell you this permit, but for short periods it's probably better just to use a meter (if you're lucky enough to find a free one). The city's feared **Dienst Parkeerbeheer (Parking Service Authority),** responsible for clamping and towing illegally parked cars, is well-staffed, hardworking, and efficient. If you don't keep your meter fed or if you park in an illegal space, you're almost sure to fall victim to the authority's search-and-destroy patrols. Their operations are swift and merciless, and the cost of transgression is high.

They don't merely write you a citation, they reinforce the ticket with a wheel-clamp (also known as a "Texas boot"), which costs 68€ to have removed, payable at one of four offices (see below). If the fine isn't paid within 24 hours, they tow your car to a car-pound at Daniël Goedkoopstraat 7 (Metro: Spaklerweg), open 24 hours a day, way out in the boonies of the southeastern Over Amstel district, and they charge you a whopping 154€ for every day it's out there. You can pay wheel-clamp fines at this office and at three other Servicepunten Stadstoezicht offices in the city: Beukenplein 50 (tram: 3, 7, 10); Jan Pieter Heijestraat 94 (tram: 1, 6, 7, 17); and Weesperstraat 105A (Metro: Weesperplein). The phone number for information (© **020/553-0333**) is the same for all four offices, and each one of the three city offices is open Monday through Friday from 8am to 6pm and Saturday from 8am to 3:30pm.

The rate for parking in the Center is 2.80€ an hour Monday through Saturday from 9am to midnight and Sunday from noon to midnight. You pay less for each hour if you pay for a block of hours at the same time: 17€ from 9am to 7pm; 11€ from 7pm to midnight; 25€ from 9am to midnight. One-day and 3-day street parking permits are available from many hotels for 15€ and 45€, respectively. You can purchase these permits from Parking Service Authority offices at Bakkerstraat 13; Ceintuurbaan 159; Nieuwezijds Kolk parking lot (off Nieuwezijds Voorburgwal); Kinkerstraat 17; and Cruquiuskade 25. Amsterdam intends to further restrict traffic through the Center, so expect even more difficulties.

FAST FACTS: Amsterdam

American Express The offices at Damrak 66 (℡ 020/504-7777; tram: 4, 9, 14, 16, 24, 25) and Van Baerlestraat 39 (℡ 020/673-8550; tram: 2, 3, 5, 12), are open Monday through Friday from 9am to 5pm, and Saturday from 9am to noon. The Damrak office provides currency exchange and books tours; the Van Baerlestraat office only books tours.

Airport See "Getting There," in chapter 1.

ATM Networks Among the centrally located automated teller machines (ATMs) accessible by cards linked to the Cirrus and PLUS networks, and the major credit cards and charge cards, are those at **ABN-AMRO Bank,** Dam 2 (tram: 4, 9, 14, 16, 24, 25) and Leidsestraat 1 (tram: 1, 2, 5), at Leidseplein; **Rabobank,** Dam 16 (tram: 4, 9, 14, 16, 24, 25); and **Fortis Bank,** Singel 548 (tram: 4, 9, 14, 16, 24, 25), at the Flower Market.

Currency See "Money," in chapter 1.

Currency Exchange The best options for changing money are the VVV tourist offices, banks, and, if you carry American Express traveler's checks, **American Express** (see above). Other fair-dealing options are **Thomas Cook,** Damrak 125 (℡ 020/620-3236; tram: 4, 9, 14, 16, 29, 24, 25), Dam 23-25 (℡ 020/625-0922; tram: 4, 9, 14, 16, 29, 24, 25), and Leidseplein 31A (℡ 020/626-7000; tram: 1, 2, 5, 6, 7, 10); and the **Grenswisselkantoor (GWK)** exchanges at Schiphol Airport (℡ 020/653-5121), Centraal Station (℡ 020/627-2731), and at some international border crossings and main train stations. These organizations can provide cash advances for holders of American Express, Diners Club, MasterCard, and Visa credit and charge cards. GWK can arrange money transfers through **Western Union.**

Hotels and bureaux de change (currency-exchange offices), which are open regular hours plus evenings and weekends, often charge a low commission (or none at all) but may give a low exchange rate—always know *exactly* how much you are going to get in your hand before agreeing to the transaction.

There are clusters of banks, such as ABN-AMRO, Rabobank, Fortis, and NMB, around the Dam, the Flower Market, and at Leidseplein.

Dentists Call the Central Medical Service (℡ 020/592-3434).

Doctors Call the Central Medical Service (℡ 020/592-3434).

Drugstores For such items as toothpaste, deodorant, and razor blades, go to a *drogerij* (drugstore), or a supermarket. See also "Pharmacies," below.

Electricity Before you weigh down your luggage with all your favorite appliances, note that the Netherlands runs on 220 volts electricity (North America uses 110 volts). So you need to take with you a small voltage transformer (available in drug and appliance stores and by mail order) that plugs into the round-holed European electrical outlet and converts the Dutch voltage from 220 volts down to 110 volts for any small appliance up to 1,500 watts. Don't try to plug an American appliance directly into a European outlet without a transformer; you may ruin your appliance and possibly even start a fire. Some American appliances (such as some electric shavers) are engineered to operate on either 110 volts or 220 volts, but even with these you usually need to buy a plug adapter for Dutch outlets.

Embassies and Consulates The **U.S. Consulate** in Amsterdam is at Museumplein 19 (© **020/575-5309;** tram: 3, 5, 12, 16), open Monday through Friday from 8:30am to noon and 1:30 to 3:30pm; the U.S. Embassy in The Hague is at Lange Voorhout 102 (© **070/310-9209**). The **U.K. Consulate-General** in Amsterdam is at Koningslaan 44 (© **020/676-4343;** tram: 2), open Monday through Friday from 9am to noon and 2 to 4pm; the U.K. Embassy in The Hague is at Lange Voorhout 10 (© **070/364-5800**).

Citizens of other English-speaking countries should contact their embassies in The Hague. **Australia:** Carnegielaan 14 (© **070/310-8200**); **Canada:** Sophialaan 7, Den Haag (© **070/311-1600**); **Ireland:** Dr. Kuyperstraat 9, Den Haag (© **070/363-0993**); **New Zealand:** Mauritskade 25, Den Haag (© **070/346-9324**).

Emergencies For police assistance, an ambulance, or the fire department, call © **112.**

Holidays January 1 (New Year's Day); Good Friday; Easter Monday; April 30 (Queen's Day/*Koninginnedag*); Ascension Day; Pentecost Monday; December 25 (Christmas) and 26. The dates for Easter, Ascension, and Pentecost change each year.

Hospitals Two hospitals with an emergency service are the **Onze Lieve Vrouwe Gasthuis,** Eerste Oosterparkstraat 179 (© **020/599-9111;** tram: 3, 7, 10), in Amsterdam Oost; and the giant **Academisch Medisch Centrum (AMC)**, Meibergdreef 9 (© **020/566-3333**; Metro: Holendrecht), in Amsterdam Zuidoost.

Information See "Visitor Information," earlier in this chapter.

Internet Access In the Center, **easyEverything** (www.easy everything.com) has two locations: Damrak 33 (© **020/ 320-8082**; tram: 1, 2, 4, 5, 9, 13, 16, 17, 24, 25); and Reguliersbreestraat 22 (© **020/320-6291**; tram: 4, 9, 14). Both are open 24 hours a day and access begins at 1.15€. A less-crowded choice is **Internet Café**, Martelaarsgracht 11 (© **020/ 627-1052**; info@internetcafe.nl; tram: 1, 2, 5, 13, 17), open Sunday through Thursday from 9am to 1am, Friday and Saturday from 9am to 3am; access is 2.75€ an hour.

Mail Postage for a postcard or ordinary letter to the U.S., Canada, Australia, New Zealand, and South Africa is .75€; to the U.K. and Ireland it's .45€.

Maps See "City Layout," earlier in this chapter.

Narcotics The use of narcotic drugs is officially illegal in the Netherlands, but Amsterdam allows the sale in licensed premises of up to 5 grams (.2 oz.) of hashish or marijuana for personal consumption, and possession of 30 grams (1.2 oz) for personal use. Not every local authority in the Netherlands is as liberal-minded as Amsterdam when it comes to smoking pot—and Amsterdam is not so tolerant that you may just light up on the street, in cafes, and on trams and trains (though enough dopey people do). The possession and use of hard drugs like heroin, cocaine, and ecstasy is an offense, and the police have swept most of the downtown heroin-shooting galleries away from the tourist centers, but even in these cases the drug abusers are considered a medical and social problem rather than purely as a law-enforcement issue. On the other hand, peddling drugs *is* a serious offense. See "Smoking Coffeeshops," in chapter 7.

Pharmacies For both prescription and non-prescription medicines, you go to an *apotheek* (pharmacy). Try **Dam Apotheek** at Damstraat 2 (© **020/624-4331**; tram: 4, 9, 14, 16, 24, 25). All pharmacies have the name and address of an all-night and Sunday pharmacy posted on the door.

Police Holland's emergency number to call for the police *(politie)*, fire department, and ambulance is © **112**. For routine matters, police headquarters are at Elandsgracht 117 (© **0900/ 8844**; tram: 7, 10, 17).

Post Office Most **post offices** are open Monday through Friday from 9am to 5pm. The post office at Singel 250-256, at the corner of Raadhuisstraat (© **020/556-3311**; tram: 13, 14, 17), is open Monday through Friday from 9am to 6pm (to 8pm Thurs), and Saturday from 9am to 3pm. To mail a large package, go to the post office at Oosterdokskade 3, a large building on the right as you face Centraal Station.

Taxes There's a value-added tax (BTW) of 6% on hotel and restaurant bills (19% on beer, wine, and liquor), and 6% or 19% (the amount depends on the product) on purchases. This tax is always included in the price. People resident outside the European Union can shop tax-free in Amsterdam. Shops that offer tax-free shopping advertise with a HOLLAND TAX-FREE SHOPPING sign in the window, and they provide you with the form you need to recover value-added tax (VAT) when you leave the European Union. Refunds are available only when you spend more than 137€ in a store. See "The Shopping Scene" in chapter 6 for more details.

Taxis See "Getting Around," earlier in this chapter.

Telephones **To call Amsterdam:** If you're calling Amsterdam from the United States:

1. Dial the international access code: 011
2. Dial the country code for the Netherlands: 31
3. Dial the area code 20 and then the number. So the whole number you'd dial would be 011-31-20-000-0000.

   To make international calls: To make international calls from Amsterdam, first dial 00 and then the country code (U.S. or Canada 1, U.K. 44, Ireland 353, Australia 61, New Zealand 64). Next you dial the area code and number. For example, if you wanted to call the British Embassy in Washington, D.C., you would dial 00-1-202-588-7800.

   For operator assistance: To make an international collect call, dial © **0800/0410**. To call collect inside Holland, dial © **0800/ 0101** (or press the "Collect" button if the phone you're using has one).

   Toll-free numbers: Numbers beginning with 0800 within Holland are toll-free, but calling a 1-800 number in the States from Holland is not toll-free. In fact, it costs the same as an overseas call.

Special numbers: Watch out for the special Dutch numbers that begin with 0900. Calls to these are charged at a far higher rate than ordinary local calls. Depending who you call, they are from .25€ to .90€ a minute.

To call the United States or Canada, dial **00** (the international access code) + **1** (the country code) + the area code + the number. Other country codes are: Australia, **61**; United Kingdom, **44**; Ireland, **353**; New Zealand, **64**.

International calls, per minute, are: **U.S.** and **Canada:** .30€; **U.K.** and **Ireland:** .25€; **Australia** and **New Zealand:** .40€. You can use pay phones in booths all around town with a KPN *telekaart* (phone card), selling for 5€, 13€, and 25€ from post offices, train ticket counters, and newsstands. Some pay phones take coins, of .05€, .10€, .20€, .50€, and 1€. Use smaller coins whenever possible, at least until you are connected with the right person, as no change is given from an individual coin and once the call has begun, excess coins will not be returned when you hang up. Should there be no answer, hang up and the coin comes back to you. On both card and coin phones, a digital reading tracks your decreasing deposit so you know when to add another card or more coins. To make additional calls when you still have a coin or card inserted, briefly break the connection, and you will get a new dial tone for another call.

The area code for Amsterdam is 020. When making local calls in Amsterdam you won't need to use the area codes shown in this book. You do need to use an area code between towns and cities. The two main formats for Dutch phone numbers are for cities and large towns, a three-digit area code followed by a seven-digit number, and for small towns and villages, a four-digit area code followed by a six-digit number.

In the Dutch telephone system, there's a sustained dial tone, and a beep-beep sound for a busy signal. Both local and long-distance calls from a pay phone are .25€ a minute. Calls placed through your hotel switchboard or dialed direct from your room phone are usually more than twice the standard rate.

To speak with an operator, call ✆ **0800.** For information inside Holland, call ✆ **0900/8008;** for international information, call ✆ **0900/8418;** for international collect calls, call ✆ **0900/0410.**

To charge a call to your calling card, call AT&T (📞 **0800/022-9111**); MCI (📞 **0800/022-9122**); Sprint (📞 **0800/022-9119**); Canada Direct (📞 **0800/022-9116**); British Telecom (📞 **0800/022-9944**).

Time Zone Holland is on Central European time (CET), which is Greenwich mean time (GMT) plus 1 hour. Amsterdam is normally 6 hours ahead of New York City time and 9 hours ahead of Los Angeles time.

Tipping The Dutch government requires that all taxes and service charges be included in the published prices of hotels, restaurants, cafes, discos, nightclubs, beauty salons/barbershops and hairdressers, and sightseeing companies. Even taxi fare includes taxes and a standard 15% tip. To be absolutely sure in a restaurant, for example, that tax and service are included, look for the words *inclusief BTW en service* (BTW is the abbreviation for the Dutch words that mean value-added tax), or ask the waiter. The Dutch are so accustomed to having these charges included that many restaurants have stopped spelling it out.

Dutch waitpersons appreciate tips and rely on them to supplement their salary. To tip as the Dutch do, in a cafe or snack bar, leave some small change; in a restaurant, leave 1€ to 2€, and up to a generous 5€ if you think the service was particularly good; for expensive tabs, you may want to leave more—or maybe less! An informal survey (I asked a taxi driver) reveals that Americans and British are the best tippers; the worst are the Dutch themselves.

Toilets Maybe you better sit down for this one. The most important thing to remember about public toilets in Amsterdam—apart from calling them *toiletten* (twa-*lett*-en) or "the WC" (*vay say*) and not restrooms or comfort stations—is not the usual male/female distinction (important though that is) but to *pay the person* who sits at the entrance. He or she has a saucer where you put your money. If you don't, you might have a visitor in the inner sanctum while you're transacting your business. Even if you have paid, in busy places, the attendant may have forgotten your face by the time you emerge and will then pursue you out of the toilet and along the street. It's tiresome, but toilets usually costs only about .1€.

If you have a toilet emergency in the Center, the very best address to find relief is the Grand Hotel Krasnapolsky (see "In the Old Center," in chapter 4). Just breeze in as if you own the "Kras," swing left past the front desk and along the corridor, past the Winter Garden restaurant, then up a short flight of stairs. Marble washbasins and what look to be gold-plated faucets are among the wonders therein.

Transit Info For information regarding tram, bus, Metro, and train services, call Ⓒ **0900/9292.**

Useful Phone Numbers Lost Property: Call Ⓒ **020/560-5858** for tram, bus, and Metro; Ⓒ **020/557-8544** for trains and stations; and Ⓒ **020/649-1433** for Schiphol Airport. Don't be optimistic about your chances. There are plenty of honest Amsterdammers, but they're generally out of town when you lose something.

U.S. Dept. of State Travel Advisory Ⓒ **202/647-5225** (manned 24 hr.). U.S. Passport Agency Ⓒ **202/647-0518.** U.S. Centers for Disease Control International Traveler's Hot Line: Ⓒ **404/332-4559.**

Water The water from the faucet in Amsterdam is safe to drink. Many people drink bottled mineral water, called generically *spa* even though it's not all from the Belgian Spa brand.

3

Where to Stay

Is your preference old-world charm combined with luxurious quarters? Glitzy modernity with every conceivable amenity? Small, intimate, family-run hotels? A historic canal house that reflects the lifestyle of centuries past? A modern, medium-size hotel on the fringe of inner-city hustle and bustle? A bare-bones room in a dormitory, which frees up scarce dollars for other purposes? Amsterdam has them all, and more. Some hotels share more than one of these characteristics: A common fusion is that of historic canal house on the outside and glitzy modernity with every conceivable amenity on the inside.

You probably have your own idea of what makes a great hotel. My advice is to let your choice reflect the kind of city Amsterdam is—democratic, adventurous, quirky, and always in search of that enigmatic Dutch quality, *gezelligheid*, which is the ambience that makes a place warm, cozy, friendly, and welcoming. You can find this quality at all prices levels, and especially among the moderately priced hotels owned by local people.

There are around 30,000 hotel and hostel beds available, 40% of which are in four- and five-star hotels. The city has moved in recent years to redress the balance in favor of hotels in the mid- and low-priced categories, but it is inevitably a slow process. If a particular hotel strikes your fancy but is out of your price range, it may pay to inquire if special off-season, weekend, specific weekday, or other packages will bring prices down to what you can afford.

Should your heart be set on, or your financial circumstances dictate, a low-end budget hotel, and you're arriving during almost any period between spring and fall, don't simply brush past the hotel and hostel touts at Centraal Station. Spending a minute to discuss pros and cons with them may save you long hours tramping the cobblestones or waiting in line at a VVV hotel reservations desk. They usually have photographs of the rooms they are offering, but don't commit to taking a place without first eyeballing the bricks-and-mortar reality.

HOTEL ORIENTATION

All hotels have been designated according to their high-season rates. If breakfast is not included, expect to pay 5€ to 15€ and up for a continental, buffet, or full breakfast, depending on the category of your hotel. Single rates are available in many hotels, though not always for a significant reduction over double occupancy. Only those hotels with rooms that all, or nearly all, have private facilities are listed here, even in the inexpensive category, unless there are compelling reasons for including a hotel where this is not the case. Only rates that apply to rooms with bathrooms are used to determine a hotel's price category. Room rates increase on average 5% annually.

If you are traveling with kids, always ask about special rates for them. Many hotels allow a child to share their parents' room free or for a small extra charge.

Many Amsterdam hotels, in all price categories, offer significant rate reductions between November 1 and March 31, with the exception of the Christmas and New Year period. The city is as much a delight then as in the tourist-packed summer months. You'll enjoy a calendar full of cultural events, the full blossoming of many traditional Dutch dishes not offered in warm weather, and the fact that streets, cafes, restaurants, and museums are filled more with locals than with visitors.

The next consideration is location: How close is a hotel to sights, restaurants, shops, or the transportation to get to them, and what sort of neighborhood is it in? There are neighborhoods that you probably want to avoid; these might include the haunts of drug or sex peddlers. Amsterdammers accept such phenomena as facts of life, and there are really no "no-go" areas. You'll probably venture into Amsterdam's shady corners in daylight or as an evening lark, but there's no reason to spend your nights in a less-than-desirable area or worry about getting back to your room safely. The hotels described here are all decent hotels in decent neighborhoods (in the case of a few on the fringes of neighborhoods that aren't quite so decent, this is mentioned in the text).

RESERVATIONS   This is a popular tourist city, especially during summer months and the tulip season, between early April and mid-May. You are advised always to make your reservation in advance. You can do this directly with any of the hotels below. They will often ask you to confirm by fax or e-mail and/or give your credit card number. Be sure you provide ample time for them to reply

A Canal-House Warning

Elevators are difficult things to shoehorn into the cramped confines of a 17th-century Amsterdam canal house and cost more than some moderately priced and budget hotels can afford. Many simply don't have them. If lugging your old wooden sea chest up six flights of narrow stairs is liable to void your life insurance policy, better make sure the elevators are in place and working.

Be prepared to climb hard-to-navigate stairways if you want to save money by lodging in a hotel without an elevator. Narrow and steep as ladders, these stairways were designed to conserve space in the narrow houses along the canals. Today they're an anomaly that'll make your stay even more memorable. If you have difficulty climbing stairs, ask for a room on a lower floor.

before you leave home. (See "Telephones" in "Fast Facts: Amsterdam," in chapter 2, before dialing; or write to the addresses given below.) In addition, you can reserve a hotel room through the **Netherlands Reservations Center (NRC),** Nieuwe Gouw 1, 1442 LE, Purmerend, Netherlands (© **029/968-9144;** fax 029/968-9154; info@hotelres.nl), and you can reserve online at the NRC's Internet site: **www.hotelres.nl**.

Or, reserve with the **Amsterdam Reservation Center** (© **077/700-0888;** reservations@amsterdamtourist.nl), which is connected with the VVV Amsterdam tourist information office. Should you arrive in Amsterdam without a reservation, VVV Amsterdam is well organized to help you, for a moderate charge of 2.50€, plus a refundable room deposit of 2.50€. This is a nice reassurance if you prefer to freelance your itinerary, though at busy periods of the year you have to expect to take potluck. They will always find you something, even at the busiest times, but it may not be what, or where, you want.

TRANSPORTATION   Most public transportation connections given are by tram (streetcar) and most, though not all, are from Centraal Station. Never use the Metro system if there is a tram stop within similar distance from your hotel: You won't get such a good view, and the Metro is a less pleasant way to travel. Inevitably, not all hotels are right by a tram stop, so if your bags are heavy you would be better off taking a taxi right from the start.

1 In the Old Center

VERY EXPENSIVE

The Grand Sofitel Demeure Amsterdam 🎭🎭 The Grand is indeed one of the grandest hotels in town. It's in a building that was a 15th-century convent, a 16th-century royal inn, the 17th-century Dutch Admiralty, and the 19th-century Town Hall. To reach the lobby, you walk through a courtyard with a fountain, then through the brass-and-wood revolving door. There are fresh flower arrangements on all the tables in the lobby and lounge area, where tea is served in the afternoon. You also find plenty of Art Deco style and stained glass windows. The black-and-white marble floors are covered with Oriental rugs. All this, and only a vigorous stone's throw from the Red Light District. The individually styled and furnished guest rooms are designed to reflect the different phases of the building's illustrious past and are about the last word in plush (though some rooms put a refreshingly simple slant on this). Most have couches and armchairs; all have a personal safe and a voice-mail answering system for the telephone. The views are good too, onto the 17th-century canals, the hotel garden, or the courtyard. You can have lunch or dinner at the Art Deco, brasserie-style Café Roux, where you see an original Karel Appel mural, the *Inquisitive Children*.

Oudezijds Voorburgwal 197 (off Damstraat), 1012 EX Amsterdam. ℂ 800/228-3000 in the U.S. and Canada, or 020/555-3111. Fax 020/555-3222. www.thegrand.nl. 182 units. 360€-395€ double; from 450€ suite; add 5% city tax. AE, DC, MC, V. Parking 25€. Tram: 4, 9, 16, 24, 25 to Spui. **Amenities:** Heated indoor pool; health club; Jacuzzi; sauna; concierge; courtesy car; secretarial services; 24-hr. room service; in-room massage; babysitting; laundry service; dry cleaning. *In room:* A/C, TV w/pay movies, dataport, minibar, coffeemaker, hair dryer, safe.

Hôtel de l'Europe 🎭🎭🎭 On a stretch of prime riverside real estate in the city center, this elegant, old establishment is one of the Leading Hotels of the World. Its pastel-red and white facade, at the point where the Amstel River flows into the city's canal network, is an iconic element in the classic view of the city. Built in 1896, the de l'Europe has a grand style and a sense of ease, a smooth combination of aged dignity and modern comforts. Rooms and bathrooms are spacious and bright, furnished with classic good taste. Some rooms have mini-balconies overlooking the river and all boast marble bathrooms. The **Excelsior** (see chapter 4 for full details), one of the toniest restaurants in town, serves breakfast, lunch, and dinner daily. **Le Relais** is a less formal setting for light lunches and dinners. Drinks and hors d'oeuvres are served daily in **Freddy's Bar** and

Kids Family-Friendly Hotels

Estheréa (p. 62)   Though most of the rooms in this canal-house hotel are rather small, all are tastefully furnished, and a few, ideal for families, are equipped with bunk beds, always a favorite with children.

Sint-Nicolaas (p. 57)   A centrally located hotel run by the warm Mesker family, which welcomes guests into a comfortable and relaxed environment that is child-friendly.

City Hostel Vondelpark   An ideal choice for families traveling on a limited budget, offering a good blend of facilities, space, easygoing atmosphere, and security, in addition to a green location in the city's famous Vondelpark at Zandpad 5, 1054 GA Amsterdam (*€* **020/589-89-96**).

Amstel Botel (p. 57)   Although it is more common to find youthful spirits traveling alone or in small groups here, there is no reason why it wouldn't work for families, and there is the added interest for the kids of being on a ship, even if it isn't going anywhere.

in summer only on **La Terrasse,** overlooking the Amstel, from 11am to 1am (weather permitting).

Nieuwe Doelenstraat 2-8 (facing Muntplein), 1012 CP Amsterdam. *€* **800/223-6800** in the U.S. and Canada, or 020/531-1777. Fax 020/531-1778. www.leurope.nl. 100 units. 335€–415€ double; suites from 445€; add 5% city tax. AE, DC, MC, V. Valet and self-parking 38€. Tram: 4, 9, 14, 16, 24, 25 to De Munt. **Amenities:** 2 restaurants (French, international); 2 bars; heated indoor pool; health club; sauna; concierge; 24-hr. room service; massage; babysitting; laundry service; dry cleaning; nonsmoking rooms. *In room:* A/C, TV w/pay movies, dataport, minibar, hair dryer, safe.

EXPENSIVE

Die Port van Cleve *€€*   Fairly oozing history and charm, this hotel is near the Royal Palace and next to Magna Plaza, a big shopping center in what used to be the city's main Post Office. The hotel itself is one of the city's oldest, and started life in 1864 as the first Heineken brewery. Over the last 100 years it has accommodated many famous guests. The ornamental facade, complete with turrets and alcoves, is original and was fully restored in 1997. Likewise, the interior has been completely renovated, and the rooms, though relatively small, have been furnished comfortably in modern yet cozy

Central Amsterdam Accommodations

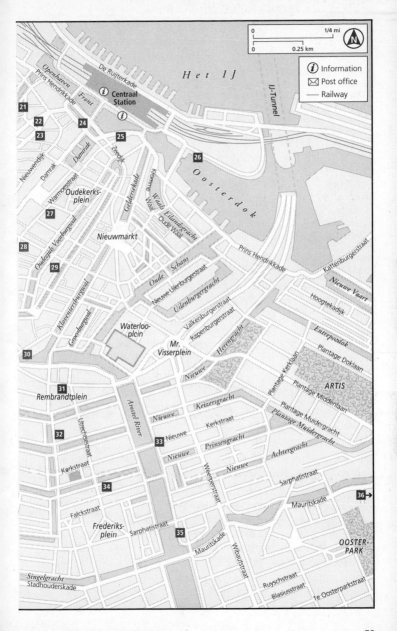

style. You won't eat much more traditionally Dutch than in the **Brasserie de Poort,** ~~and you can drink in the~~ **Bodega de Blauwe Parade** watched over by Delft blue tiles.

Nieuwezijds Voorburgwal 176-180 (behind the Royal Palace), 1012 SJ Amsterdam. ℭ 020/624-4860. Fax 020/622-0240. www.dieportvancleve.com. 120 units. TV. 215€-295€ double; 350€-525€ suite; add 5% city tax. AE, DC, MC, V. No parking. Tram: 1, 2, 5, 13, 17 to the Dam. **Amenities:** Restaurant (Dutch/international); bar; cafe; concierge; business center; limited room service; babysitting; laundry service; dry cleaning; nonsmoking rooms; executive rooms. *In room:* TV w/pay movies, hair dryer, safe.

Hotel Amsterdam ☆☆

Just 400m (1,308 ft.) from Centraal Station, this hotel, from 1911 and still owned by descendants of the original proprietors, has an 18th-century facade. Its rooms are supermodern, though, featuring thick carpets and ample wardrobe space. The entire hotel underwent renovation, completed in April 2001. Rooms at the front of the hotel tend to get more light, but are also subjected to more street noise; some have balconies. The in-house **De Roode Leeuw** restaurant serves typical Dutch cuisine and daily two-course menus. The glassed-in heated terrace overlooking the Dam is a pleasant and relaxing spot for a beer (open daily 11am-11:30pm).

Damrak 93-94 (beside the Dam), 1012 LP Amsterdam. ℭ 020/555-0666. Fax 020/620-4716. www.hotelamsterdam.nl. 80 units. 225€-250€ double. AE, DC, MC, V. No parking. Tram: 4, 9, 14, 16, 24, 25 to the Dam. **Amenities:** Restaurant (Dutch); business center; 24-hr. room service; laundry service; dry cleaning; nonsmoking rooms; executive rooms; in-house movies. *In room:* A/C, TV w/pay movies, dataport, minibar, coffeemaker, hair dryer, safe.

NH Barbizon Palace Hotel ☆☆

This sparkling establishment meets every criterion for the ideal Amsterdam hotel. It was built behind the facades of 19 traditional canal houses. Inside, it's fully modern, loaded with amenities, and efficient; it's also centrally located, within walking distance of Centraal Station and the Dam. Many of the rooms feature split-level designs and antique oak beams. A Roman forum may come to mind as you step into the hotel; the lobby is a long promenade of highly polished black-and-white marble floor tiles, with a massive skylight arching above. The excellent Restaurant **Vermeer** earns frequent praise from food critics. **Hudson's,** serving light food, and a late breakfast of juice, two eggs, a *broodje,* and coffee or tea from 10:30am to noon, is also pretty good.

Prins Hendrikkade 59-72 (facing Centraal Station), 1012 AD Amsterdam. ℭ **800/ 327-1177** in the U.S. and Canada, or 020/556-4564. Fax 020/624-3353. www. goldentuliphotels.nl/gtbpalace. 275 units. 275€-380€ double; add 5% city tax. AE, DC, MC, V. Parking 25€. Tram: 1, 2, 4, 5, 9, 13, 16, 17, 24, 25 to Centraal Station. **Amenities:** 2 restaurants (Dutch/international); bar; health club with Jacuzzi and sauna; concierge; car-rental desk; business center; salon; 24-hr. room service; babysitting; laundry service; dry cleaning. *In room:* A/C, TV w/pay movies, minibar.

NH Grand Hotel Krasnapolsky 🌟🌟

Living it up at the Hotel Krasnapolsky, one of Amsterdam's landmark hotels, is no great trick. The Krasnapolsky is on the Dam, facing the Royal Palace. It began life as the Wintertuin (Winter Garden) restaurant, where Victorian ladies and gentlemen sipped wine and nibbled pancakes beneath the hanging plants and lofty skylight ceiling—the Wintertuin still dominates the ground floor. The place was founded in 1866 by a Polish tailor turned entrepreneur. Its original 100 rooms had parquet floors, central heating, and electric lights—the first hotel in Holland to have them. Over the past century the "Kras" has spread over four buildings on several different levels. The sizes and shapes of the rooms vary, with some tastefully converted into individually decorated apartments. Renovations have added a new wing featuring a Japanese garden and a Dutch roof garden. The hotel's side streets lead into the Red Light District, which may not be the ideal direction to take for a casual evening stroll. There are several great dining possibilities here. The Winter Garden is the most elegant place in Amsterdam for lunch. **Brasserie Reflet** specializes in French cuisine, and there are two fine Japanese restaurants: **Edo** and **Kyo.** Certainly the most novel is the Bedouin banquet dinner at the **Shibli,** Friday through Sunday.

Dam 9 (facing Royal Palace), 1012 JS Amsterdam. ℭ **020/554-9111.** Fax 020/622-8607. www.nh-hotels.com. 468 units. 290€-340€ double; 450€-700€ suite; add 5% city tax. AE, DC, MC, V. Valet parking and self-parking 35€. Tram: 4, 9, 14, 16, 24, 25 to the Dam. **Amenities:** 4 restaurants (French, Bedouin buffet, 2 Japanese); lounge; bar; health club; concierge; business center; salon; 24-hr. room service; babysitting; laundry service; dry cleaning; nonsmoking rooms; executive rooms. *In room:* A/C, TV w/pay movies, dataport, minibar, coffeemaker, hair dryer, iron, safe.

Victoria Hotel 🌟

You can survive quite nicely without taking taxis if you stay here, as close as you can be to Centraal Station, where most of the city's trams begin and end their routes, and where you can board a train to other parts of Holland and to Schiphol Airport. To emphasize the point, the hotel offers individual guests free first-class return train travel between Schiphol and Centraal

Station. Since 1890, the elegant Victoria has been a turreted landmark at the head of Damrak. It overlooks the canal-boat piers and the stack of bikes parked outside the station. It can be noisy and tacky out on busy, neon-lit Damrak, but you won't notice that inside. Its original spacious rooms have been recently redecorated and refurnished, and the windows replaced with double-glazed panes. Rooms in the adjacent new block inevitably lack some of the atmosphere of the old. The idea of its proprietors is to give you a five-star hotel at four-star rates. All this and location, too. You can enjoy dinner or a quick lunch in the Scandinavian-look **Seasons Garden** restaurant, or take cocktails at the **Tasman Bar** and tea at the **Brasserie Vic's** glassed-in terrace beside Damrak.

Damrak 1-5 (facing Centraal Station), 1012 LG Amsterdam. ⓒ **800/670-PARK** in the U.S. and Canada, or 020/627-1166. Fax 020/627-4259. www.parkplazaeurope. com. 305 units. 315€–365€ double; 470€–505€ suite; add 5% city tax. AE, DC, MC, V. No parking. Tram: 1, 2, 4, 5, 9, 13, 16, 17, 24, 25 to Centraal Station. **Amenities:** Restaurant (international); continental cafe; bar; small heated indoor pool; health club and spa; business center; limited room service; massage; babysitting; laundry service; same-day dry cleaning; nonsmoking rooms. *In room:* A/C, TV w/pay movies, minibar, hair dryer.

MODERATE

Avenue Hotel ⓡ   About 2 minutes from Centraal Station, this recently renovated and extended establishment has some of the style and amenities of its neighbor, the Crowne Plaza (above), at less than half the price. Part of the premises is a converted Golden Age warehouse that belonged to the V.O.C., the United East India Company. The rooms aren't huge, but they are bright and have clean furnishings, good-size bathrooms, some with a double sink.

Nieuwezijds Voorburgwal 33 (near Centraal Station), 1012 9599 Amsterdam. ⓒ **020/530-9530.** Fax 020/530-3946. www.emb.hotels.nl. 78 units. 105€–164€ double. Rates include buffet breakfast. AE, DC, MC, V. Limited street parking. Tram: 1, 2, 5, 13, 17 to Nieuwezijds Kolk. **Amenities:** Bar/brasserie; bike rental; dry cleaning. *In room:* TV w/pay movies, dataport, hair dryer.

Rho Hotel   Once you find it, you'll bless this hotel for its easy convenience. Tucked away in a side street just off the National Monument on the Dam, the Rho is housed in a building that once was the offices of a gold company and before that housed a theater dating from 1908 in the space that now holds the reception desk and breakfast area. There are elevators; the rooms are modern and comfortable, having been recently renovated; the price is right; and the location, quiet yet central, is one of the best in town. All rooms have fans, and car rental and tour bookings are available at the reception desk, as are the hotel's own bikes for rent. Who could ask for more?

Nes 5-23 (at the Dam), 1012 KC Amsterdam. (C) **020/620-7371.** Fax 020/620-7826. www.rhohotel.com. 170 units. 95€-145€ double. Rates include buffet breakfast. AE, MC, V. Parking 20€. Tram: 4, 9, 14, 16, 24, 25 to the Dam. **Amenities:** Bar, nonsmoking rooms. In room: TV, minibar, hair dryer, safe.

Sint-Nicolaas & Kids

Named after Amsterdam's patron saint, this hotel is conveniently near the Centraal Station, in a prominent corner house with a dark facade. It's a typical family hotel with an easygoing atmosphere, and children are welcome. Originally the building was occupied by a factory that manufactured ropes and carpets from sisal imported from the then Dutch colonies. It was converted into a hotel in 1980. The rather basic furnishings are more than compensated for by the ideal location and the Mesker family's friendliness.

Spuistraat 1A (at Nieuwendijk), 1012 SP Amsterdam. (C) **020/626-1384.** Fax 020/623-0979. www.hotelnicolaas.nl. 24 units. 95€-115€ double. Rates include continental breakfast. AE, DC, MC, V. Limited street parking. Tram: 1, 2, 5, 13, 17 to Martelaarsgracht. **Amenities:** Bar. In room: TV, hair dryer, safe.

Tulip Inn Dam Square & Value

This hotel is another example of putting an old Amsterdam building to good use housing tourists. This time the old building, behind the Nieuwe Kerk, was a distillery—and a magnificent building it is. Its granite details accentuate the brickwork and massive curve-topped doors with elaborate hinges. Inside, the rooms are all you'll want: modern, bright, comfortable, and attractively priced.

Gravenstraat 12-16 (at the Dam), 1012 NM Amsterdam. (C) **800/344-1212** in the U.S. and Canada, or 020/623-3716. Fax 020/638-1156. www.tulipinndamsquare. com. 38 units. 150€ double. Rates include continental breakfast. AE, DC, MC, V. No parking. Tram: 1, 2, 4, 5, 9, 13, 14, 16, 17, 24, 25 to the Dam. **Amenities:** Bar; dry cleaning. In room: A/C, TV, dataport, coffeemaker, hair dryer.

INEXPENSIVE

Amstel Botel & Kids

Where better to experience a city on the water than on a boat-hotel? Its cabins are spread out over four decks connected by elevator. Be sure to ask for a room with a view on the water, not on the uninspiring quay. The boat is popular largely because of its location and rates, and for that extra something added by sleeping on a boat. Turn left out of Centraal Station, pass the bike rental, and you see it floating in front of you. This moored boat-hotel has 352 beds in cabins on four decks, connected by an elevator. The bright, modern rooms are no-nonsense but comfortable, the showers

---

Tips Summer Stays: Reserve Ahead

July and August are tough months for finding hotel rooms in Amsterdam, and you are advised to reserve as far ahead as possible for this period. If you have problems getting a room, contact the VVV Amsterdam tourist information office, which can generally arrange a room somewhere though it might not be in the kind of hotel you are looking for and you might need to pay more for a room in a better-class hotel.

It can be particularly hard to find hoteliers willing to give away rooms for a single night when that might cost them a longer booking. What to do? In this circumstance a last-minute search might be called for, since a hotel that's had a last-minute cancellation would be more likely to consider single-night occupancy, but in general a last-minute search is the wrong approach.

---

small. To get here, leave the station and turn left, passing the bike rental—the Botel is painted white and directly in front of you.

Oosterdokskade 2-4 (at Centraal Station), 1011 AE Amsterdam. © **020/626-4247.** Fax 020/639-1952. 175 units. 75€-86€ double. AE, DC, MC, V. Limited street parking. Tram: 1, 2, 4, 5, 9, 13, 16, 17, 24, 25 to Centraal Station. **Amenities:** Concierge; dry cleaning. *In room:* TV w/in-house movie channel.

Winston ☆ Formerly a backpackers' hotel, the Winston moved upscale by asking local artists to create paintings, photographs, and other works of what you might call art, for the halls, rooms, doors, and bathrooms. The project brought an element of whimsy to what was a rather bland lodging, giving it the character of an artist's hangout. Combine this with a location on edgy Warmoesstraat, which borders the Red Light District, and you have a place with a reputation for being hang-loose and alternative. It's not entirely justified: The proprietors reserve the right to eject guests who take this too literally. Within these limits, they've done a good job of creating a democratic facility aimed mostly at young people. If you're not keen on being on a main route for charged-up groups heading into and out of the city's sin district, or on the street's sex shops and noisy bars, this won't be the place for you to rest your head. In addition to being ad hoc spaces for art exhibits, the guest rooms are sparely furnished in a modern style, vary in size, holding from two to six beds, and are clean and well-maintained. None of them have anything like a view that's worth looking out the window for. Bathrooms are small, but have all the requisite facilities, and most of those rooms that have no full bathroom do have a shower. The downstairs bar is a fun meeting place and has live music on weekends.

Warmoesstraat 129 (off Damrak), 1012 JA Amsterdam. © **020/623-1380.** Fax 020/639-2308. www.winston.nl. 69 units, 25 with bathroom. 87€-92€ double with bathroom, 85€ double without bathroom. Rates include continental breakfast. AE, DC, MC, V. No parking. Tram: 4, 9, 14, 16, 24, 25 to the Dam. **Amenities:** Bar. *In room:* TV.

2 Along the Canal Belt
VERY EXPENSIVE

Blakes Amsterdam 🏵🏵🏵   The exceptional service at this intimate boutique hotel wins justified raves from its primarily American and British guests, and the Asian-influenced decor—courtesy of proprietor and British designer Anouska Hempel—is arguably the most stylish in town. Housed in a 17th-century landmark, Blakes began life as a theater (Antonio Vivaldi once conducted here) and its serene black-and-white lounge still sports the theater's original brick floor. All of the guest rooms and suites have the usual array of luxury amenities and are individually decorated in different colors and themes; room no. 5, for example, is a blue Japanese-style room with a deep soaking tub and traditional sliding screens. The excellent location, in the heart of the Canal Belt, puts you within walking distance of the Leidseplein, Museumplein, and the Bloemenmarkt. My one complaint: Style here occasionally trumps substance—the water fountain-style sinks in a few of the rooms look grand, but the design makes them somewhat hard to use.

Keizersgracht 384 (near Huidenstraat). 1016 GB Amsterdam. © **020/530-2010.** Fax 020/530-2030. www.slh.com/netherlands/amsterdam/hotel_amsbla.html. 41 units. 350€-660€ double; 800€-1,250€ suite; add 5% city tax. AE, DC, MC, V. Valet and self parking 20€. Tram: 1, 2, 5 to Spui. **Amenities:** Restaurant (Asian/international); lounge; bar; bike rental; boat rental; concierge; 24-hr. room service; laundry service; dry cleaning. *In room:* A/C, TV/VCR w/pay movies, minibar, hair dryer, safe, CD player, bathrobe.

Hotel Pulitzer Amsterdam 🏵🏵🏵   The recently renovated Pulitzer has spread through 25 old canal houses, giving it frontage on the historic Prinsengracht and Keizersgracht canals. The houses date from the 17th and 18th centuries and adjoin one another, side by side and garden to garden. You walk between two houses to enter the lobby, or climb the steps of a former merchant's house to enter the ever-crowded and cheerful bar. With the exception of bare beams or brick walls here and there, history stops at the Pulitzer's many thresholds. Rooms are modern, with wickerwork furnishings, and impart an airy, expansive feeling to spaces that seem to have been shoehorned into the building. The rooms with the best views look out over either the canals or the hotel garden. The Pulitzer is big on culture, with its own art gallery, and every August the hotel sponsors a popular classical music concert performed by musicians on barges in the canal. As icing on the cake, the Pulitzer owns a restored saloon cruiser dating from 1909, which awaits your pleasure at the hotel's own jetty. The **Rendezvous Lounge** has a canal-side entrance and serves lunch and snacks. Pulitzer's Bar is for a quiet drink.

Prinsengracht 315-331 (near Westermarkt), 1016 GZ Amsterdam. ✆ **800/325-3589** in the U.S. and Canada, or 020/523-5235. Fax 020/627-6753. www.luxury collection.com/pulitzer. 230 units. 490€-590€ double; 1,025€ suite; add 5% city tax. AE, DC, MC, V. Valet parking 37€, self-parking 18€. Tram: 13, 14, 17 to Westermarkt. **Amenities:** Restaurant (Dutch/international); bar; cafe; concierge; business center; 24-hr. room service; babysitting; laundry service; dry cleaning; non-smoking rooms. *In room:* A/C, TV w/pay movies, dataport, minibar, coffeemaker, hair dryer, safe.

EXPENSIVE

Ambassade 🐞🐞 Perhaps more than any other hotel in Amsterdam, this one, in ten 17th- and 18th-century canal houses on the Herengracht and Singel canals, re-creates the feeling of living in an elegant canal house. The pastel-toned rooms are individually styled and their size and shape vary according to the character of the individual houses. Each year one of the houses is completely renovated. Everyone who stays at the Ambassade enjoys the view each morning with breakfast in the bi-level, chandeliered breakfast room or each evening in the adjoining parlor, with Persian rugs and a stately grandfather clock ticking away. To get to some guest rooms, you cope with a typically Dutch steep and skinny staircase, though other rooms are accessible by elevator. For the nimble-footed who can handle the stairs, the rewards are a spacious room with large multipane windows overlooking the canal.

Herengracht 335-353 (near Spui), 1016 AZ Amsterdam. ✆ 020/555-0222. Fax 020/555-0277. www.ambassade-hotel.nl. 59 units. 180€ double; 250€-315€ suite; 285€ apartment. AE, DC, MC, V. Limited street parking. Tram: 1, 2, 5 to Spui. **Amenities:** Bike rental; 24-hr. room service; massage at nearby float center; babysitting; laundry service; dry cleaning. *In room:* TV, hair dryer, safe.

Dikker & Thijs Fenice ⟨R⟩   On the Prinsengracht, at the intersection of the lively Leidsestraat, is this small and homey hotel, whose smart but cozy character is indicated by the marble-rich lobby. The stylish facade has hosted Dikker & Thijs here since 1921. Upstairs, the spacious and tastefully styled rooms are clustered in groups of two or four around small lobbies, which makes the Dikker & Thijs feel more like an apartment building than a hotel. Welcoming touches are flowers in the rooms, a subtle but elegantly modern Art Deco decor, and double-glazed windows to eliminate the noise rising up from Leidsestraat at all hours of the day and night. But some rooms are clearly in need of renovation. Those at the front have a super view of the classy Prinsengracht. The **Prinsenkelder** restaurant and bar serves good French and Italian dinners, and the adjacent cellar bar is worth a visit.

Prinsengracht 444 (at Leidsestraat), 1017 KE Amsterdam. ⓒ **020/620-1212.** Fax 020/625-8986. www.dtfh.nl. 42 units. 195€-345€ double. Rates include buffet breakfast. AE, DC, MC, V. Limited street parking. Tram: 1, 2, 5 to Prinsengracht. **Amenities:** Restaurant (international); bar; bike rental; concierge; room service; in-room massage; babysitting; laundry service; dry cleaning; nonsmoking rooms. *In room:* TV, dataport, minibar, hair dryer.

MODERATE

Agora ⟨R⟩   Old-fashioned friendliness is the keynote at this efficiently run and well-maintained lodging, a block from the Flower Market. Proprietors Yvo Muthert and Els Bruijnse like to keep things friendly and personal. Although the hotel occupies a canal house built in 1735, it has been fully restored in an eclectic style. Furniture from the 1930s and 1940s mixes with fine mahogany antiques. Bouquets greet you as you enter, and a distinctive color scheme creates an effect of peacefulness and drama at the same time. They have installed an abundance of overstuffed furniture; nearly every room has a puffy armchair you can sink into after a wearying day of sightseeing. Upgrading of the bathrooms is proceeding apace and all beds have been recently renewed. Rooms with a canal view cost the most, but the extra few euros are worth it, though the hustle and bustle out on the street can make them somewhat noisy by day; the large family room has three windows overlooking the Singel. Those rooms that don't have a canal view look out on a pretty garden at the back.

Singel 462 (at Koningsplein), 1017 AW Amsterdam. ⓒ **020/627-2200.** Fax 020/627-2202. www.hotelagora.nl. 16 units, 13 with bathroom. 90€-127€ double with bathroom, 72€ double without bathroom. Rates include buffet breakfast. AE, DC, MC, V. Limited street parking. Tram: 1, 2, 5 to Koningsplein. *In room:* TV, hair dryer.

Amsterdam Wiechmann ⭐   It takes only a moment to feel at home in the antiques-adorned Amsterdam Wiechmann. Owned by American T. Boddy and his Dutch wife, Nicky, for a number of years, the Wiechmann is a classic, comfortable, casual sort of place, in spite of the suit of armor you encounter just inside the front door. Besides, the location is one of the best you find in this or any price range: 5 minutes in one direction is the Kalverstraat shopping street; 5 minutes in the other, Leidseplein. Most of the rooms are standard, with good-size twin beds or double beds, and some have big bay windows. Furnishings are elegant, and Oriental rugs grace many of the floors in the public spaces. The higher-priced doubles have antique furnishings, and many have a view of the Prinsengracht. The breakfast room has hardwood floors, lots of greenery, and white linen cloths on the tables. There is a lounge and bar.

Prinsengracht 328-332 (at Looiersgracht), 1016 HX Amsterdam. © 020/626-3321. Fax 020/626-8962. www.hotelwiechmann.nl. 40 units. 120€-140€ double. Rates include continental breakfast. MC, V. Limited street parking. Tram: 1, 2, 5 to Prinsengracht. **Amenities:** Bar. *In room:* TV, safe.

Canal House ⭐   A contemporary approach to reestablishing the elegant canal-house atmosphere has been taken by the American proprietor of the Canal House Hotel. This small hotel below Raadhuisstraat is in three adjoining houses that date from 1630; they were gutted and rebuilt to provide private bathrooms and filled with antiques, quilts, and Chinese rugs. Fortunately, it's blessed with an elevator (though one that does not stop at every floor, so you may still have to walk a short distance up or down stairs), along with a (steep) staircase that still has its beautifully carved old balustrade, and overlooking the back garden, which is illuminated at night, a magnificent breakfast room that seems to have been untouched since the 17th century. Plus, on the parlor floor, the proprietor has created a cozy Victorian-era saloon. It is, in short, a home away from home.

Keizersgracht 148 (near Leliegracht), 1015 CX Amsterdam. © 020/622-5182. Fax 020/624-1317. www.canalhouse.nl. 26 units. 150€-190€ double. Rates include continental breakfast. DC, MC, V. Limited street parking. Tram: 13, 14, 17 to Westermarkt. **Amenities:** Lounge; limited room service. *In room:* hair dryer.

Estheréa ⭐⭐ *Kids*   The Estheréa has been owned by the same family since its beginnings and is built within the walls of neighboring 17th-century canal houses. The family touch shows in careful attention to detail and a breezy but professional approach. It offers the blessed advantage of an elevator, a rarity in these old Amsterdam homes. In the 1930s, the proprietors spent a lot of money on wood paneling and other structural additions; more recent proprietors have had the good sense to leave all of it in place. While it will look dated to some, the wood bedsteads and dresser-desks in fact lend warmth to the recently renovated and upgraded rooms. The room sizes vary considerably according to their location in the canal houses, and a few are quite small, though not seriously so. Most of the rooms will accommodate two, but some rooms have more beds, which make them ideal for families. The excellent small Greek restaurant **Traîterie Grekas,** next door (see chapter 4 for full details), provides room-service meals.

Singel 303-309 (near Spui), 1012 WJ Amsterdam. © 020/624-5146. Fax 020/623-9001. www.estherea.nl. 75 units. 154€-260€ double; add 5% city tax. AE, DC, MC, V. Limited street parking. Tram: 1, 2, 5, to Spui. **Amenities:** Bar; bike rental; concierge; limited room service; babysitting; laundry service; dry cleaning; non-smoking rooms. *In room:* TV, minibar, hair dryer, safe.

Rembrandt Residence

Following the example of the Hotel Pulitzer, the Rembrandt Residence was built anew within old walls. In this case the structures are a wide 18th-century building on a canal above Raadhuistraat and four small 16th-century houses directly behind it on the Singel canal. The look of the place is best described as basic, but rooms tend to be large (in all sizes and shapes). Some still have their old fireplaces (not working) with elegant wood or marble mantels. And as you walk around, occasionally you see an old beam or pass through a former foyer on the way to your room. Hair dryers are available at the reception desk.

Herengracht 255 (at Hartenstraat), 1016 BJ Amsterdam. © 020/623-6638. Fax 020/625-0630. www.bookings.nl/hotels/rembrandt. 111 units. 100€-160€ double; 220€ executive room. AE, DC, MC, V. Limited street parking. Tram: 1, 2, 5, 13, 14, 17 to the Dam. *In room:* TV.

Seven Bridges ✦✦

Proprietors Pierre Keulers and Gunter Glaner have made the Seven Bridges, which gets its name from its view of seven arched bridges, one of Amsterdam's gems. Each room is individual. There are antique furnishings (Art Deco, Biedemeyer, Louis XVI, rococo), handmade Italian drapes, hand-painted tiles and wood-tiled floors, and Impressionist art posters on the walls. The biggest room, on the first landing, can accommodate up to four and has a huge bathroom with marble floor, double sinks, a fair-size shower, and a separate area for the lavatory (the sink and shower even have gold-plated taps). The room is enormous, with high ceilings, a big mirror over the fireplace, an Empire onyx table and antique leather armchairs, and an array of potted plants. Attic rooms have sloped ceilings and exposed wood beams, and there are big, bright basement rooms done almost entirely in white.

Reguliersgracht 31 (at Keizersgracht), 1017 LK Amsterdam. ℂ 020/623-1329. 8 units. 110€–200€ double. Rates include full breakfast. AE, MC, V. Limited street parking. Tram: 16, 24, 25 to Keizersgracht. *In room:* TV, hair dryer.

Singel Hotel ⚘ Style marries tradition in the elegant little Singel, near the head of the Brouwersgracht in one of the most pleasant and central locations in Amsterdam. Three renovated canal houses have been united in harmony to create this hotel. The decor is bright and welcoming. The modernly furnished rooms are spacious for a small hotel. Some of the rooms have an attractive view of the Singel canal. An elevator services the building's four floors.

Singel 13 (near Centraal Station), 1012 VC Amsterdam. ℂ 020/626-3108. Fax 020/620-3777. www.lempereur-hotels.nl. 32 units. 120€–150€ double. Rates include buffet breakfast. AE, DC, MC, V. Limited street parking. Tram: 1, 2, 4, 5, 9, 13, 16, 17, 24, 25 to Centraal Station. *In room:* TV, hair dryer.

Toren ⚘ The Toren is a sprawling enterprise that encompasses two buildings, separated by neighboring houses. With so many rooms, it's a better bet than most canal-house hotels during the tourist seasons in Amsterdam. Clean, attractive, and well maintained, the Toren promises private facilities with every room, though in a few cases that means a private bathroom located off the public hall (with your own private key, however). There's a bridal suite here, complete with a blue canopy and a Jacuzzi. There's also a little private guesthouse off the garden that's done up in Laura Ashley prints. All this and a canalside location, too.

Keizersgracht 164 (near Leliegracht), 1015 CZ Amsterdam. ℂ 020/622-6352. Fax 020/626-9705. www.toren.nl. 43 units. 120€–205€ double; 230€ suite; add 5% city tax. AE, DC, MC, V. Limited street parking. Tram: 13, 14, 17 to Westermarkt. **Amenities:** Bar; room service; babysitting; laundry service; dry cleaning. *In room:* TV w/pay movies, fax, dataport, minibar, coffeemaker, hair dryer, safe.

INEXPENSIVE

Hoksbergen ⚘ At a tranquil point on the historic Singel canal, this inexpensive hotel in a 300-year-old canal house is not flashy or elegant, but it's bright and fresh and recently renovated, which makes it appealing to budget-conscious travelers who don't want to swap creature comforts for euros. Its central location makes it easy to get to all the surrounding sights and attractions. Rooms at the front have a canal view.

Singel 301 (near Spui), 1012 WH Amsterdam. ℂ 020/626-6043. Fax 020/638-3479. www.hotelhoksbergen.com. 14 units. 76€–90€ double. Rates include continental breakfast. AE, DC, MC, V. Limited street parking. Tram: 1, 2, 5 to Spui. *In room:* TV.

Keizershof 𝒜   Owned by the genial De Vries family, this hotel in a four-story canal-house from 1672 has six rooms named after movie stars—though a greater claim to fame is that members of the Dutch royal family were regular visitors in its prehotel days. Several other touches make a stay here memorable. From the street-level entrance a wooden spiral staircase built from a ship's mast leads to the beamed rooms. Note that there's no elevator. There is, however, a television and a grand piano in the cozy lounge. In good weather, breakfast, which includes excellent omelets and pancakes, is served in the flower-bedecked courtyard. Because the hotel, which is non-smoking, has so few rooms, you need to book well ahead.

Keizersgracht 618 (at Nieuwe Spiegelstraat), 1017 ER Amsterdam. ℂ 020/622-2855. Fax 020/624-8412. www.vdwp.nl/keizershof. 6 units, 3 with bathroom. 90€ double with bathroom, 70€–75€ double without bathroom. Rates include full breakfast. MC, V. Limited street parking. Tram: 16, 24, 25 to Keizersgracht. *In room:* Coffeemaker, hair dryer, safe, no phone.

Prinsenhof 𝒜   A modernized canal house near the Amstel River, this hotel offers rooms with beamed ceilings and basic yet reasonably comfortable beds. The place has been recently refurbished, and new showers and carpets installed. Front rooms look out onto the Prinsengracht, where colorful houseboats are moored. Breakfast is served in an attractive blue-and-white decorated dining room. The proprietors, Rik and André van Houten, take pride in their hotel and will make you feel welcome. There's no elevator, but a pulley hauls your luggage up and down the stairs.

Prinsengracht 810 (at Utrechtsestraat), 1017 JL Amsterdam. ℂ 020/623-1772. Fax 020/638-3368. www.hotelprinsenhof.com. 10 units, 3 with bathroom. 80€ double with bathroom, 60€ double without bathroom. Rates include continental breakfast. AE, MC, V. Limited street parking. Tram: 4 to Prinsengracht.

3 Around Leidseplein

VERY EXPENSIVE

Crowne Plaza Amsterdam-American 𝒜𝒜𝒜   One of the most fascinating buildings on Amsterdam's long list of monuments is this fanciful, castlelike mix of Venetian Gothic and Art Nouveau, which has been both a prominent landmark and a popular meeting place for Amsterdammers since 1900. While the exterior of the American must always remain an architectural treasure (and curiosity) of turrets, arches, and balconies, in accordance with the regulations of the National Monument Care Office, the interior of the hotel (except that of the cafe, which is also protected) is modern and chic, though at times a bit gaudy. Rooms are subdued and refined, superbly furnished, and while some have a view of the Singelgracht, others overlook kaleidoscopic Leidseplein. They are always pink and bright, which perhaps appeals to the international rock stars, who often stay here. The location, in the thick of the action and near many major attractions, is one of the best in town. The famous **Café Americain** is one of the most elegant eateries in Europe (see chapter 5). There is also the **Bar Americain,** which has a closed-in terrace looking out on Leidseplein.

Leidsekade 97 (at Leidseplein), 1017 PN Amsterdam. © 020/556-3000. Fax 020/556-3001. www.amsterdam-american.crowneplaza.com. 174 units. 290€-405€ double; 470€-505€ suite; add 5% city tax. AE, DC, MC, V. No parking. Tram: 1, 2, 5, 6, 7, 10 to Leidseplein. **Amenities:** Restaurant (Continental); bar; exercise room; sauna; concierge; 24-hr. room service; in-room massage; laundry service; same-day dry cleaning. *In room:* A/C, TV w/pay movies, dataport, minibar, coffeemaker, hair dryer, iron, safe.

MODERATE

Orfeo One of the city's longest-standing gay lodgings has for more than 30 years been providing basic, practical facilities and friendly, helpful service at low rates. The front desk is in a cozy and sociable lounge and there is a marble-floored breakfast room. Only three guest rooms have a full bathroom, some with charming beamed ceilings; others share shower and/or toilet. One of the perks is a small in-house Finnish sauna; and the largest concentration of city-center restaurants is right on the doorstep.

Leidsekruisstraat 14 (off Leidseplein), 1017 RH Amsterdam. © 020/623-1347. Fax 020/620-2348. www.hotelorfeo.com. 17 units, 3 with bathroom. 105€-122€ double with bathroom, 79€-83€ double without bathroom. Rates include continental breakfast. AE, MC, V. Limited street parking. Tram: 1, 2, 5 to Prinsengracht. *In room:* TV, minibar, hair dryer, safe.

4 Around Rembrandtplein

EXPENSIVE

NH Schiller Hotel 🕿🕿 A historic Amsterdam gem, now fully restored, this hotel boasts a blend of Art Nouveau and Art Deco in its public spaces that is reflected in tasteful decor and furnishings in the rooms. Its sculpted facade, wrought-iron balconies, and stained-glass windows stand out on the often brash Rembrandtplein. **Café Schiller,** next door to the hotel, is one of the trendiest watering holes in town. The hotel takes its name from the painter Frits Schiller, who built it in 1912. His outpourings of artistic expression, in the form of 600 portraits, landscapes, and still lifes, are displayed in the halls, rooms, stairwells, and public areas; and their presence fills this hotel with a unique sense of vitality, creativity, and personality. Perhaps the happiest outcome of the revitalization of the Schiller is the new life it brings to the hotel's gracious oak-paneled dining room and to the Café Schiller, one of Amsterdam's few permanent, and perfectly situated, sidewalk cafes. Experience classic French and Dutch cuisine and the hotel's own beer, Frisse Frits, in the Art Nouveau **Brasserie Schiller** (see chapter 4 for more details), or join the in crowd next door for a drink amid the Art Deco splendor of the Café Schiller.

Rembrandtplein 26-36, 1017 CV Amsterdam. ℂ 020/554-0700. Fax 020/624-0098. www.nh-hotels.nl/nhschiller. 92 units. 220€-270€ double; from 300€ suite. AE, DC, MC, V. Limited street parking. Tram: 4, 9, 14 to Rembrandtplein. **Amenities:** Restaurant (Dutch); 2 bars; health club; 24-hr. room service; babysitting; laundry service; dry cleaning. *In room:* TV, minibar, coffeemaker, hair dryer.

5 In the Jordaan

INEXPENSIVE

Acacia 𝒢   Not on one of the major canals, but in the Jordaan, facing a small canal, just a block from the Prinsengracht, the Acacia, shaped like a slice of cake, is run by Hans and Marlene van Vliet, a friendly couple who have worked hard to make their hotel welcoming, clean, and well kept, and are justifiably proud of the result. Simple, clean, and comfortable, the rooms have recently been equipped with new beds, writing tables, and chairs. They all have canal views. Breakfast is served in a triangular breakfast room. With windows on two sides, a nice view of the canal, and a breakfast of cold cuts, cheese, a boiled egg, and a choice of coffee or tea, it's a lovely way to start the morning. Two houseboats for guests on nearby Lijnbaansgracht add an authentic local touch—but what might seem like the earth moving for you may be only the wake from a passing boat roiling the water and setting your houseboat bobbing.

Lindengracht 251 (at Lijnbaansgracht), 1015 KH, Amsterdam. ℂ 020/622-1460. Fax 020/638-0748. 18 units. 85€ double; 120€ houseboat double. Rates include continental breakfast. MC, V (5% charge). Limited street parking. Tram: 3 to Nieuwe Willemstraat. *In room:* TV.

Van Onna   Consisting of three canal houses, this hotel has grown over the years, but genial owner Loek van Onna continues to keep his prices reasonable. Mr. van Onna has lived here since he was a boy and will gladly tell you about the building's history. Accommodations vary considerably, with the best rooms in the newest building. However, the oldest and simplest rooms also have a great deal of charm. Whichever building you wind up in, ask for a room in front overlooking the canal.

Bloemgracht 102-104 and 108 (off Prinsengracht), 1015 TN Amsterdam. © 020/626-5801. 39 units, 30 with bathroom. 45€ double with bathroom, 35€ double without bathroom. Rates include continental breakfast. No credit cards. Limited street parking. Tram: 13, 14, 17 to Westermarkt. **Amenities:** Lounge.

6 Around Museumplein & Vondelpark

EXPENSIVE

Bilderberg Hotel Jan Luyken 🏛🏛 One block from the Van Gogh Museum and from the elegant Pieter Cornelisz Hooftstraat shopping street, the Jan Luyken is best described as a small hotel with many of the amenities and facilities of a big hotel. Everything here is done with perfect attention to detail. The Jan Luyken maintains a balance between its sophisticated lineup of facilities (double sinks and bidets, elevator, lobby bar with fireplace, and meeting rooms for business) and an intimate and personalized approach that's appropriate to this 19th-century residential neighborhood. That residential feel extends to the rooms, which look much more like a well-designed home than a standard hotel room. The proprietors are proud of the atmosphere they've created, and are constantly improving the look of the hotel.

Jan Luykenstraat 58 (near the Rijksmuseum), 1071 CS Amsterdam. © 800/641-0300 in the U.S. and Canada, or 020/573-0730. Fax 020/676-3841. www.jan luyken.nl. 62 units. 180€-295€ double; add 5% city tax. AE, DC, MC, V. Limited street parking. Tram: 2, 5 to Hobbemastraat. **Amenities:** Winebar; spa; concierge; 24-hr. room service; in-room massage; babysitting; laundry service; dry cleaning; nonsmoking rooms. *In room:* A/C, TV, dataport, minibar, hair dryer, iron, safe.

MODERATE

Acro 🏛 The Acro, in a town house on a fairly quiet street near Vondelpark and close to the main museums, tends to appeal especially to young travelers. The hotel is modern on the inside, with crisp-and-clean bedspreads and furniture and walls all colored light blue-gray. Most rooms have twin beds—some have three and some four. You find more ambience in the hotel bar than in many street cafes. The Acro is definitely value for your money.

Jan Luykenstraat 44 (near the Rijksmuseum), 1071 CR Amsterdam. ℂ **020/662-5538.** Fax 020/675-0811. 65 units. 125€ double. Rates include continental breakfast. AE, DC, MC, V. Parking 25€. Tram: 2, 3, 5, 12 to Van Baerlestraat. **Amenities:** Bar. *In room:* TV, hair dryer.

AMS Toro   On the fringes of Vondelpark in a quiet residential district, this beautiful hotel in a completely renovated mansion dating from 1900 is one of Amsterdam's top moderately priced choices. Both on the inside and the outside, it is as near as you can get in Amsterdam to staying in a country villa. The house is furnished and decorated with taste, combining Louis XIV and Liberty styles and featuring stained-glass windows and Murano chandeliers. The guest rooms are worthy of being featured in *Better Homes & Gardens.* The house also affords guests a private garden and terrace. It's about a 10-minute walk through Vondelpark to Leidseplein.

Koningslaan 64 (off Oranje Nassaulaan), 1075 AG Amsterdam. ℂ **020/673-7223.** Fax 020/675-0031. 22 units. www.ams.nl. 185€ double. AE, MC, V. Limited street parking. Tram: 2 to Valeriusplein. **Amenities:** Laundry service; dry cleaning, nonsmoking rooms. *In room:* TV, minibar, hair dryer, safe.

Atlas   Off Van Baerlestraat, the Atlas is a converted house with a convenient location for shoppers, concertgoers, and museum lovers. The staff backs up the homey feel with attentive service. The guest rooms are small but tidy, decorated attractively in gray with blue comforters on the beds and a welcoming basket of fruit on the desk. Leather chairs fill the front lounge, which has a grandfather clock ticking in the corner.

Van Eeghenstraat 64 (near Vondelpark), 1071 GK Amsterdam. ℂ **020/676-6336.** Fax 020/671 7633. 23 units. 110€ double. Rates include continental breakfast. AE, DC, MC, V. Limited street parking. Tram: 2, 3, 5, 12 to Van Baerlestraat. **Amenities:** Restaurant; bar; room service; dry cleaning/laundry service. *In room:* TV; a hair dryer is available at the reception desk.

De Filosoof 𝒦𝒦 *Finds*   On a quiet street facing Vondelpark, this hotel might be the very place if you fancy yourself as something of a philosopher king or queen. One of the proprietors, a philosophy professor, has chosen posters, painted ceilings, framed quotes, and unusual objects to represent philosophical and cultural themes. Each room is dedicated to a mental maestro—Goethe, Wittgenstein, Nietzsche, Marx, and Einstein are among those who get a look-in—or are based on motifs like Eros, the Renaissance, astrology, and women. Rooms in an annex across the street are larger; some open onto a private terrace. Recent all-round improvements in service and facilities have raised the hotel's local rating.

Anna van den Vondelstraat 6 (off Overtoom, at Vondelpark), 1054 GZ Amsterdam. © 020/683-3013. Fax 020/685-3750. www.hotelfilosoof.nl. 38 units. 92€-122€ double. Rates include buffet breakfast. AE, MC, V. Limited street parking. Tram: 1, 6 to Jan Pieter Heijestraat. **Amenities:** Lounge. *In room:* TV, hair dryer, safe.

Piet Hein Facing Vondelpark, and close to the city's most important museums, this appealing, well-kept hotel is in a villa named after a 17th-century Dutch admiral who captured a Spanish silver shipment. Its spacious rooms are well furnished and the staff is charming and professional. Half the rooms overlook the park, two second-floor double rooms have semicircular balconies, and the honeymoon suite has a water bed. The lower-priced rooms are in an annex behind the main hotel. Hair dryers are available on request.

Vossiusstraat 52-53 (off Van Baerlestraat), 1071 AK Amsterdam. © 020/662-7205. Fax 020/662-1526. www.hotelpiethein.com. 65 units. 115€-155€ double. Rates include continental breakfast. AE, DC, MC, V. Limited street parking. Tram: 3, 5, 12 to Van Baerlestraat. **Amenities:** Bar; concierge; limited room service; laundry service; dry cleaning; nonsmoking rooms. *In room:* TV w/pay movies.

Vondel Named after the famous 17th-century Dutch poet Joost Van den Vondel, this five-floor hotel opened in late 1993 and has since become one of the leading three-star hotels in Amsterdam. Each room is named after one of Vondel's poems, like Lucifer or Solomon. Three of the rooms (all with soundproof windows) are on the first floor and are ideal for travelers with disabilities. The furniture is solid, the rooms are spacious, and the service is good. This is a comfortable place, conveniently located in a quiet and popular area close to the museum area and Leidseplein.

Vondelstraat 28-30 (off Stadhouderskade), 1054 GE Amsterdam. © 020/612-0120. Fax 020/685-4321. 74 units. 170€-205€ double; 275€ suite. Rates include continental breakfast. AE, DC, MC, V. Limited street parking. Tram: 1, 6 to Eerste Constantijn Huygensstraat; 3, 12 to Overtoom. *In room:* TV, minibar, hair dryer.

Zandbergen Beside Vondelpark, this place nearly outdoes the Amstel in its use of shiny brass handrails and door handles. Rebuilt in 1979, and modernized since then, the Zandbergen has been efficiently divided into a variety of room types and sizes by the use of simple but attractive brick wall dividers between rooms. Wall-to-wall carpets and a color scheme based on bright tones of sand and blue-gray make the rooms seem more spacious and inviting, and all are outfitted with some flair and have good comfortable beds. There's also a great family-size room with a garden patio for between two and four guests. Recent improvements include new bathrooms and air-conditioning in the reception and breakfast area.

Willemsparkweg 205 (at Vondelpark), 1071 HB Amsterdam. ℭ **020/676-9321.** Fax 020/676-1860. www.hotel-zandbergen.com. 21 units. 130€ double. Rates include buffet breakfast. AE, DC, MC, V. Limited street parking. Tram: 2 to Emmastraat. **Amenities:** Laundry service; dry cleaning; nonsmoking rooms. *In room:* TV, dataport, minibar, coffeemaker, hair dryer.

INEXPENSIVE

Museumzicht   This hotel in a Victorian house across from the back of the Rijksmuseum is ideal for museum-goers on a budget. The breakfast room commands an excellent view of the museum with its numerous stained-glass windows. Robin de Jong, the proprietor, has filled the rooms with an eclectic furniture collection, from 1930s English wicker to 1950s pieces. There's no elevator and the staircase up to reception is pretty steep.

Jan Luykenstraat 22 (near the Rijksmuseum), 1071 CN Amsterdam. ℭ **020/671-2954.** Fax 020/671-3597. 14 units, 3 with bathroom. 58€ double without bathroom, 80€ double with bathroom. Rates include continental breakfast. AE, DC, MC, V. Limited street parking. Tram: 2, 5 to Hobbemastraat. *In room:* No phone.

Owl ✿   If small but chic and reasonably priced seems to describe the sort of hotel you prefer, you'll be pleased to learn about the Owl, located in the pleasant residential area around Vondelpark, behind the Marriott. One of Amsterdam's best buys, the Owl Hotel has been owned by the same family since 1972 and is bright, tidy, and well kept. Rooms are not very big but are not cramped, and have all been renovated recently. The bathrooms are tiled floor to ceiling. There's also a pleasant lounge/bar overlooking a small garden.

Roemer Visscherstraat 1 (off Stadhouderskade), 1054 EV Amsterdam. ℭ **020/618-9484.** Fax 020/618-9441. www.owl-hotel.demon.nl. 34 units. 92€-112€ double. Rates include buffet breakfast. AE, DC, MC, V. Limited street parking. Tram: 1, 6 to Stadhouderskade. **Amenities:** Bar; concierge; limited room service; babysitting; laundry service; dry cleaning. *In room:* TV, hair dryer.

P. C. Hooft ✿   Imagine staying on Amsterdam's most upscale shopping street, amid chic boutiques and classy restaurants, for no more than you'd pay in any other budget hotel in town. One of the spiffiest little budget lodgings in town, the P. C. Hooft seems to have picked up a sense of style from the smart shops on the street without picking up their tendency toward upscale pricing. The guest rooms are bright and tidy, and the building houses a coffeeshop, which is a handy spot to stop for a quick bite before you hit the sights or the shops. You have to climb quite a few stairs to enjoy your stay, though. Most rooms have been updated. The breakfast room, guaranteed to wake you up, is painted wild shades of orange and blue.

Pieter Cornelisz Hooftstraat 63 (near the Van Gogh Museum), 1071 BN Amsterdam. ℂ 020/662-7107. Fax 020/675-8961. 16 units, 3 with bathroom. 55€ double with bathroom, 45€ double without bathroom. Rates include continental breakfast. MC, V. Limited street parking. Tram: 2, 5 to Hobbemastraat. *In room:* TV.

Wynnobel 𝒦 *Finds* Just around the corner from the boutiques on Pieter Cornelisz Hooftstraat and only a few minutes' walk from the Rijksmuseum, the hotel overlooks a corner of Vondelpark and is owned by the Wynnobel family, who always make sure the hotel is clean and their guests are happy. One way they achieve this is by serving you breakfast in bed, if you want it. In addition, Pierre, the head of the family, plays some perfectly acceptable Gershwin, Cole Porter, and Chopin on the piano. The large rooms are furnished with old-fashioned or antique pieces. A steep but striking central stairway leads to the hotel's four floors.

Vossiusstraat 9 (at Vondelpark), 1071 AB Amsterdam. ℂ 020/662-2298. 12 units, none with bathroom. 60€-75€ double. Rates include continental breakfast. No credit cards. Limited street parking. Tram: 2, 5 to Hobbemastraat. **Amenities:** Lounge. *In room:* No phone.

7 In Amsterdam East

VERY EXPENSIVE

Amstel Inter-Continental Amsterdam 𝒦𝒦𝒦 The stately Amstel, grande dame of Dutch hotels since its opening in 1867, offers the ultimate in luxury. This is the Rolls Royce of Amsterdam hotels, a place for visiting royalty and superstars hiding from eager fans. Its only possible fault is that it may seem to run a bit *too* smoothly. The hotel sports a mansard roof and wrought-iron window guards, a graceful Grand Hall, and rooms that boast all the elegance of a country manor, complete with antiques and genuine Delft blue porcelain. The Italian marble bathrooms have separate toilets and showers. The staff notes each guest's personal preferences for their next visit. The French La Rive restaurant is one of the hallowed temples of Amsterdam cuisine (see chapter 4 for details). The **Amstel Lounge, Amstel Bar & Brasserie,** and terraces overlooking the river are more informal.

Prof. Tulpplein 1 (at the Torontobrug over the Amstel River), 1018 GX Amsterdam. ℂ 800/327-1177 in the U.S. and Canada, or 020/622-6060. Fax 020/622-5808. http://amsterdam.interconti.com. 79 units. 470€-550€ double; from 750€ suite; add 5% city tax. AE, DC, MC, V. Tram: 6, 7, 10 to Weesperplein. **Amenities:** Restaurant (French); lounge; bar-brasserie; heated indoor pool; health club; Jacuzzi; sauna; concierge; limo; 24-hr. room service; massage; laundry service; dry cleaning. *In room:* A/C, TV w/pay movies, minibar.

MODERATE

Bridge Hotel 🐸🐸   The bridge in question is the famous Magere Brug (Skinny Bridge) over the Amstel River. The small and tastefully decorated hotel likely provides its guests with more space per euro than any other hotel in town. Its pine-furnished rooms seem like studio apartments, with couches, coffee tables, and easy chairs arranged in lounge areas in such a way that there's plenty of room left between them and the beds for you to do your morning exercises.

Amstel 107-111 (near Theater Carré), 1018 EM Amsterdam. ℂ 020/623-7068. Fax 020/624-1565. www.thebridgehotel.nl. 36 units. 85€-130€; double. Rates include continental breakfast. AE, DC, MC, V. Limited street parking. Tram: 6, 7, 10 to Weesperplein. **Amenities:** Bar. *In room:* TV.

Hotel Arena 🐸   A converted Roman Catholic orphanage from 1890 houses a friendly, stylish, youth-oriented hotel. For all that the exterior bears a passing resemblance to Dracula's castle, the interior proves they really knew how to do an orphanage in those days. Monumental marble staircases, cast-iron banisters, stained-glass windows, marble columns, original murals—all have been faithfully restored. Spare modern rooms, some sporting timber roof beams and wooden floors, line long high-ceilinged corridors on two floors. Each room is individually decorated and styled by up-and-coming young Dutch designers. Some are split-level. Meeting and reception facilities, and spaces for art exhibits and other cultural events, signal a shift away from the Arena's history as a backpackers' rendezvous to a lodging with broader appeal. You still see kids toting backpacks, but they're a better class of backpack than those that clog corridors in the city's hostels and cheap hotels. The continental cafe-restaurant **To Dine** looks a little like an upgraded cafeteria on the inside, but has a great alfresco terrace in the garden and an attached bar, **To Drink.** Hotel guests get a discount on concerts and dance nights in the nightclub **Tonight,** which puts up music from the 1960s onward in the old orphanage chapel. The Arena is a bit removed from the center, but isn't too far away, and the traffic is two-way, with youthful revelers heading out here to the nightspot and the outdoor cafe.

's-Gravesandestraat 51 (at Mauritskade), 1092 AA Amsterdam. ℂ 020/850-2410. Fax 020/850-2415. www.hotelarena.nl. 121 units. 102€-149€ double, 149€-173€ split-level double. Rates include buffet breakfast. AE, DC, MC, V. Free parking. Tram: 7, 10 to Korte 's-Gravesandestraat. **Amenities:** Restaurant (Continental); bar; executive rooms. *In room:* TV.

8 In Amsterdam South

EXPENSIVE

Bilderberg Garden Hotel 👁👁👁   This is the smallest and most personal five-star hotel in town. Because of its excellent **Mangerie de Kersentuin** restaurant, the Garden considers itself a "culinary hotel," an idea that extends to the rooms, whose color schemes are salad-green, salmon-pink, cherry-red, and grape-blue—and you can choose whichever suits you best. The rooms themselves are furnished and equipped to the highest standards and with refined taste; only executive rooms have coffeemakers. Bathrooms are in marble, and each is equipped with a Jacuzzi tub. The Garden's spectacular lobby has a wall-to-wall fireplace with a copper-sheathed chimney. The French Mangerie de Kersentuin (Cherry Orchard) restaurant, a member of Les Etappes du Bon Goût, has an international reputation (see chapter 4 for full details) and moderate prices. The **Kersepit** (Cherry Pit) is a cozy bar with an open fireplace and a vast range of Scotch whiskeys.

Dijsselhofplantsoen 7 (at Apollolaan), 1077 BJ Amsterdam. 📞 **0800/641-0300** in the U.S. and Canada, or 020/570-5600. Fax 020/570-5654. www.gardenhotel.nl. 124 units. 325€ double; 370€ executive double; add 5% city tax. AE, DC, MC, V. Limited street parking. Tram: 5, 24 to Apollolaan. **Amenities:** Restaurant (French/Mediterranean); bar; concierge; business center; access to nearby health club; 24-hr. room service; in-room massage; babysitting; laundry service; same-day dry cleaning; nonsmoking rooms; executive rooms. *In room:* A/C, TV w/pay movies, fax, dataport, minibar, hair dryer, safe.

MODERATE

Apollofirst 👁   The small and very elegant Apollofirst, a family owned hotel set amid the Amsterdam school architecture of Apollolaan, advertises itself as the "best quarters in town in the town's best quarter." Their claim may be debatable, but the Venman family's justifiable pride in their establishment is not. All the accommodations of this intimate hotel are quiet, spacious, and grandly furnished. Bathrooms are fully tiled, and rooms at the back of the hotel overlook the well-kept gardens of the hotel and its neighbors, and the summer terrace where guests can have a snack or a cocktail. The hotel's elegant **Restaurant Chambertin** is a French *fin de siècle* affair.

Apollolaan 123 (off Minervalaan), 1077 AP Amsterdam. 📞 **020/577-3800.** Fax 020/675-0348. www.apollofirst.nl. 40 units. 125€-170€ double; 275€ suite. Rates include continental breakfast. AE, DC, MC, V. Limited street parking. Tram: 5, 24 to Apollolaan. **Amenities:** Bar; 24-hr. room service; laundry service; dry cleaning. *In room:* TV.

INEXPENSIVE

Van Ostade Bicycle Hotel 🐕🐕   The young proprietors of this establishment have hit on an interesting idea: They cater to visitors who wish to explore Amsterdam on bikes and they are helpful in planning biking routes through and around the city. You can rent bikes for 5€ daily, no deposit, and stable your trusty steed indoors. The recently renovated rooms have new carpets and plain but comfortable modern furnishings; some have kitchenettes and small balconies, and there are large rooms for families. The hotel is a few blocks from the popular Albert Cuyp street market, in the somewhat raggedy De Pijp neighborhood. An old bike hangs on the hotel's facade, and there are always bikes parked in front.

Van Ostadestraat 123 (off Ferdinand Bolstraat), Amsterdam 1072 SV. ℰ **020/679-3452.** Fax 020/671-5213. www.bicyclehotel.com. 16 units, 8 with bathroom. 99€ double with bathroom, 61€-70€ double without bathroom. Rates include continental breakfast. No credit cards. Parking 20€. Tram: 24, 25 to Ceintuurbaan. **Amenities:** Bike rental. *In room:* TV.

4

Where to Dine

If cities get the cuisine they deserve, this one's ought to be liberal, multiethnic, and adventurous. Guess what? It is. As a port and trading city with a true melting-pot character, Amsterdam has absorbed culinary influences from far, wide, and yonder, and rustled them all up to its own satisfaction. More than 50 different national cuisines are served at its restaurants. Better yet, many of these eateries satisfy the sturdy Dutch insistence on getting maximum value out of each guilder spent.

From elegant 17th-century dining rooms to cozy canalside bistros, to exuberant taverns with equally exuberant Greek attendants to exotic Indonesian rooms attended by turbaned waiters, to the *bruine kroegjes* (brown cafes) with their smoke-stained walls and friendly table conversations, the eateries of Amsterdam confront the tourist with the exquisite agony of being able to choose only one or two from their vast numbers each day. Dutch cooking, of course, is part of all this, but you won't be stuck with *biefstuk* (beefsteak) and *kip* (chicken) every night, unless you want to be. Dutch practicality has also produced a wide selection of restaurants in all price ranges.

There are a few distinctively **Dutch foods** whose availability is seasonal. Among them: asparagus, beautifully white and tender, in May; "new" herring, fresh from the North Sea and eaten raw, in May or early June (great excitement surrounds the first catch of the season, part of which goes to the queen and the rest to restaurateurs amid spirited competition); and Zeeland oysters and mussels (*Zeeuwsoesters* and *Zeeuwsmosselen*), from September to March.

Since a 15% service charge is automatically included in the prices shown on the menus, you needn't leave a tip beyond the amount shown on the tab—but if you want to do as the Dutch do, round up to the next euro or two, or in the case of a large check, up to the next 5 or 10 euros.

On the weekends, unless you eat especially early or late, reservations are generally recommended at top restaurants and at those on the high end of the moderate price range. A call ahead to check is a good idea at any time in Amsterdam, where restaurants are often

Tips **Good-Eats Cafes**

For good, low-cost food, look out for examples of that Dutch dining institution, the _eetcafé_ (pronounced _ayt_-caff-ay). Many of these places—some of which are reviewed below—are essentially brown cafes (bars) with a hardworking kitchen attached. The food is generally unpretentious, mainstream Dutch (though some are more adventurous), and the price for their _dagschotel_ (plate of the day), which might come with meat, vegetable, and salad all on one large plate, is usually in the 6€ to 10€ range.

---

small and may be crowded with neighborhood devotees. Note that restaurants with outside terraces are always in big demand on pleasant summer evenings; make a reservation, if the restaurant will let you—if not, get there early or forget it.

Dutch national dishes tend to be of the ungarnished, hearty, wholesome variety—solid, stick-to-your-ribs stuff. A perfect example is _erwtensoep,_ a thick pea soup cooked with ham or sausage that provides inner warmth against cold Dutch winters and is filling enough to be a meal by itself. Similarly, _hutspot,_ a potato-based "hotchpotch," or stew, is no-nonsense nourishment that becomes even more so with the addition of _klapstuk_ (lean beef).

Seafood, as you might imagine in this traditionally seafaring country, is always fresh and simply—but well—prepared. Fried sole, oysters from Zeeland, mussels, and herring (fresh in May, pickled other months) are most common. In fact, if you happen to be in Holland for the beginning of the herring season, it's an absolute obligation—at least once—to interrupt your sidewalk strolls for a "green" (raw) herring with onions from a fish stall. Look for signs saying HOLLANDSE NIEUWE. These fish stalls are a great resource for snacks of baked fish, smoked eel, and seafood salads, taken on the run.

Far-ranging Dutch explorers and traders brought back recipes and exotic spices, and the popular Indonesian _rijsttafel_ (rice table), a feast of 15 to 30 small portions of different dishes eaten with plain rice, has been a national favorite ever since it arrived in the 17th century. If you've never experienced this minifeast, it should definitely be on your "must eat" list for Holland. Should you part company with the Dutch and their love of Indonesian food, you'll find the cuisines of

Secrets of the Rijsttafel

The Indonesian feast **rijsttafel** is Holland's favorite meal and has been ever since the Dutch United East India Company captains introduced it to the wealthy burghers of Amsterdam in the 17th century. The rijsttafel (literally "rice table") originated with Dutch plantation overseers in Indonesia, who liked to sample selectively from Indonesian cuisine. It became a kind of tradition, one upheld by Indonesian immigrants to Holland who opened restaurants and, knowing the Dutch fondness for rijsttafel, made it a standard menu item. Rijsttafels are only a small part of the menu in an Indonesian restaurant, and there is a trend among the Dutch to look down on them as being just for tourists; the Dutch generally have a good understanding of Indonesian cuisine and prefer to order an individual dish rather than the mixed hash of flavors of a rijsttafel. However, rijsttafels remain popular, and many Chinese, Japanese, Vietnamese, and Thai restaurants in Holland have copied the idea.

Rijsttafel is an acquired taste, and unless you already have a stomach for both Chinese and Indian cooking, you may not like much of what you eat. But to be in Holland and not at least try a rijsttafel is as much a pity as it would be to miss seeing Rembrandt's *The Night Watch* while you had the chance. Besides, with more than 20 different dishes on the table, you're bound to find a few you enjoy.

The basic concept of a rijsttafel is to eat a bit of this and a bit of that, blending the flavors and textures. A simple, unadorned bed of rice is the base and the mediator between spicy meats and bland vegetables or fruits,

China, France, Greece, India, Italy, Japan, Spain, Turkey, Yugoslavia, and several other nationalities well represented.

1 In the Old Center
VERY EXPENSIVE
Excelsior ★★★ CONTINENTAL   One of Amsterdam's most famous restaurants derives its reputation from critically acclaimed cuisine and superb service. It's more than a little formal—more than

between sweet-and-sour tastes, and soft-and-crunchy textures. Although a rijsttafel for one is possible, this feast is better shared by two or by a table full of people. In the case of a solitary diner or a couple, a 17-dish rijsttafel will be enough food; with four or more, order a 24- or 30-dish rijsttafel and you can experience the total taste treat.

Before you begin to imagine 30 dinner-size plates of food, it's important to mention that the dishes used to serve an Indonesian meal are small and the portions served are gauged by the number of people expected to share them. Remember, the idea is to have tastes of many things rather than a full meal of any single item. Also, there are no separate courses in an Indonesian rijsttafel. Once your table has been set with a row of low, Sterno-powered plate warmers, all 17 or 24 or 30 dishes arrive all at one time, like a culinary avalanche, the sweets along with the sours and the spicy, so you're left to plot your own course through the extravaganza. (Beware, however, of one very appealing dish of sauce with small chunks of what looks to be bright-red onion—that is *sambal badjak,* or simply *sambal,* and it's hotter than hot.)

Among the customary dishes and ingredients of a rijsttafel are *loempia* (classic Chinese-style egg rolls); *satay,* or *sateh* (small kabobs of pork, grilled and served with a spicy peanut sauce); *perkedel* (meatballs); *gado-gado* (vegetables in peanut sauce); *daging smoor* (beef in soy sauce); *babi ketjap* (pork in soy sauce); *kroepoek* (crunchy, puffy shrimp toast); *serundeng* (fried coconut); *roedjak manis* (fruit in sweet sauce); and *pisang goreng* (fried banana).

a lot formal, by Amsterdam standards—but people who like this kind of thing will like this kind of thing. Crystal chandeliers, elaborate moldings, crisp linens, fresh bouquets of flowers, and picture windows with great views on the Amstel River, help to give this refined place a baronial atmosphere. Respectable attire (jackets for men) is required. If your budget cannot compete with that of the royalty or showbiz stars that often dine here, try the Excelsior's

Central Amsterdam Dining

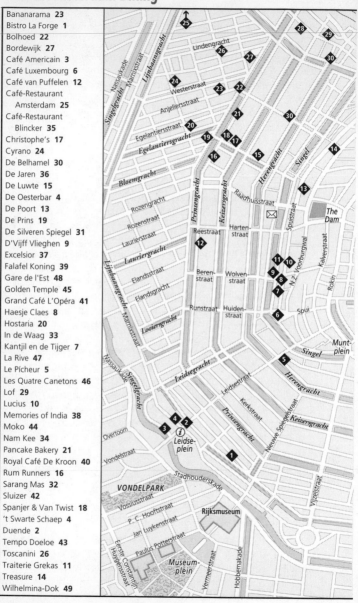

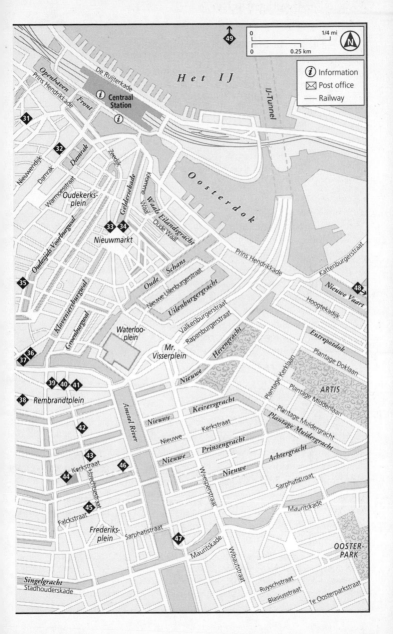

Moments In Search of Gezelligheid

When in Amsterdam, do as the Dutch do: Look for some-place *gezellig*, and treasure it if you find it.

So what is *gezellig*, or *gezelligheid* (the state of being *gezellig*)?

Ah . . . it's a simple idea, yet one that underlines every-day life; one of those imprecise, enigmatic, and finally untranslatable-in-a-single-word concepts for a mood and an attitude that you'll recognize right away when you find it, and then you'll say with quiet satisfaction, "Ah, this place looks *gezellig*."

So what *is* it then?

The special *something* that makes a place comfortable, congenial, cozy, familiar, friendly, intimate, memorable, tolerant, warm, and welcoming. Dutch, in fact. You find it in abundance in brown cafes; in a candle-lit restaurant where the atmosphere is unforced and there's a view of a softly illuminated canal; in a Dutch home where you are made to feel one of the family; even on a packed-to-the-gills tram where everyone is in good humor and sees the funny side of the situation.

The great thing about gezelligheid is that it's free. Box some up and take it home with you.

three-course *menu du théàtre*, which makes fine dining a little more affordable. It includes such choices as smoked eel with dill (a Dutch specialty) or marinated sweetbreads of lamb with salad for starters, fillet of halibut with caper sauce or fillet of veal with leek sauce as main courses, and desserts such as orange pie with frozen yogurt or raspberry bavaroise with mango sauce. A meal here is a lovely way to start an evening at the ballet or the opera, especially as live—and soft—music is played on the grand piano every evening to get you into the mood.

In the Hôtel de l'Europe, Nieuwe Doelenstraat 2-8 (facing Muntplein). ☎ 020/531-1777. Reservations recommended on weekends. Main courses 27.75€-38.50€; fixed-price menus 42€-75€. AE, DC, MC, V. Mon-Fri 7-11am, 12:30-2:30pm, 7-10:30pm; Sat-Sun 7-11am, 7-10:30pm. Tram: 4, 9, 14, 16, 24, 25 to Muntplein.

EXPENSIVE

D'Vijff Vlieghen 🦆🦆 MODERN DUTCH   Among the most famous restaurants in town, the "Five Flies" occupies five canal houses (hence the name). In fact, it's an Amsterdam institution. "Who wants to eat in an institution?" I can hear you say, but I don't think you'll find any reason to knock this one. The decor is Old Dutch, though each of the nine separate dining rooms has a different character. There's the Rembrandt Room, which has five original etchings by the artist, the Glass Room, with a collection of Golden Age handmade glassware, and the Knight's Room, adorned with 16th-century armor and accoutrements, to name just three. The chef is out to convey the culinary excellence inherent in many traditional Dutch recipes and products, but in an updated, French-influenced "New Dutch" form, and employing organic ingredients so far as is possible. You can enjoy quite a mouthful by choosing the *geroosteerde tamme eend op een bedje van appeltjes en tuinboontjes overgroten met een vinaigrette van rode en groene pepers* (roasted tame duck on a layer of apples and broad beans drizzled with a vinaigrette of red and green peppers). Or select from an extensive range of fish, game, and vegetarian options. And what better way to end your meal than with one of 40 brands of *jenever* (Dutch gin), including the restaurant's own.

Spuistraat 294-302 (at Spui). ✆ **020/530-4060.** Main courses 21€-29.50€; seasonal menu 31€-52€. AE, DC, MC, V. Daily 5:30pm-midnight. Tram: 1, 2, 5 to Spui.

De Silveren Spiegel 🦆🦆 DUTCH/FRENCH   The owner of this traditional old restaurant, one of the best known in Amsterdam, has introduced a fresh approach. The two houses that form the premises were built in 1614 for a wealthy soapmaker, Laurens Jansz Spieghel. It's typically Old Dutch inside, with the bar downstairs and more dining rooms where the bedrooms used to be. The whole place emanates a traditionally Dutch tidiness that's very welcoming. There's a garden in back. The menu has been updated and now offers new, finely prepared seafood and meat dishes, such as baked sole fillets with wild spinach, and trilogy of lamb with ratatouille—but just as in the old days, the lamb is still Holland's finest, from Texel, and traditional Zaanse mustard is never far away.

Kattengat 4-6 (off Singel). ✆ **020/624-6589.** Main courses 24.50€-29.50€; fixed-price menus 37.50€-44.50€. AE, MC, V. Daily 6-11pm (open for lunch by reservation). Tram: 1, 2, 5, 13, 17 to Martelaarsgracht.

Lucius ⍟ SEAFOOD   Lucius, which means "pike" in Latin, has earned a reputation for fine seafood at fairly reasonable prices. Oysters and lobsters imported from Norway and Canada are the specialties. The three-course menu is also very popular. Among the half dozen or so choices featured on the chalkboard menu, you might find fish soup to start, followed by grilled plaice, Dover sole, bass, or John Dory. The spectacular seafood plate includes 6 oysters, 10 mussels, clams, shrimp, and half a lobster. The long, narrow dining room is cooled by ceiling fans and features an aquarium. In summer, chairs are placed out on the sidewalk.

Spuistraat 247 (near Spui). ℂ **020/624-1831.** Main courses 19.50€-40€; fixed-price menus 29.50€-35€. AE, DC, MC, V. Daily 5pm-midnight. Tram: 1, 2, 5 to Spui.

MODERATE

De Jaren ⍟ CONTINENTAL   One of the city's largest cafes, the recently refurbished, brightly lit De Jaren is fashionable without being pretentious. It occupies a solid-looking, spacious building on two stories (with unusually high ceilings) that served originally as bank. Many students from the nearby university who are tired of cafeteria food lunch here, and it's popular with the media crowd. De Jaren's unique selling point is not so much the fashionable set that hangs out here, but its marvelous open-air terrace beside the Amstel River, a place in the sun that is much in demand in fine weather. Occupants of those prime-time seats settle into them with a firmness of purpose that looks as if they meant to settle there permanently, but it's still worth checking out the outdoor deck, in case one of them might have fallen—or been pushed—into the river. You can enjoy everything from a cup of coffee, a beer, or a glass of *jenever* (gin) to a good salad, spaghetti Bolognese, and rib eye steak. And you can peruse the English-language newspapers while you do it.

Nieuwe Doelenstraat 20-22 (near Muntplein). ℂ **020/625-5771.** Main courses 7.50€-14.50€; fixed-price menus 9.50€-14.50€. V. Sun-Thurs 10am-1am, Fri-Sat 10am-2am. Tram: 4, 9, 14, 16, 24, 25 to Muntplein.

De Poort ⍟⍟ DUTCH/INTERNATIONAL   This restaurant, in a former beer hall, has been offering its steaks and typically Dutch dishes for more than 100 years. Its beamed and tiled Dutch-tavern dining room has recently been fully restored along with its parent hotel. De Poort still maintains a tradition that has become legendary among its patrons: Each of its steaks is numbered, and if the number on yours is a round thousand, you're the winner of a free bottle of wine. They've already served more than 6 million steaks! The restaurant is equally noted for its Dutch pea soup.

In the Hotel Die Port van Cleve, Nieuwezijds Voorburgwal 176-180 (behind the Dam). ℂ 020/624-0047. Main courses 15€-22€; monthly Dutch Province menu 28.50€ ; fixed-price menu 31.50€. AE, DC, MC, V. Daily 7am-10:30pm. Tram: 1, 2, 5, 13, 14, 17 to the Dam.

Haesje Claes ℛ DUTCH   If you're yearning for a cozy Old Dutch environment and hearty Dutch food at moderate prices, try this inviting place. Lots of nooks and crannies decorated with Delftware and wooden barrels, brocaded benches and traditional Dutch hanging lamps with fringed covers give an intimate, comfortable feel to the setting. The menu covers a lot of ground, from canapés to caviar, but you have the most luck with Dutch stalwarts ranging from omelettes to tournedos, and taking in *hutspot* (stew), *stampot* (mashed potatoes and cabbage), and various fish stews, including those with IJsselmeer *paling* (eel), along the way.

Spuistraat 273-275 (at Spui). ℂ 020/624-9998. Main courses 14€-20€; tourist menu 18.50€. AE, DC, MC, V. Daily noon-10pm. Tram: 1, 2, 5 to Spui.

In de Waag ℛ CONTINENTAL   This cafe-restaurant is called In de Waag because it's in the Waag (see, you *can* speak Dutch). And what is the Waag? In medieval times it was the St. Antoniespoort Gate in the city walls; by the Golden Age, it had become a weigh house: De Waag. Dissections were once carried out on the top floor. Nowadays, dissections are of a culinary nature, as the castlelike structure holds one of Amsterdam's most stylish cafe-restaurants, in an area that's becoming hipper by the minute. It's an indelibly romantic place, the long banquet-style tables ablaze with candlelight in the evening. You can mix easily with other diners. The breast of Barbary duck with sesame-cracker and sherry dressing is pretty good, as is the vegetarian Kashmir bread with braised vegetables and coriander-yogurt sauce.

Nieuwmarkt 4. ℂ 020/422-7772. Main courses 14.50€-19.50€. AE, DC, MC, V. Daily 10am-1am. Metro: Nieuwmarkt.

Kantjil en de Tijger ℛℛ INDONESIAN   Unlike the many Indonesian restaurants in Holland that wear their ethnic origins on their sleeves, literally, with waitstaff decked out in traditional costume, the Antelope and the Tiger is chic, modern, and cool. Moreover, it attracts customers who like their Indonesian food not only chic, modern, and cool, but good, as well. The two best sellers in this popular place are *nasi goreng Kantjil* (fried rice with pork kabobs, stewed beef, pickled cucumbers, and mixed vegetables), and the 20-item *rijsttafel* for two. Other choices include stewed chicken in soja sauce, tofu omelette, shrimp with coconut dressing, Indonesian pumpkin, and mixed steamed vegetables with peanut-butter sauce. Finish off your meal with the multilayered cinnamon cake or (try this at least once) the coffee with ginger liqueur and whipped cream.

Spuistraat 291 (beside Spui). © 020/620-0994. Reservations recommended on weekends. Main courses 11.50€-15.50€; rijsttafels 37.50€-47.50€ for two. AE, DC, MC, V. Daily 4:30-11pm. Tram: 1, 2, 5 to Spui.

Le Pêcheur 🍴 SEAFOOD   Both popular and appealing, in a frenetic neighborhood where establishments are more commonly either one or the other, Le Pêcheur has long combined elegant simplicity of presentation with a steely focus on freshness and taste. Flowers adorn the tables set on a marble floor, beneath a muraled ceiling, and there's a courtyard garden for summer dining. Dishes are prepared in Dutch, continental and international styles. In season, come for the *coquilles St-Jacques* scallops, the mussels and oysters from the southern Dutch province of Zeeland, and the house-smoked salmon. You could also try poached brill with onion sauce, fried wolf-fish with light mustard sauce, or sashimi. Tournedos of beef cooked to your liking are available for those who don't like seafood.

Reguliersdwarsstraat 32 (behind the Flower Market). © 020/624-3121. Main courses 17.50€-22.50€; fixed-price menu 33.50€. AE, MC, V. Mon-Fri noon-midnight, Sat 5pm-midnight. Tram: 1, 2, 5 to Koningsplein.

Lof 🍴🍴 *Finds* CONTINENTAL   It's hard to pin down this fashionable, vaguely French/Italian eatery. For one thing, there's no menu. Its youthful chefs describe their creations as *cuisine spontane*—they go to the markets, spontaneously pick out whatever's fresh and takes their fancy, and equally spontaneously figure out what to do with it back at base. The results are invariably splendid. Oysters are a regular feature among three or four starters; then, choose from three main courses: meat, fish, and vegetarian; and finish with a *torte*. You dine on one of two levels, at plain tables in a cozy setting with bare brick walls, and a view of proceedings in the open kitchen.

Haarlemmerstraat 62 (near Centraal Station). © 020/620-2997. Main courses 9.50€-18.50€, fixed-price menus 25.50€-37.50€. No credit cards. Tues-Sun 6-11pm. Tram: 1, 2, 4, 5, 9, 13, 16, 17, 24, 25 to Centraal Station.

Sarang Mas INDONESIAN   This intimate Indonesian restaurant is near the canal-boat piers, so you get a nice view while you dine on traditional Indonesian dishes, including a decent selection of rijsttafels. The pink, white, and green color scheme is a refreshing and contemporary alternative to the usual basic decor found in Indonesian restaurants. The big drawback is location: Damrak is central enough but is also the center of "tacky" Amsterdam; Sarang Mas is surrounded by sex boutiques, souvenir shops, fast-food joints, and video-game parlors. Still, the ruckus ends at the restaurant door, and Sarang Mas hasn't let its standards slip by being in a tourist ghetto.

Damrak 44 (near Centraal Station). © 020/622-2105. Main courses 12.50€-20€; rijsttafels 26.50€-32.50€. AE, DC, MC, V. Daily 11:30am-11pm. Tram: 4, 9, 14, 16, 24, 25 to the Dam.

Treasure ★★ CHINESE   In a city with a passion for Indonesian food, it can be difficult to find traditional Chinese cuisine, let alone good traditional Chinese cuisine. Don't despair—make a beeline for Treasure, a legend in its own lunchtime (and dinnertime), rated among the best restaurants in Amsterdam by *Avant Garde*. It offers a wide array of classic Chinese choices in a classic Chinese setting, with lots of lanterns, watercolor paintings, and Chinese scripts. You can eat dishes from any of the four main styles of Chinese cooking—Beijing, Shanghai, Cantonese, and Szechuan. Look for specialties such as Beijing duck, Szechuan-style prawns (very spicy), and steamed dumplings.

Nieuwezijds Voorburgwal 115-117 (near the Dam). © 020/623-4061. Main courses 9€-13.50€; fixed-price menus 14.50€ 37.50€. AF, MC, V. Daily noon-11pm. Tram: 1, 2, 5, 13, 14, 17 to the Dam.

INEXPENSIVE

Blincker CONTINENTAL   To find this cafe-restaurant, turn into Nes (which runs parallel to Rokin) from the Dam, then turn left after the Frascati Theater. This intimate restaurant in the Frascati Theater building attracts actors, journalists, artists, and other assorted bohemians. At night the place is jammed with people around the bar. The simple but tasty fare includes lamb chops with garlic, pancakes with cheese and mushrooms, homemade pasta, and cheese fondue.

St. Barberenstraat 7 (off Rokin). © 020/627-1938. Main courses 5€-15€. AE, DC, MC, V. Mon-Sat 4pm-1am. Tram: 4, 9, 16, 24, 25 to Rokin.

Café Luxembourg ★★ INTERNATIONAL "One of the world's great cafes," wrote *The New York Times* about this stylish grand cafe. Unlike other cafes in Amsterdam, which often draw a distinctive clientele, Luxembourg attracts all kinds of people because it offers amazingly large portions of food at reasonable prices. Soups, sandwiches, and such dishes as meat loaf are available. A special attraction is that some of the dishes are specials like the Chinese dim sum and the saté ajam (Indonesian grilled chicken in a peanut sauce). It's a good place to do breakfast with the day's papers. You're encouraged to linger in this relaxing place and read one of the many international newspapers. In summer there's sidewalk dining.

Spui 22-24 (at Spui). ✆ **020/620-6264.** Salads and specials 8.50€-11€; lunch 4€-8.50; main courses 8€-17.50€. AE, DC, MC, V. Sun-Thurs 9am-1am, Fri-Sat 9am-2am. Tram: 1, 2, 5 to Spui.

Nam Kee ★ CHINESE Not many Dutch restaurants have made a name for themselves in the movies, but Nam Kee played a notable supporting role in the 2002 red-hot romance flick *De Oesters van Nam Kee (The Oysters of Nam Kee),* based on a novel of the same name. In the heart of the city's small but growing Chinatown, Nam Kee has a long interior with few obvious graces, little in the way of decor, and for sure no plastic Ming Dynasty knickknacks. People come here to pay modestly for food that is both authentic and excellent, from a menu with 140 items written on it. The steamed oysters with black bean sauce and the duck with plum sauce are to die for. Judging by the number of ethnic Chinese customers clicking chopsticks around, Nam Kee does okay when it comes to homeland credibility. The service is fast—not quite so fast that you'll still be eating off your plate while the waitperson is bringing it to the dishwasher, but not far away. On the bright side, this means you don't have long to wait for a table, popular though the restaurant is.

Zeedijk 111-113 at Nieuwmarkt. ✆ **020/624-3470.** Main courses 6€-15.75€. AE, DC, MC, V. Daily 11:30am-midnight. Metro: Nieuwmarkt.

2 Along the Canal Belt

EXPENSIVE

Christophe ★★ MODERN FRENCH The star of this Michelin-star show is owner and chef Jean-Christophe Royer, who combines influences from his youth in Algeria and southwest France with his experience at top restaurants in New York, Baltimore, and

Massachusetts, and a penchant for Mediterranean flourishes, to create an updated and unpretentious version of classic French cuisine. Royer serves sensuous, sophisticated food in an elegant setting featuring dark cherry-wood paneling, thick carpets, rice-paper lamp shades, stately cacti by the windows, and floral paintings by contemporary Dutch artist Martin van Vreden. The food is similarly refined, using traditional Mediterranean ingredients—figs, truffles, olives, and saffron—in exciting new ways. Try the roasted milk-fed Pyreneean lamb, or roasted turbot in a light curry sauce, and finish with a light tart of prunes in Armagnac.

Leliegracht 46 (between Prinsengracht and Keizersgracht). ℰ 020/625-0807. Main courses 27.50€-32.50€; fixed-price menus 42.50€-52.50€. AE, DC, MC, V. Tues-Sat 6:30-10:30pm. Tram: 13, 14, 17 to Westermarkt.

MODERATE

Bolhoed 𝒦𝒦 VEGETARIAN   Forget the corn-sheaf 'n' brown-rice image affected by so many vegetarian restaurants, that worthy but dull message: "This stuff is good for you." Instead, garnish your healthful habits with a dash of zest. Latin style, world music, a changing program of ethnic exhibitions, evening candlelight, and a fine view of the canal from each of its two cheerful rooms distinguish a restaurant for which *vegetarian* is a tad too wholesome-sounding. Service is delivered with equal amounts of gusto and attention. Try such veggie delights as *ragoût croissant* (pastry filled with leeks, tofu, seaweed, and curry sauce), and *zarzuela*. If you want to go whole hog, so to speak, and eat vegan, most of Bolhoed's dishes can be so prepared on request, and in any case, most are made with organically grown produce.

Prinsengracht 60-62 (near Noordermarkt). ℰ 020/626-1803. Main courses 11.50€-14.50€. No credit cards. Sun-Fri noon-11pm, Sat 11am-11pm. Tram: 13, 14, 17 to Westermarkt.

Café van Puffelen DUTCH/CONTINENTAL   A big café-restaurant near the Westerkerk. Among the menu dishes that show flair, creativity, and a seemingly inexhaustible supply of ingredients, you can try fried butterfish with a tarragon, coriander, and pesto cream sauce served on bacon and tomato spaghetti; and the main course Salad van Puffelen, served with tandoori chicken, smoked turkey, smoked salmon, roast veal and Cajun shrimps. Other choices include vegetable platters and mozzarella with tomato. Save room for the delicious handmade chocolates that are house specialties.

Prinsengracht 377 (facing Lauriergracht). © **020/624-6270**. Main courses 14.50€-19.50€. AE, DC, MC, V. Mon-Thurs 3pm-1am, Fri 3pm-2am, Sat noon-2am, Sun noon-1am. Tram: 13, 14, 17 to Westermarkt.

De Belhamel 🎯🎯 *Finds* CONTINENTAL   Soft classical music complements a graceful Art Nouveau setting at this two-level restaurant overlooking the photogenic junction of the Herengracht and Brouwersgracht canals. The tables fill up quickly most evenings, so make reservations or go early. The menu changes seasonally, but if you're like me, you'll hope that something like, or as good as, this will be on the list: puffed pastries layered with salmon, shellfish, crayfish tails, and chervil beurre-blanc to start; and beef tenderloin in Madeira sauce with zucchini rösti and puffed garlic for a main course. You can also get vegetarian dishes. Try for a window table and take in the superb canal views. Although generally excellent, De Belhamel does have two minor flaws: The waitstaff is occasionally a bit too laid-back, and when it is full, as it often is, the acoustic peculiarities of the place can drive the noise level up to about that of a boiler factory.

Brouwersgracht 60 (at Herengracht). © **020/622-1095**. Main courses 18€-20€; fixed-price menu 32€. AE, MC, V. Sun-Thurs 6-10pm, Fri-Sat 6-10:30pm. Tram: 1, 2, 5, 13, 17 to Martelaarsgracht.

De Luwte 🎯🎯 FUSION   *Graceful* is the term that seems best to sum up this fine restaurant, though that quality never descends into stiffness. It gets its grace from Florentine wall murals, floor-to-ceiling Art Deco lamps, drapes, hangings, ceiling mirrors painted with flowers and vines, a candle on each table, and not least from an elegant canalside location. And it avoids being starchy by a characteristic Amsterdam exuberance and buzz. In either of the twin rooms, try for one of the window tables that look out on the canal. The menu ranges across the globe for inspiration. Look out for items such as the vegetarian coconut curry crepes filled with spinach, lentils, and nuts; and stir-fried guinea fowl with nuts and *bok choy.*

Leliegracht 26-28 (between Keizersgracht and Herengracht). © **020/625-8548**. Main courses 16€-18€. AE, MC, V. Daily 6-11pm. Tram: 13, 14, 17 to Westermarkt.

Golden Temple 🎯 VEGETARIAN   In its fourth decade of tickling meat-shunning palates, this temple of taste is still one of the best vegetarian (and vegan) options in town. The first thing you notice when you enter is that you can actually *see* the place—the veil of cigarette smoke that obscures most Amsterdam restaurants has been lifted here by a nonsmoking policy that adds a heavenly touch all on its own. If anything, the limpid atmosphere is a tad too hallowed, an effect enhanced by an absence of decorative flourishes that may be Zen-like in its purity but leaves you wishing for something, anything, to look at other than your fellow veggies while you wait to be served. The menu livens things up, with its unlikely roster of Indian, Middle Eastern, and Mexican dishes. This could make for an interesting game of mix-and-match if only the small print didn't all but instruct you to keep them apart. The food is ace, delicately spiced and flavored, and evidently prepared by loving hands. Multiple-choice platters are a good way to go. For the Indian *thali*, you select from constituents like *sag paneer* (homemade cheese), vegetable *korma*, and *raita* (cucumber and yogurt dip); the Middle Eastern platter has stalwarts like falafel, chickpea-and-vegetable stew, and vegetable *dolmas*. Side dishes range across items as varied as guacamole, couscous, and *pakora*. The homemade ice cream is a finger-licking good way to wind up.

Utrechtsestraat 126 (close to Frederiksplein). (✆ **020/626-8560**. Main courses 6.50€-9.50€; mixed platter 12€. MC, V. Daily 5-10pm. Tram: 4 to Prinsengracht.

Moko ✿ FUSION/POLYNESIAN Experimental and trendy, Moko—the name refers to a Maori facial tattoo—has garnered mixed reviews since it replaced the beloved Kort on this prime canalside site in 2001. Be ready to go out on a limb, foodwise, and to write the experience down to, well, to experience, should it get hacked off behind you. After 10pm, you'll need to integrate music from a live DJ, who does his stuff in a lounge area beyond the central, boat-shaped cocktail bar, not right among the finely decorated dining tables. The food mixes influences from Australia, New Zealand, Asia, and Oceania with north European and Mediterranean dishes, in a free-style yet rarely overindulgent manner. Moko occupies a converted 17th-century, white-painted timber church, the Amstelkerk, but here endeth the churchly connection. Eating, design, and music intersect in a colorful, if somewhat impersonal high-tech space, in which natural materials combine with Maori accents and images. Three coral-reef fish tanks add a touch of South Seas verisimilitude. The menu changes frequently, but these main courses provide a flavor of what's on offer: *Spiced zwaardvis en tonijn met tamari en wasabi-mayonnaise* (spiced swordfish and tuna with tamari-broth and wasabi mayonnaise), and *tomaten-risotto cake met veldchampignons, rucola en tomatenjam* (tomato risotto with portobello mushrooms, rucola and sun-dried-tomato paste). On warm summer evenings, try to get a table outdoors, on a wide, open square beside the Prinsengracht canal.

Amstelveld 12 (at Prinsengracht). ⓒ **020/626-1199.** Reservations not accepted. Main courses 16€-20€ AE, DC, MC, V. May-Oct Mon-Fri 11:30am-1am, Sat-Sun 11:30am-2am; Nov-Apr Tues-Sat 11:30am-1am, Sat-Sun 11:30am-2am. Tram: 4 to Prinsengracht.

Rum Runners ⓡ CARIBBEAN   In the former coach house of the Westerkerk (yes, the church) is Rum Runners, a two-level, laid-back, tropical kind of place where the atmosphere and cuisine are inspired by the Caribbean. Two gigantic bamboo birdcages greet you as you enter. You sit beneath gently circling ceiling fans and among towering potted palms that stretch to the lofty rafters. At night, the reggae beat of the music often lasts until the wee hours. Try asopao, a Caribbean rice dish, or a Caribbean barbecue. You can also just drink cocktails to your heart's content and fill up on some of the best guacamole in town.

Prinsengracht 277 (beside Anne Frankhuis). ⓒ **020/627-4079.** Main courses 11.50€-17.50€; fixed-price menus 17.50€-22.50€. AE, DC, MC, V. Mon-Thurs 2pm-1am, Fri-Sun 2pm-2am. Tram: 13, 14, 17 to Westermarkt.

Sluizer ⓡ CONTINENTAL/SEAFOOD   Two notable restaurants (sadly, not for the price of one), stand side by side in convivial harmony. No. 45 is an old-fashioned brasserie with an eclectic menu that has a slightly French bias, in such items as *entrecôte Dijon* (steak with mustard sauce) and *poulet à la Provençal* (chicken with olives, sage, rosemary, and tomato). Next door, at nos. 41-43, the vaguely Art Deco *Visrestaurant* (Fish restaurant) has at least 10 specials daily, ranging from simple cod or eel to *coquille St-Jacques* (scallops), crab casserole, Dover sole, halibut, and octopus. Meat dishes, such as beef stroganoff and chicken supreme, also appear on the menu.

Utrechtsestraat 41-43 and 45 (between Herengracht and Keizersgracht). ⓒ **020/ 622-6376** (Continental) or 020/626-3557 (seafood). Main courses 11.75€-29.75€; optional menu 14.50€. AE, DC, MC, V. Mon-Fri noon-2:30pm and 5pm-1am, Sat-Sun 5pm-1am. Tram: 4 to Utrechtsestraat.

Spanjer & Van Twist ⓡⓡ *Finds* CONTINENTAL   This place would almost be worth the visit for its name alone, so it's doubly gratifying that the food is good, too. The interior is typical *eetcafé* style, with the day's specials chalked on a blackboard, a long table with newspapers at the front, and the kitchen visible in back. High standards of cooking, however, put this place above others of the kind. The eclectic menu changes seasonally, but to give an idea of its range, I've come fork-to-face in the past with Thai fish curry and *pandan* rice; *saltimbocca* of trout in white-wine sauce; and artichoke mousseline with tarragon sauce and green asparagus. In fine weather, you can eat on an outdoors terrace beside the tranquil Leliegracht canal.

Leliegracht 60 (off Keizersgracht). © 020/639-0109. Reservations not accepted. Main courses 11.75€–14.75€. MC, V. Daily 10am–1am (only light snacks after 11pm). Tram: 13, 14, 17 to Westermarkt.

Tempo Doeloe 🎄🎄 INDONESIAN   For authentic Indonesian cuisine, from Java, Sumatra, and Bali—which doesn't leave out much—this place is hard to beat. Though its local reputation goes up and down with the tide, it's invariably busy. You dine in a *batik* ambience that's Indonesian, but restrained, and a long way short of being kitsch. The attractive decor and the fine china are unexpected pluses. Try the many little meat, fish, and vegetable dishes of the three different *rijsttafel* (rice table) options, from the 15-plate vegetarian *rijsttafel sayoeran,* and the 15-plate *rijsttafel stimoelan,* to the sumptuous 25-plate *rijsttafel istemewa.* In the big one, you get dishes like *gadon dari sapi* (beef in a mild coconut sauce and fresh coriander), *ajam roedjak* (chicken in a strongly seasoned sauce of chile peppers and coconut), *sambal goreng oedang* (small shrimps with Indonesian spices), and *atjar* (sweet-and-sour Indonesian salad). For great individual dishes, go for the *nasi koening,* or any of the vegetarian options. Finish with the *spekkoek,* a layered spice cake. One caution: When something on the menu is described as *pedis,* meaning hot, that's *exactly* what it is. A fire extinguisher would be a useful table accessory for these dishes; for an equally effective, and better-tasting alternative, order a *witbier* (white beer). But the chef doesn't rely only on killer spices; many of the flavors are subtle and refined.

Utrechtsestraat 75 (between Prinsengracht and Keizersgracht). © 020/625-6718. Main courses 18€–22.50€; *rijsttafel* 24€31.50€; fixed-price menu 27€–43€. AE, DC, MC, V. Mon–Sat 6–11:30pm. Tram: 4 to Keizersgracht.

INEXPENSIVE

De Prins 🎄🎄 *Value* DUTCH/FRENCH   This companionable restaurant, housed in a 17th-century canal house, has a smoke-stained, brown-cafe style and food that could easily grace a much more expensive place. De Prins offers an unbeatable price-to-quality ratio for typically Dutch/French menu items, and long may it continue to do so. The youthful clientele is loyal and enthusiastic, so the relatively few tables fill up quickly. This is a quiet neighborhood place—nothing fancy or trendy, but quite appealing in a human

Family-Friendly Restaurants

Pancake Bakery *(see below)*   I have yet to meet a kid who doesn't love pancakes, and this restaurant at Prinsengracht 191 (📞 020/625-1333) is *the* best pancake source in town. Pancakes come with various inventive toppings (sweet and savory). Suitably colorful ornaments such as umbrellas and clowns accompany child-oriented meals and desserts. Toys, children's chairs, and special menus complete the picture. There are also pancakes big enough to satisfy the most adult of tastes.

De Rozenboom   The tiny De Rozenboom, Rozenboomsteeg 6 (📞 020/622-5024), in an alley leading to the Begijnhof, serves hearty Dutch meals and has a special children's menu. Eating here is like having dinner in a doll's house.

L'Enfant Terrible   This cafe at De Genestetstraat 1 (📞 020/612-2032) is in a quiet residential area, not far from Leidseplein. In front is a large play room. You can take a break and have a coffee on your own, or have lunch or dinner together with the children. There's even a playpen for the very young. The cafe also offers a babysitting service (maximum 3 hours).

way. There's a bar on a slightly lower level than the restaurant. From March to September, De Prins spreads a terrace out onto the canalside.

Prinsengracht 124 (at Leliegracht). 📞 020/624-9382. Main courses 6€-12.50€ ; dish of the day 9.90€; specials 23.50€-27.50€. AE, DC, MC, V. Daily 10am-1am. Tram: 13, 14, 17 to Westermarkt.

Pancake Bakery 🎭🎭 *(Kids)* PANCAKES   This two-story canal-house restaurant serves almost nothing but pancakes—an appropriate choice for any meal. The satisfyingly large pancakes come adorned with all sorts of toppings, both sweet and spicy, including Cajun chicken (on the spicy end of the taste spectrum), ice cream and liqueur (on the sweet end), and curried turkey with pineapple and raisins (for a little bit of both). The decor is simple, with winding staircases and exposed beams contributing to the pleasant ambience,

KinderKookKafé 🄰 Children are the chefs and waiters at this small restaurant at Oudezijds Achterburgwal 193 (☎ 020/625-3527). With the help of some adults, they prepare dinner on Saturday and bake cookies and pies for high tea on Sunday. If your kids want to, they can join the kitchen brigade; or you can all just relax and enjoy the meal. Kids must be at least 8 years old to help with the Saturday dinner, and 5 for the Sunday bake.

New York Pizza When your kids are longing for that all-American Italian food, head to New York Pizza, Amsterdam's answer to Pizza Hut, bright, clean, and decorated in Italy's national colors—red, white, and green. You can order three different kinds of pizza—traditional, deep pan, or whole meal. Branches are at Damrak 59 (☎ 020/639-0494; tram: 4, 9, 16, 24, 25); Spui 2 (☎ 020/420-3538; tram: 1, 2, 5); Reguliersbreestraat 15-17 (☎ 020/420-5585; tram: 4, 9, 14, 16, 24, 25); Damstraat 24 (☎ 020/422-2123; tram: 4, 9, 14, 16, 24, 25); and Leidsestraat 23 (☎ 020/622-8689; tram: 1, 2, 5).

and the windows provide a pretty view over the Prinsengracht. In the summertime, you can dine outside at long wooden tables, but beware: All the syrup, honey, and sugar being passed around tends to attract bees and hornets. Nonetheless, the Pancake Bakery remains a firm local favorite, especially among children.

Prinsengracht 191 (at Prinsenstraat). ☎ 020/625-1333. Reservations required for large groups. Pancakes 4€-10€. AE, MC, V. Daily noon-9:30pm. Tram: 13, 14, 17 to Westermarkt.

Traîterie Grekas 🄰 GREEK With just five tables and a small sidewalk terrace in summertime, Grekas would be more of a frustration than anything else, except that its main business is its take-out service. If you're staying at one of the hotels in this neighborhood (particularly next door at the Estheréa, to which Grekas provides room service), this place can even become your local diner. The food is fresh and authentic, and you can choose your meal like you would in Mykonos, by pointing to the dishes you want. If there are no free tables, you can always take your choices back to your room, or eat alfresco on the canalside. Menu items are standard Greek but with a freshness and taste that are hard to beat. The moussaka and pasticcio are heavenly; the roast lamb with wine, herbs, olive oil, and bouillon is excellent; the calamari in the calamari salad seems to have come straight out of Homer's wine-dark sea; and there's a good Greek wine list, too. Takeout dishes cost a euro or two less.

Singel 311 (near Spui). ✆ 020/620-3590. Main courses 9€-11.25€. No credit cards. Wed-Sun 5-10pm. Tram: 1, 2, 5 to Spui.

3 Around Leidseplein

EXPENSIVE

De Oesterbar SEAFOOD   De Oesterbar, which is more than 50 years old, is the best-known and most popular fish restaurant in Amsterdam. Its seafood is delivered fresh twice daily. The decor is a delight: all white tiles with fish tanks bubbling at your elbows on the street level, and Victorian brocades and etched glass in the more formal dining room upstairs. The menu is a directory of Dutch seafood dishes, but it also includes a few meat selections. Choices include *sole Danoise* with the tiny Dutch shrimp; *sole Véronique* with muscadet grapes; stewed eel in wine sauce; and the assorted fish plate of turbot, halibut, and fresh salmon.

Leidseplein 10. ✆ 020/623-2988. Main courses 23.80€-32.95€. AE, DC, MC, V. Daily noon-1am. Tram: 1, 2, 5, 6, 7, 10 to Leidseplein.

MODERATE

Café Americain ✦ CONTINENTAL   The lofty dining room here is a national monument of Dutch Art Nouveau. Since its opening in 1900, the place has been a hangout for Dutch and international artists, writers, dancers, and actors. Seductress/spy Mata Hari held her wedding reception here in her pre-espionage days. Leaded

---

⸨Fun Fact⸩ **The Knives Are Out**

In the 1960s, satirist Gerrit Komrij described the Café Americain's famously brusque waiters as "unemployed knife-throwers."

windows, newspaper-littered reading tables, bargello-patterned velvet upholstery, frosted-glass chandeliers from the 1920s, and tall carved columns are all part of the dusky sit-and-chat atmosphere. Seafood specialties include monkfish, perch, salmon, and king prawns; meat dishes include rack of Irish lamb and rosé breast of duck with creamed potatoes. Jazz lovers can stock up on good music and good food at the Sunday jazz brunch.

In the American Hotel, Leidsekade 97 (at Leidseplein). ✆ 020/556-3232. Main courses 16€-21€. AE, DC, MC, V. Daily 10:30am-midnight. Tram: 1, 2, 5, 6, 7, 10 to Leidseplein.

4 Around Rembrandtplein

MODERATE

Grand Café l'Opéra INTERNATIONAL   The main advantage of l'Opéra is that beyond its beautiful Art Nouveau facade it has probably the best and most restrained terrace in Rembrandtplein, though others are more centrally located on the square. On busy days in good weather, the Art Deco interior is a cool and quiet brasserie-style retreat, but of course on such days no one wants to go inside. The food in this cafe-restaurant is fine, if nothing to write home about. The menu items include such standards as salads, steak and mushrooms, croquettes, and mussels, and even Thai chicken curry for variation. Service, though friendly, is at times a little erratic.

Rembrandtplein 27-29. ✆ 020/620-4754. Main courses 13.50€-17.50€. AE, DC, MC, V. Sun-Thurs 10am-1am, Fri-Sat 10am-2am. Tram: 4, 9, 14 to Rembrandtplein.

Memories of India ✿ INDIAN   The owner earned his spurs in the crowded London market for Indian cuisine and then brought his award-winning formula to Amsterdam. That formula is simple, really: Serve top-flight Indian cuisine in a setting that gives traditional Indian motifs a modern slant, charge moderate prices, and employ an attentive staff. Memories has won plenty of friends since it opened its doors a few years ago. The restaurant somehow manages to combine the hallowed silence of diners intent on their plates with a buzz of friendly conversation. Takeout service is available.

Reguliersdwarsstraat 88. ✆ 020/623-5710. Main courses 14.50€-19.50€; fixed-price menus 15.50€-22.50€. AE, DC, MC, V. Daily 5-11:30pm. Tram: 4, 9, 14 to Rembrandtplein.

Royal Café de Kroon ✿ INTERNATIONAL   The "Royal Café" tag may be a tad overdone, but de Kroon comes close to justifying it.

Tips **Late-Night Eateries**

Since the majority of restaurant kitchens in Amsterdam are closed by 10:30pm, it's good to keep these late-night addresses handy in case the munchies strike: **De Knijp, Rum Runners,** and **Sluizer** (see p. 100, 92, and 92); and **Gary's Muffins,** Reguliersdwarsstraat 53.

Along with the Café Schiller opposite, it has gone a long way toward raising the often tacky standards of Rembrandtplein. A fanciful mix of Louis XVI-style and tropical decor makes an eclectic but restful setting for the palm court orchestra that plays here on Sunday. De Kroon also has a superb enclosed balcony with a great view on the bustling square. The diverse, international menu choices range from snacks to three-course meals, and a good continental breakfast.

Rembrandtplein 17. ✆ 020/625-2011. Snacks 4€-12€; fixed-price menu 29.50€. AE, MC, V. Sun–Thurs 10am-1am, Fri–Sat 10am-2am. Tram: 4, 9, 14 to Rembrandtplein.

INEXPENSIVE

Falafel Koning *Finds* MIDDLE-EASTERN   This tiny gem of a restaurant really needs a category all to itself: "Almost Cost-Free" comes to mind. The specialty of the house will set you back a mere 3€. It's falafel, but don't laugh—it's probably the best falafel this side of the River Jordan: mashed chick peas mixed with herbs, rolled in a ball along with what must be some magic ingredient, fried, and served in pita bread with salad. The snack bar is capable of seating about eight people at a push, plus more at a few tables outside when the sun shines.

Reguliersteeg 2 (off Reguliersstraat, opposite the Theater Tuschinski). ✆ 020/421-1423. Snacks and light meals 3€-6€. Daily 10am-1am. Tram: 4, 9, 14 to Rembrandtplein.

5 In the Jordaan

EXPENSIVE

Bordewijk *𝕽𝕽* FRENCH   This pleasantly located restaurant is often regarded as one of the best in the city. The decor is tasteful, with green potted plants offsetting the severity of the white walls and metallic black tables. Service is relaxed yet attentive, and on mild summer evenings you can't beat dining alfresco on the canal-side terrace. But the real treat is the food. An innovative chef accents

French standards with Mediterranean and Asian flourishes to create an elegant fusion of flavors. The menu changes often, but might include salted rib roast with bordelaise sauce, serrano ham marinated in wine and vinegar and served with fresh pasta, pigeon cooked in the style of Bresse, or even Japanese-style raw fish. Dinner is followed by a fine selection of cheeses. The wine list is superb.

Noordermarkt 7 (at Prinsengracht). © 020/624-3899. Main courses 22.50€-25.50€; fixed-price menu 32.50€-42.50€. AE, MC, V. Tues-Sun 6:30-10pm. Tram: 1, 2, 5, 13, 17 to Martelaarsgracht.

MODERATE

Bananarama FILIPINO   There used to be four Filipino restaurants in Amsterdam, but now only Bananarama (formerly at Mango Bay) remains—a clear case of survival of the fittest. This slice of the Philippines occupies the front room of a canal house in the heart of the Jordaan. Diners enjoy delicately flavored dishes amid festive and colorful surroundings, with tropical flowers and a mural depicting an island paradise. The food also evokes the south Pacific: Entrees include prawns simmered in coconut milk with hints of ginger, coriander, and lemongrass; and beef marinated in honey and soy sauce. Cocktails are equally exotic. One favorite, a dangerous but tasty mixture of mango, passion fruit, lemon juice, and brandy, is humorously titled "Imelda's Shoes Plus or Minus 3,000 Ingredients."

Westerstraat 91 (off Prinsengracht). © 020/638-1039. Reservations recommended on weekends. Main courses 12.50€-15.50€; fixed-price menus 15.50€-19.50€. AE, DC, MC, V. Daily 6pm-midnight. Tram: 3, 10 to Marnixstraat.

Hostaria 𝄇 ITALIAN   This lively street lined with cafes and restaurants might remind you of Italy. On long summer evenings, even the ubiquitous Amsterdam cyclists have trouble picking their way through the many pedestrians out for a stroll. The Hostaria adds a little piece of authentic Italy to the scene, serving delicate homemade pasta and *secondi piatti* such as veal stuffed with Italian sausage, or duck cooked Roman style. Try the excellent *zuppa di gamberone con l'acquetta* (a plate of prawns and shellfish from the market).

Tweede Egelantiersdwarsstraat 9 (off Egelantiersgracht). © 020/626-0028. Main courses 14.50€-18.50€. No credit cards. Tues-Sun 7-10pm. Tram: 13, 14, 17 to Westermarkt.

Toscanini 𝄇 SOUTH ITALIAN   This small restaurant has a warm and welcoming ambience and excellent southern Italian food.

It's popular with the artists and bohemians who inhabit this neighborhood. Toscanini has the type of unembellished country-style decor, and an open kitchen, that speak of authenticity, as does the fresh homemade food. Service is congenial but can be slow, though that doesn't seem to deter the loyal regulars, who clamor for such specialties as the delicious veal lasagna and *fazzoletti,* green pasta stuffed with ricotta, mozzarella, and mortadella. For dessert, the Italian ice cream is as good as it looks.

Lindengracht 75 (off Brouwersgracht). © 020/623-2813. Main courses 15€-19€. AE, DC, MC, V. Daily 6-10:30pm. Tram: 3, 10 to Marnixplein.

6 Around Museumplein & Vondelpark

EXPENSIVE

Bodega Keyzer ✶✶ CONTINENTAL   Whether or not you attend a concert at the Concertgebouw, you may want to visit its next-door neighbor, Bodega Keyzer. An Amsterdam landmark since 1903—old-timers say it hasn't changed a whit through the years—the Keyzer has enjoyed a colorful joint heritage with the world-famous concert hall. Among the many stories still told here is the one about the night a customer mistook a concert soloist for a waiter and tried to order some whisky from him. The musician, not missing a beat, lifted his violin case and said graciously, "Would a little Paganini do?" The traditional dark-and-dusky decor and highly starched pink linens add elegance to the place. The menu leans heavily to fish from Dutch waters and, in season, to game specialties, such as hare and venison. (Note that at this writing, Bodega Keyzer was closed for refurbishment and the phone number was out of service. The restaurant was due to re-open in the summer of 2003—and I keep my fingers crossed that all proceeds according to plan.)

Van Baerlestraat 96 (beside the Concertgebouw). © 020/671-1441. Main courses 19.50€-34.50€; fixed-price menu 33€. AE, DC, MC, V. Mon-Sat 9am-midnight, Sun 11am-midnight. Tram: 2 to Willemsparkweg; 3, 5, 12 to Van Baerlestraat; 16 to De Lairessestraat.

MODERATE

De Knijp ✶ DUTCH/FRENCH   One of the advantages of this fine restaurant is that it's open late—its kitchen is still taking orders when chefs at many other Amsterdam restaurants are sound asleep back home. This would not count for much, of course, if the food weren't good, but De Knijp is definitely worth staying up late for, or worth stopping by for after a performance at the nearby

Concertgebouw. The menu is not wildly inventive, but you might try such specialties as carpaccio with pesto, poached salmon with tarragon sauce, and goose breast with pink pepper sauce. Look also for friendly, if sometimes a little worn-out, service (this is a hard-working place), and an intimate bistro ambience, with lots of wood and tables on two levels.

Van Baerlestraat 134 (near the Concertgebouw). ℂ 020/671-4248. Reservations required for lunch and for more than 5 people. Main courses 14.50€-19.50€; fixed-price menus 24.50€-34.50€. AE, DC, MC, V. Mon-Fri noon-3pm; daily 5:30pm-1:30am. Tram: 3, 5, 12, 24 to Museumplein; 16 to Concertgebouwplein.

Sama Sebo 𝒜𝒜 INDONESIAN   Many Amsterdammers consider Sama Sebo the best Indonesian restaurant in town, which means that the place is often filled with locals. A 23-plate *rijsttafel* that sets a standard the others try to match is served in a very Indonesian environment of rush mats and *batik.* Some of its components are hot-and-spicy but in general the effect comes from and effective blending of spices and sauces rather than from the addition of rocket-fuel to the mix. You can make your own mini-*rijsttafel* by putting together a selection from the a la carte menu, or take one big menu dish, like the *nasi goreng* or *bami goreng,* or even settle for just a snack. When the restaurant is busy, as it often is, you can either think of the quarters as convivial or cramped. A sidewalk terrace is equally as area-challenged as the interior. The takeout service is a good option if you want to eat in your hotel room, or maybe even to snack on a bench on nearby Museumplein.

Pieter Cornelisz Hooftstraat 27 (close to the Rijksmuseum). ℂ **020/662-8146.** Main courses 13.50€-19.50€; rijsttafel 25€. AE, DC, MC, V. Mon-Sat noon-2pm and 6-10pm. Tram: 2, 5 to Hobbemastraat.

Vertigo 𝒜𝒜 MEDITERRANEAN   If the name of this animated cafe/restaurant suggests a high location, the reality is far less giddy—in terms of altitude, at least. The reference is to Hitchcock's classic movie. In the vaulted basement of a monumental, late 19th-century villa, Vertigo shares premises with the Film Museum. Hence the portraits of screen legends on the walls and the classic scenes of movie dining on the menu. On summer days, the outside terrace on the edge of Vondelpark is a favored time-out spot for in-line skaters and joggers, and on hot days a restricted menu is served here; you can expect to share your table and make instant acquaintance of just about everyone within earshot. At other times, you can enjoy the southern-European-inspired cuisine in an intimate, candle-lit setting

---

Tips **Picnic Pick**

You can pick up almost anything you might want for a picnic, from cold cuts to a bottle of wine, at the **Albert Heijn supermarket,** at the corner of Leidsestraat and Koningsplein, near Spui (Tram: 1, 2, 5), open Monday to Friday from 9am to 8pm and Saturday from 9am to 6pm. Then head over to Vondelpark, only a 15-minute walk. If it's summer, you might even catch a free concert at the outdoor theater there.

---

inside. The menu, which changes every 6 to 8 weeks, has a choice of fish, meat, and vegetarian options, plus some fresh pasta varieties. If you see grilled breast of guinea fowl on the menu again, my advice is to go for it!

Vondelpark 3 (at the Film Museum). © 020/612-3021. Reservations recommended on weekends. Main courses 14.50€–21.50€. AE, MC, V. Daily 10am–1am. Tram: 1, 6 to Eerste Constantijn Huygensstraat; 2, 3, 5, 12 to Van Baerlestraat.

Wildschut CONTINENTAL Wildschut is one of those places that keeps its chic reputation through thick and thin. The cafe-restaurant occupies a curved dining room at the junction of Van Baerlestraat and Roelof Hartstraat. Amsterdam's bold and beautiful like to see and be seen on the fine terrace in summer or amid the smoke in the brasserie-style interior in winter. It gets crowded here on Friday and Saturday evenings, so be prepared to join the standing throng while waiting for a table. The food is straightforward but good, ranging from BLTs, to vegetarian lasagna, to American rib eye with green pepper sauce. If at all possible, try to wear something that gets you noticed—but not too much, if you get the idea.

Roelof Hartplein 1-3 (off Van Baerlestraat). © 020/676-8220. Main courses 8€–14.50€; fixed-price menu 24.50€. MC, V. Mon–Thurs 9am–1am, Fri 9am–3am, Sat 10:30am–3am, Sun 9:30am–midnight. Tram: 3, 12, 24 to Roelof Hartstraat; 5 to Joh. M. Coenenstraat.

7 In Amsterdam East

VERY EXPENSIVE

La Rive FRENCH/MEDITERRANEAN Cradling a pair of prestigious Michelin stars, La Rive is Amsterdam's undoubted high temple of the culinary arts, combining regional French cuisines with influences from around the Mediterranean and a taste of adventure from even further afield. Royalty, leading politicians, show business stars, and captains of industry dine here—and you don't even need to rub shoulders with them, so discreetly far apart are the tables placed. The dining room overlooks the Amstel River, and in summer, it opens onto a terrace along the embankment with a superb view of the goings-on on the water. The interior atmosphere suggests a small private library called into service for a dinner party. The walls are paneled in cherry and punctuated with tall cabinets filled with books and brass objects. Along one wall is a row of particularly romantic private booths that overlook the other tables and provide a view through the tall French windows to the water. The impeccable service and wine cellar are in the finest modern French traditions. Specialties include grilled baby abalone with citrus-pickled onion puree and garlic juice, turbot and truffles with trimmings, and grill-roasted rack of lamb with dates and Zaanse mustard.

In the Amstel Inter-Continental Amsterdam Hotel, Professor Tulpplein 1 (off Weesperstraat). ⓒ **020/622-6060**. Main courses 25€-65€; fixed-price menus 67.50€-99€. AE, DC, MC, V. Mon-Fri noon-2pm; Mon-Sat 6:30-10:30pm. Tram: 6, 7, 10 to Sarphatistraat.

MODERATE

Gare de l'Est ✿✿ FRENCH/MEDITERRANEAN   A distinctive detached house, with a conservatory extension and a large sidewalk terrace, originally a coffeehouse for workers at the docks, is an altogether good reason for making a trip to a part of town that is by no means fashionable. As the restaurant's name indicates, the cuisine is French, traditional, though with Mediterranean touches. Service is both relaxed and knowledgeable, and as the fixed-price menu is excellent value for money any surprises appear on your plate rather than on the check. The strict five-course formula (starter, salad, main course of meat or fish, cheese, and dessert) leaves no room for choice—except for the main course—but plenty for market-fresh ingredients and culinary creativity. How does this sound: *pulpo estofado et risotto nero* (ink-fish stew and black rice) as a starter, and roast lamb with gazpacho and farfalle as a main course?

Cruquiusweg 9 (at the East Harbor). ⓒ **020/463-0620**. Reservations recommended on weekends. Fixed-price menu 27.50€. No credit cards. Daily 6-11pm. Tram: 7, 10 to Zeeburgerdijk.

8 In Amsterdam South

MODERATE

De Kas ✿✿ CONTINENTAL   People who dine in glass houses shouldn't throw stones. But if you have the trouble I had reserving

for this oh-so-trendy eatery in a greenhouse—calling in March for June and being told that August is the earliest available date—you might want to bring along some rocks. Assuming the feeding frenzy slacks off enough to make calling worthwhile, you'll be able to see and be seen, both outside and inside. The converted 1926 greenhouse with smokestack on open ground in South Amsterdam is light, breezy, and spacious, though the atmosphere's maybe a tad too precious. You get just a couple of variations on a 3-course, dailychanging fixed menu, with cheeseboard extra. Mediterranean-style greens and herbs come fresh from an adjacent working hothouse and the restaurant's own farm, and meat is sourced daily from nearby animal-friendly, eco-producers. Service is attentive enough that the waitstaff seem to be acquainted personally with every item on your plate.

Kamerlingh Onneslaan 3 (close to Amstel Station). ℂ 020/462-4562. Reservations required. Fixed-price lunch 27.25€; fixed-price dinner 35€. AE, DC, MC, V. Open Mon-Fri noon-3pm and 6:30-10pm, Sat 6:30-10pm. Tram: 9 to Hogeweg.

INEXPENSIVE

Artist LEBANESE   Owners Ralfo and Simon have brought a little piece of the eastern Mediterranean to Amsterdam South and presented it in a simple, authentic way at low cost with good taste guaranteed. Members of the city's Lebanese community are often seated at the tables here—always a good sign for an ethnic restaurant. Specialties include Lebanese *meze* and a selection of small dishes that adds up to a big meal, including *falafel, couscous,* and even Lebanese pizza. Many of the dishes here are vegetarian.

Tweede Jan Steenstraat 1 (off Van Woustraat). ℂ 020/671-4264. Main courses 4.50€-9.50€; fixed-price menu (*meze*) 9.50€. AE, DC, MC, V. Daily 5-11pm. Tram: 4 to Van Woustraat.

9 In Amsterdam West

MODERATE

Café-Restaurant Amsterdam ✦✦✦ *(Finds* CONTINENTAL Think of it as *Amsterdam: the Restaurant,* because it's quite a performance. Based in a century-old water-pumping station, complete with diesel-powered engine, the Amsterdam has taken this monument of Victorian industrial good taste and made of it a model of contemporary good eats. You dine amidst a buzz of conviviality in the large, brightly lit, former pumping hall, which had been so carefully tended by the water workers that some of its elegant decoration didn't even need repainting. Service is friendly and the food is good and moderately priced. The fried sweetbreads are popular. If you're feeling flush, spring for a double starter of half lobster with six Zeeland oysters. The Amsterdam is a little bit out from the Center, but easily worth the tram ride.

Watertorenplein 6 (off Haarlemmerweg). © 020/682-2666. Reservations recommended on weekends. Main courses 9.50€-19.50€. AE, DC, MC, V. Daily 11am-midnight. Tram: 10 to Van Hallstraat.

10 In Amsterdam North

MODERATE

Wilhelmina-Dok ✿✿ CONTINENTAL   Amsterdam is making increasing use of its vast harbor for living and working space, as the old cargo-handling installations are erased. You can dive right into the middle of this trend at this waterside eatery in Amsterdam Noord, across the IJ ship channel from Centraal Station. Getting there involves a 5-minute ferry ride followed by a 5-minute walk, but the ferry is at least free. The cafe-restaurant, which opened in 2000, is a slightly wacko-looking place on three floors (the chandeliered top-floor Kapiteinskamer [Captain's Cabin] is for groups only). Plain wood, candlelit tables, wood floors, and oak cabinets give the interior an old-fashioned maritime look, and large windows serve up views across the canal-barge-speckled channel to the cruiseship Passenger Terminal Amsterdam on the south shore. Breezy is one way to describe the impact of the prevailing westerlies, but tables on the outdoor terrace are sheltered from the wind in a glass-walled enclosure. The menu favors organic products. A couple of good choices are the *zwaardvis van de grill met saffranrisotto* (grilled swordfish with saffron rice) and the *kalfslende van de grill met gemarineerde aubergine en flageolottensalade en pesto* (grilled veal cutlets with marinated aubergines, flageolet salad, and pesto). Or, you can settle back with just a beer and a snack. On Monday evenings in August, movies are shown on an outdoor screen.

Nordwal 1 (at IJplein). © 020/632-3701. Main courses 15€-16.50€. AE, DC, MC, V. Mon-Fri noon-midnight, Sat-Sun noon-1am. Ferry: IJveer from Pier 8 behind Centraal Station to the dock at IJplein, then go right along the dike-top path.

5

Exploring Amsterdam

Amsterdam offers sightseers an almost bewildering embarrassment of riches. There are miles and miles of canals to cruise and hundreds of narrow streets to wander, almost 7,000 historic buildings to see in the city center, more than 40 museums of all types to visit, diamond cutters and craftspeople to watch as they practice generations-old skills—the list is as long as every tourist's individual interests, and then some.

The city has 160 canals—more than Venice—with a combined length of 76km (47 miles), spanned by 1,281 bridges. So the first thing you should do is join the 2.5 million people every year that take a ride around the canals on one of the 70 canal tour-boats. Why? Because the water-level view of those gabled canal houses and the picturesque bridges lends meaning and color to everything else you do during your stay. Amsterdam's 17th-century Golden Age becomes a vivid reality as you glide through the waterways that were largely responsible for those years of prosperity. You view the canal houses from canal level, just as they were meant to be seen. This is also the best way to see Amsterdam's large and busy harbor. (See "Organized Tours," later in this chapter.)

1 The Big Four

Rijksmuseum 𝄞𝄞𝄞 *Note:* Most of the Rijksmuseum is due to be closed for a whopping 5 years, from late 2003 to mid-2008, for renovation. During the period of partial closure, key paintings from the 17th-century Dutch Golden Age collection can be viewed in the museum's own Philips Wing, and other elements of the collection will likely be on view at other venues in the city. During the renovation period, you can find a complete review of the Rijksmuseum at www.frommers.com.

Stadhouderskade 42 (behind Museumplein, halfway between Leidseplein and Weteringplantsoen). ℂ 020/670-7047. Admission 8.50€ adults, free for children under 18. Daily 10am-5pm. Tram: 2, 5 to Hobbemastraat; 6, 7, 10 to Weteringschans.

Van Gogh Museum ✫✫✫ Thanks to the chauvinism of his family—in particular, his brother's wife and a namesake nephew—nearly every painting, sketch, print, etching, and piece of correspondence that Vincent van Gogh ever produced has remained in his native country, and since 1973, the collection has been housed in its own museum. To the further consternation of van Gogh admirers and scholars elsewhere in the world, all but a few of the drawings and paintings that are not in the museum's keeping hang at the Kröller-Müller Museum in the Hoge Veluwe National Park near Arnhem.

You can trace this great artist's artistic and psychological development by viewing more than 200 of his paintings displayed simply and in chronological order according to the seven distinct periods and places of residence that defined his short career. (He painted for only 10 years and was on the threshold of success when he committed suicide in 1890, at age 37.)

One particularly splendid wall, on the second floor, has a progression of 18 paintings produced during the 2-year period when Vincent lived in the south of France, generally considered to be his artistic high point. It's a symphony of colors and color contrasts that includes *Gauguin's Chair; The Yellow House; Self-Portrait with Pipe and Straw Hat; Vincent's Bedroom at Arles; Wheatfield with Reaper; Bugler of the Zouave Regiment;* and one of the most famous paintings of modern times, *Still Life Vase with Fourteen Sunflowers,* best known simply as *Sunflowers.* By the time you reach the vaguely threatening painting of a flock of black crows rising from a waving cornfield, you can almost feel the mounting inner pain the artist was finally unable to bear.

A new wing, elliptical and partly underground, designed by Japanese architect Kisho Kurokawa, opened on Museumplein in June 1999 to house temporary exhibits of work by van Gogh and other artists.

Paulus Potterstraat 7 (at Museumplein). ✆ **020/570-5200.** Admission 7€ adults, 2.50€ children 13-17, children under 13 free. Daily 10am-6pm. Tram: 2, 3, 5, 12 to Van Baerlestraat.

Stedelijk Museum ✫✫ *Note:* The Stedelijk is due to close from January 1, 2003, to March 2005 for renovation and the construction of two new wings. The following review stands in case something should happen to delay these plans. During the period of closure, elements from the museum's collection can be viewed at other venues in the city. The city's modern art museum is the place

Central Amsterdam Attractions

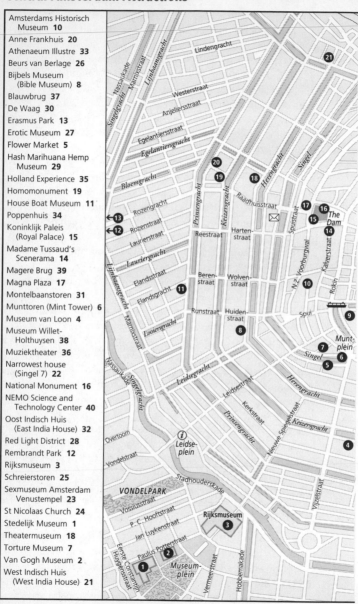

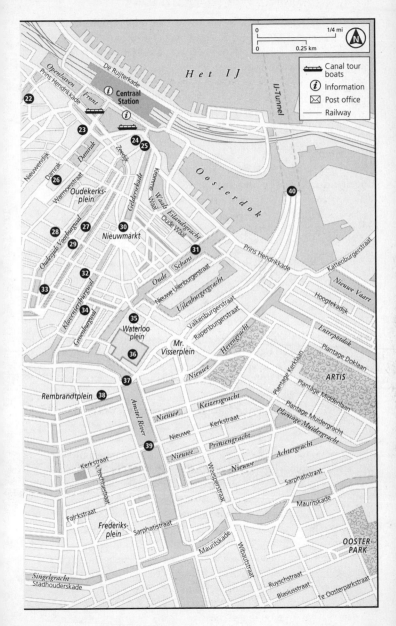

to see works by such Dutch painters as Karel Appel, Willem de Kooning, and Piet Mondrian, alongside works by the French artists Chagall, Cézanne, Picasso, Renoir, Monet, and Manet and by the Americans Calder, Oldenburg, Rosenquist, and Warhol. The Stedelijk centers its collection around the De Stijl, Cobra, post-Cobra, nouveau réalisme, pop art, color-field painting, zero, minimalist, and conceptual schools of modern art. It houses the largest collection outside Russia of the abstract paintings of Kasimir Malevich.

Architect Alvaro Siza has drawn up plans for restoring the old building as closely as possible to its original 1895 neo-Renaissance appearance, and constructing an extension on Museumplein, but no start date for the project has been announced.

Paulus Potterstraat 13 (at Museumplein). © 020/573-2737. Admission 5€ adults, 2.50€ children 7-17 and seniors, children under 7 free. Daily 11am-5pm. Closed Jan 1. Tram: 2, 5 to Van Baerlestraat; 3, 12, 16 to Museumplein.

Anne Frankhuis ✸✸✸ In summer you may have to wait an hour or more to get in, but no one should miss seeing and experiencing this house, where eight people from three separate families lived together in near total silence for more than 2 years during World War II. The hiding place Otto Frank found for his family and friends kept them safe until, tragically close to the end of the war, it was raided by Nazi forces, and its occupants were deported to concentration camps. It was in this house that Anne kept her famous diary as a way to deal with both the boredom and her youthful jumble of thoughts, which had as much to do with personal relationships as with the war and the Nazi terror raging outside her hiding place. Visiting the rooms where she hid is a moving and eerily real experience.

The rooms of the building, which was an office and warehouse at that time, are still as bare as they were when Anne's father returned, the only survivor of the eight *onderduikers* (divers, or hiders). Nothing has been changed, except that protective Plexiglas panels have been placed over the wall where Anne pinned up photos of her favorite actress, Deanna Durbin, and of the little English princesses Elizabeth and Margaret. As you tour the small building, it's easy to imagine Anne's experience growing up in this place, awakening as a young woman, and writing down her secret thoughts in a diary.

Get there as early as you can to avoid the lines—this advice isn't as useful as it used to be, because everybody is both giving it and heeding it, but it should still save you some waiting time. An alternative strategy if you're in town from April to August, when the museum is open to 9pm, is to go in the evening, as it is invariably quiet then—till now at any rate. A typical Amsterdam canal house, this has very steep interior stairs. Next door at no. 265-267 is a new wing for temporary exhibits. You can see a bronze sculpture of Anne at nearby Westermarkt.

Prinsengracht 263 (beside Westermarkt). © 020/556-7100. Admission 6.50€ adults, 3€ children 10-17, children under 10 free. Apr-Aug daily 9am-9pm; Sept-Mar daily 9am-7pm; Jan 1 and Dec 25 noon-5pm. Closed Yom Kippur. Tram: 13, 14, 17 to Westermarkt.

2 More Museums & Galleries

Amsterdams Historisch Museum (Amsterdam Historical Museum) Few cities in the world have gone to as much trouble and expense to display and explain their history, and few museums in the world have found as many ways to make such dry material as population growth and urban development as interesting as the latest electronic board game. Don't say you have little interest in Amsterdam's history. This fascinating museum, in the huge 17th-century Burger Weeshuis, the restored former City Orphanage, gives you a better understanding of everything you see

---

C A New Museumplein

Three of the big four—Rijksmuseum, Van Gogh Museum, and Stedelijk Museum—are conveniently clustered around Museumplein, a big open square just south of the old city. The square has been totally transformed in recent years, and motorized through-traffic has been abolished.

Most of the rebuilt square consists of open green areas bordered by avenues of linden trees and gardens, which can be used for major outdoor events. Walkways and bike paths pass through. At the north end are sports and play areas, and a long pond that serves as an ice-skating rink in winter.

I have to say that, compared to the old Museumplein's raggedy appeal, I find the new model to be a charm-free zone, something from the Antiseptic School of urban design.

Museumplein Area & Amsterdam South Attractions

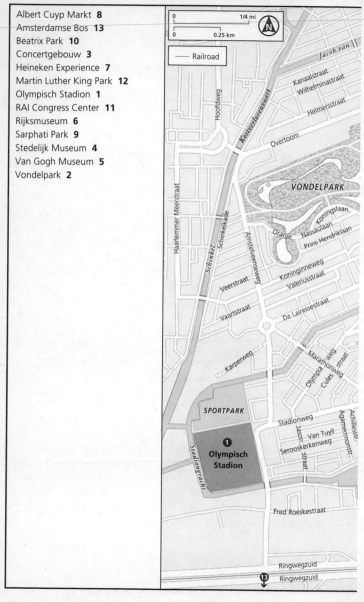

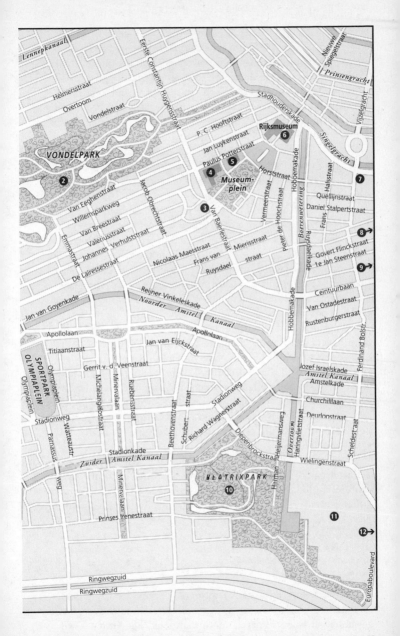

Lennepkanaal

Helmersstraat

Overtoom

Vondelstraat

Eerste Constantijn Huygensstraat

Nieuwe Spiegelstraat

Prinsengracht

Stadhouderskade

Vizelgracht

P. C. Hoofstraat

Jan Luykenstraat

Paulus Potterstraat

Rijksmuseum ❻

VONDELPARK

❷

❹ ❺

Museum-plein

❸ Van Baerlestraat

Horststraat

Hobbemakade

Singelgracht

❼

Hallsstraat

Quellijnstraat

Daniel Stalpertstraat

Frans

❽ →

Govert Flinckstraat

1e Jan Steenstraat

❾ →

Van Eeghenstraat

Willemsparkweg

Jacob Obrechtstraat

Van Breestraat

Valeriusstraat

Johannes Verhulststraat

De Lairessestraat

Emmastraat

Nicolaas Maesstraat

Frans van

Mierisstraat

straat

Ruysdael

Vermeerstraat

Pieter de Hoochstraat

Barentszweg

Ruysdaelkade

Ceintuurbaan

Van Ostadestraat

Rustenburgerstraat

Reijnier Vinkeleskade

Noorder Amstel Kanaal

Jan van Goyenkade

Hobbemakade

Ferdinand Bolstr.

Apollolaan

Titiaanstraat

Jan van Eijckstraat

Apollolaan

Jozef Israelskade

Amstel Kanaal

Amstelkade

SPORTPARK OLYMPIAPLEIN

Olympiaplein

Gerrit v. d. Veenstraat

Michelangelostraat

Minervalaan

Ruebensstraat

Stadionweg

Churchilllaan

Deurloostraat

Stadionweg

Parnassus

Watteaustr.

weg

Beethovenstraat

Schubert

straat

Richard Wagnerstraat

Diepenbrockstraat

Heijermansweg

Overtoom

Haringvlietstraat

Wielingenstraat

Scheldestraat

Stadionkade

Zuider Amstel Kanaal

Minervalaan

BEATRIXPARK

❿

Herman

⓫

⓬ →

Prinses Irenestraat

Europaboulevard

Ringwegzuid

Ringwegzuid

when you go out to explore the city on your own. Gallery by gallery, century by century, you learn how a small fishing village founded around 1200 became a major sea power and trading center.

The main focus is on the city's 17th century golden age, a period when Amsterdam was the richest city in the world, and some of the most interesting exhibits are of the trades that made it rich. You can also view many of the famous paintings by the Dutch masters in the context of their time and place in history.

There's a fascinating and beautiful scale model from around 1677 of the then new Stadhuis (Town Hall) on the Dam, now the Royal Palace, with some of its outer walls and the roof removed to give you a bird's-eye look inside.

A small room is given over to the story of local hero Jan Carel Josephus van Speyk, a Dutch naval officer during the 1830 rebellion by Belgium against Dutch rule. A boarding party of Belgian patriots who aimed to commandeer his warship in the Scheldt River off Antwerp reckoned without Van Speyk's "Don't give up the ship" disposition. He dropped his lit cigar into the ship's gunpowder magazine, setting off an explosion that blew him, the vessel, and the rebel boarders into the air and into history.

Among many other historic items are four beautiful late-15th-century altar cushions depicting the Miracle of the Host in 1345.

You can pop into Café 't Mandje, a typical, if tiny, Amsterdam neighborhood bar. Sadly, you can't order a beer or a *jenever*, since the "cafe" is a museum exhibit. But you really can visit the museum's **David & Goliath** cafe, which has a high-beamed ceiling and lofty wooden statues of David and Goliath, salvaged from an amusement park that was a feature of Amsterdam's landscape for nearly 250 years until 1862.

When you leave the Historical Museum, cut through the **Schuttersgalerij (Civic Guard Gallery),** a narrow, two-story skylit chamber bedecked with a dozen large, impressive 17th-century group portraits of militiamen. The hours are the same as for the museum, and admission is free.

Kalverstraat 92, Nieuwezijds Voorburgwal 359, and Sint-Luciënsteeg 27 (next to the Begijnhof). © **020/523-1822.** Admission 6€ adults, 4.50€ seniors, 3€ children 6-16, children under 6 free. Mon-Fri 10am-5pm; Sat-Sun 11am-5pm. Closed Jan 1, Apr 30, Dec 25. Tram: 1, 2, 4, 5, 9, 14, 16, 24, 25 to Spui.

Bijbels Museum (Biblical Museum) &   Taking the Good Book as a starting point, you move on to explore biblical history and geography in objects, images, and installations. The setting—twin patrician canal houses from 1662, designed by noted architect

---

Tips Money Savers

One way to save money—and not just on admission to museums and attractions—is to buy the VVV Amsterdam tourist office's **Amsterdam Pass** (see "Your Passport to Amsterdam," in chapter 2).

Remember that many museums and other attractions offer reduced admission to seniors, students, and children.

If you should happen to be in the Netherlands on **National Museum Weekend,** April 12 and 13, 2003, you're in luck. Most museums in the country have free admission at this time and others charge greatly reduced admission.If museums are high on your sightseeing agenda—and you're a resident of the Netherlands—you might find a **Museumjaarkaart (Museum Year Pass)** to be a good investment. At 30€ for adults, 25€ for those over 54, and 15€ for those under 25, the pass gives a year's free admission to 350 museums throughout the land. You can purchase it from VVV tourist offices and from many museums.

Philips Vingboons, and with a lovely courtyard garden—would be worth visiting for its historical interest alone. In 1717, Jacob de Wit painted its main ceiling with mythological scenes. The museum collection includes models of ancient Jerusalem, the Temple of Solomon, and the Tabernacle; archaeological finds from Israel, Palestine, and Egypt; and paintings of biblical scenes. Among the Bibles on display are the first Bible printed in the Low Countries, dating from 1477, and the first edition of the authorized Dutch translation, from 1637.

Herengracht 366-368 (near Spui). ℭ **020/624-2436.** Admission 5€ adults, 2.50€ children 6-17, children under 6 free. Mon-Sat 10am-5pm; Sun 1-5pm. Tram: 1, 2, 5 to Spui.

Joods Historisch Museum (Jewish Historical Museum) ℜ

In 1987, this museum opened in the restored Ashkenazi Synagogue complex, a cluster of four former synagogues, in the heart of what was once Amsterdam's thriving Jewish Quarter. It's home to a collection of paintings, decorations, and ceremonial objects confiscated during World War II and patiently reestablished in the postwar period. Through its objects, photographs, artworks, and interactive displays, the museum tells three intertwining stories—of Jewish identity, Jewish religion and culture, and Jewish history in the

Netherlands. It presents the community in both good times and bad and provides insights into the Jewish way of life over the centuries. Leave time to appreciate the beauty and size of the buildings themselves, which include the oldest public synagogue in Europe. This is a museum for everyone—Jewish or otherwise. There are frequent temporary exhibits of international interest.

Tip: The museum cafe is a great place to have a cup of coffee and a pastry, or a light meal (kosher, too). It's quiet, inexpensive, and the food is good.

Jonas Daniël Meijerplein 2-4 (at Waterlooplein). © 020/626-9945. Admission 5€ adults, 3€ seniors, 2.50€ children 13-17, 1.50€ children 6-12, children under 6 free. Daily 11am-5pm. Closed Yom Kippur. Tram: 9, 14 to Waterlooplein.

Museum Het Rembrandthuis ⊛ To view the greatest masterpieces by Rembrandt van Rijn, you must visit the Rijksmuseum (when it re-opens), but in this house you find a more intimate sense of the artist himself. Bought by Rembrandt in 1639 when he was Amsterdam's most fashionable portrait painter, the house, which has 10 rooms, is a shrine to one of the greatest artists the world has ever known. In this house, Rembrandt's son Titus was born and his wife, Saskia, died. The artist was bankrupt when he left it in 1658. (The militia company of Captain Frans Banning Cocq portrayed in *The Night Watch* hated the artistic freedom Rembrandt had exercised on their group portrait and this helped to ruin his previously brilliant career.) Not until 1906 was the building rescued from a succession of subsequent owners and restored as a museum.

In 1998, a modern wing for temporary exhibits was added; restoration completed in 1999 has returned the old house to the way it looked when Rembrandt lived and worked there. Further work in 2000 has restored the artist's cabinet of art and curiosities, his combined living room and bedroom, and the studio he and his pupils used. The rooms are furnished with 17th-century objects and furniture that, as far as possible, match the descriptions in Rembrandt's 1656 petition for bankruptcy. His printing press is back in place, and you can view 250 of his etchings and drawings hanging on the walls. These include self-portraits and landscapes; several relate to the traditionally Jewish character of the neighborhood, such as the portrait of Rabbi Menassah ben Israel, who lived across the street and was an early teacher of another illustrious Amsterdammer, Baruch Spinoza. Opposite Rembrandthuis, appropriately, stands the Amsterdamse Hogeschool voor de Kunsten (Amsterdam High School for the Arts).

Jodenbreestraat 4 (behind Waterlooplein). ℂ **020/520-0400**. Admission 7€ adults, 5€ students, 1.50€ children 6-15, children under 6 free. Mon-Sat 10am-5pm; Sun and holidays 1-5pm. Tram: 9, 14 to Waterlooplein.

Museum Van Loon   The history of this magnificent patrician house, one of a matched pair dating from 1672, is a long saga of ne'er-do-well spouses and ailing orphans, of misguided inheritances and successive bankruptcies. The elegant home was owned by the Van Loon family from 1884 to 1945. On its walls hang more than 80 family portraits, including those of Willem van Loon, one of the founders of the Dutch United East India Company; Nicolaes Ruychaver, who liberated Amsterdam from the Spanish in 1578; and another, later, Willem van Loon, who became mayor in 1686. Among other treasures are a family album in which you can see tempera portraits of all living Van Loons painted at two successive dates (1650 and 1675), and a series of commemorative coins struck to honor seven different golden wedding anniversaries celebrated between the years 1621 and 1722. The house's completely restored period rooms are filled with richly decorated paneling, stucco work, mirrors, fireplaces, furnishings, porcelain, medallions, chandeliers, rugs, and more. The garden has carefully tended hedges and a coach house modeled on a Greek temple.

Keizersgracht 672 (near Vijzelstraat). ℂ **020/624-5255**. Admission 4.50€ adults, 3€ students, children 12 and under free. Fri-Mon 11am-5pm. Tram: 16, 24, 25 to Keizersgracht.

Museum Willet-Holthuysen   This museum offers another rare opportunity to visit an elegant 17th-century canal house, with a beautiful garden. This particular house, built in 1687, was renovated several times before its last inhabitant gave it and its contents to the city in 1889. Among the most interesting rooms are a Victorian-era bedroom on the second floor, a large reception room with tapestry wall panels, and an 18th-century basement kitchen that's still so completely furnished and functional you could swear the cook had merely stepped out to go shopping.

Herengracht 605 (near the Amstel River). ℂ **020/523-1822**. Admission 4€ adults, 2€ children 6-16, children under 6 free. Mon-Fri 10am-5pm; Sat-Sun 11am-5pm. Closed Jan 1, Apr 30, Dec 25. Tram: 4, 9, 14 to Rembrandtplein.

Scheepvaartmuseum (Maritime Museum) 🐠🐠   A bonanza for anyone who loves ships and the sea, the museum overlooks the busy harbor, and is appropriately housed in a former Amsterdam Admiralty arsenal, from 1656. Room after room is filled with boats and ship models, seascape and ship paintings, navigational instruments, prints, and old maps, including a 15th-century Ptolemaic atlas and a sumptuously bound edition of the *Great Atlas, or Description of the World,* produced over a lifetime by Jan Blaeu, the master cartographer of Holland's Golden Age. All the exhibits chronicle the country's abiding ties to the sea through commerce, fishing, yachting, exploration, and war. Among the important papers on display are several pertaining to the Dutch colonies of Nieuwe Amsterdam (New York City) and Nieuwe Nederland (New York), including a receipt for the land that now surrounds the New York State capital at Albany.

A full-size replica of the Dutch United East India Company ship *Amsterdam,* which foundered off Hastings, England, in 1749 on her maiden voyage to the fabled Spice Islands (Indonesia), is moored at the wharf, as is a replica of the *Stad Amsterdam,* a three-masted iron clipper from 1854 (it may eventually be moved to Java Island in the harbor). Other ships you can see are a steam icebreaker, a motor lifeboat, and a herring lugger; the historic Royal Barge and two towing barges are housed indoors.

You can reach the museum by taking a 20-minute walk along the historical waterfront, the Nautisch Kwartier.

Kattenburgerplein 1 (at the Eastern Dock). © 020/523-2222. Admission 7€ adults, 4€ children 6-18, children under 6 free. Tues-Sat 10am-5pm (also Mon mid-June to mid-Sept); Sun noon-5pm. Bus: 22, 32 to Kattenburgerplein.

Theatermuseum   The Netherlands Theater Institute occupies a group of adjoining 17th-century canal houses, two of which house this imaginative museum. No. 168, known as Het Witte Huis (the White House) for its whitish-gray, neoclassical sandstone facade, was built in 1638 by Philips Vingboons and sports the city's first neck gable. Dazzling interior ornamentation from around 1730 includes a spiral staircase, intricate stuccowork, and painted ceilings by Jacob de Wit. The elaborate Bartolotti House at no. 170-172, built in 1617 and 1618 by Hendrick de Keyser, famous for its ornate redbrick gable and Dutch Renaissance facade, has illuminated ceilings and other interior decoration by Jacob de Wit. In the museum, you find costumes, maquettes, masks, puppets, photographs, paintings, miniature theaters, and theatrical backdrops, covering all forms of theater, including opera and children's theater. Hands-on experience includes creating your own stage and sound effects. Book ahead for hands-on workshops for children (7-12) on Wednesday, Saturday, and Sunday afternoons.

Herengracht 168 (at Leliegracht). $\mathcal{C}$ 020/551-3300. Admission 3.85€ adults, 1.95€ seniors/children 7-16, children under 7 free. Tues-Fri 11am-5pm; Sat-Sun 1-5pm. Tram: 13, 14, 17 to the Dam.

Tropenmuseum (Tropical Museum) ★★
One of the city's most intriguing museums belongs to the Royal Institute for the Tropics, a foundation devoted to the study of the cultures of tropical areas around the world. Its focus reflects Holland's centuries as a landlord in such areas as Indonesia; Surinam (on the northern coast of South America); and the islands of St. Maarten, Saba, St. Eustatius, Aruba, Bonaire, and Curaçao in the West Indies. The Tropical Institute building complex alone is worth the trip to Amsterdam East; its heavily ornamented 19th-century facade is an amalgam of Dutch architectural styles: turrets, stepped gables, arched windows, delicate spires, and the monumental galleried interior court (a popular spot for concerts).

Of the exhibits, the most interesting are the walk-through model villages and city-street scenes that, except for the lack of genuine inhabitants, seem to capture a moment in the daily life of such places as India and Indonesia; the displays of tools and techniques used to produce *batik,* the distinctively dyed Indonesian fabrics; and displays of the tools, instruments, and ornaments that clutter a tropical residence. There's a permanent exhibit on people and environment in West Asia and North Africa.

Part of the premises is given over to the children-only Kindermuseum TM Junior.

Linnaeusstraat 2 (at Mauritskade). $\mathcal{C}$ 020/568-8215. Admission 6.80€ adults, 3.40€ children 6-17, children under 6 free. Daily 10am-5pm. Closed Jan 1, Apr 30, May 5, Dec 25. Tram: 7, 9, 10, 14 to Mauritskade.

Woonboot Museum (Houseboat Museum)
In Amsterdam, no one ever tosses away an old boat. You see many houseboats moored along the canals, on the river, and in the harbor of Amsterdam, but you won't be able to get aboard most of them unless you know the owner. The *Hendrika Maria,* a former commercial sailing ship built in 1914, is an exception. You can visit the original deckhouse where the skipper and his family lived, the cupboard bed in which they slept, and the cargo hold, now equipped as remarkably spacious and comfortable living quarters. How do you get the boat's bottom cleaned? Might you sink? What happens in winter? These and other questions are answered in models, photographs, and books.

Opposite Prinsengracht 296 (near Elandsgracht). ℭ **020/427-0750.** Admission 2.50€ adults, 2.05€ children under 152cm (59 in.). Mar-Oct Wed-Sun 11am-5pm; Nov-Dec and Feb Fri-Sun 11am-5pm. Tram: 13, 14, 17 to Westermarkt.

3 Historic Buildings & Monuments

Beurs van Berlage (Old Stock Exchange)   Designed by architect Hendrik Petrus Berlage and built between 1896 and 1903, the Stock Exchange, a massive edifice of colored brick and stone enclosing three arcades roofed in glass and iron, represented a revolutionary break with 19th-century architecture. Though it's no longer the stock exchange, it's still well worth visiting as the prime example of Amsterdam School architecture, which was contemporaneous with the work of Frank Lloyd Wright in America. Today, the Beurs is used as a space for concerts, conferences, and exhibits.

Note on its facade a relief of two fishermen and a dog in a boat, depicting a legend of Amsterdam's foundation, and a modern sculpture of Count Gijsbrecht II van Amstel, who in 1204 built Amsterdam's first castle, at the Dam, set in a corner of the building facing Beursplein. This pleasant square is dotted with plane trees and 19th-century wrought-iron streetlamps. The modern Effectenbeurs (Stock Exchange) is on the eastern side of the square.

Beursplein 7 (near the Dam). ℭ **020/626-8936.** Admission 3.75€ adults, 2.50€ children 5-16, children under 5 free. Mon-Fri 9am-5pm. Tram; 4, 9, 14, 16, 24, 25 to the Dam.

De Waag (Weigh House)   Built in the 14th century, the city's only surviving medieval fortified gate later became a guild house. Among the guilds lodged here was the Surgeon's Guild, immortalized in Rembrandt's painting *The Anatomy Lesson* (1632), which depicts a dissection in the rarely open upper-floor Theatrum Anatomicum. Today the Waag is a multimedia center for exhibits, theater, and music performances. The reading table in its cafe features not only newspapers, as is common in Amsterdam, but also Internet access and a selection of CD-ROMs.

Nieuwmarkt. ℭ **020/557-9898.** Free admission (but some exhibits charge admission). Sun-Thurs 10am-1am; Fri-Sat 10am-2am. Metro: Nieuwmarkt.

Koninklijk Paleis (Royal Palace) 🏛🏛   One of the heavier features of the Dam is the solid, neoclassical facade of the Royal Palace (1648-55). Designed by Jacob van Campen—the Thomas Jefferson of the Dutch Republic—as a Stadhuis (Town Hall) to replace the frumpy and decayed old Gothic one that in 1652 did everyone a favor by burning down, it was designed to showcase the city's burgeoning prosperity; its interior is replete with white Italian marble. Poet Constantijn Huygens called the new Town Hall the "Eighth Wonder of the World."

Not until 1808, when Napoléon Bonaparte's younger brother Louis reigned as king of the Netherlands, did it become a palace, filled with Empire-style furniture courtesy of the French ruler. Since the return to the throne in 1813 of the Dutch House of Orange, this has been the official palace of the reigning king or queen of the Netherlands. Few of them, however, have used it for more than an occasional state reception or official ceremony (such as the inauguration of Queen Beatrix, who prefers living at Huis ten Bosch in The Hague), or as their *pied-à-terre* in the capital.

In the Vierschaar (Tribunal), magistrates pronounced death sentences watched over by images of Justice, Wisdom, and Mercy. Atlas holds up the globe in the high-ceilinged Burgerzaal (Citizens Chamber), and maps inlaid on the marble floor show Amsterdam as the center of the world. Ferdinand Bol's painting *Moses the Lawgiver* hangs in the Schepenzaal (Council Chamber), where the aldermen met. On the pediment overlooking the Dam, Flemish sculptor Artus Quellien carved a baroque hymn in stone to Amsterdam's maritime preeminence, showing figures symbolizing the oceans paying the city homage. The weathervane on the cupola takes the form of a Dutch sailing ship.

Tip: Don't miss the excellent video presentation (in English) that's shown continuously (usually in the Magistrate's Court on the 2nd floor).

Dam. ℂ 020/620-4060. Admission 4€ adults, 3€ children 5-12, children under 5 free. Easter and June-Oct daily 11am-5pm; Nov to mid-Dec and mid-Feb to May generally Tues-Thurs 12:30-5pm (opening days and hours are highly variable; check before going). Closed mid-Dec to mid-Feb. Tram: 1, 2, 4, 5, 9, 13, 14, 16, 17, 24, 25 to the Dam.

OTHER HISTORIC SIGHTS

You may come away thinking Amsterdam is one big historic monument. Still, some buildings are more historic and monumental than others and therefore more worth going out of your way for. You won't have to go far out of your way to see **Centraal Station.** Built on an artificial island in the IJ inlet of the Zuider Zee (now the IJsselmeer), between 1884 and 1889, the station was thoroughly disliked by Amsterdammers at the time. Now it's an attraction in its own right, partly for its extravagant Dutch neo-Renaissance facade, partly for the liveliness that permanently surrounds it. The left one of the two central towers has a gilded weathervane; on the right one there's a clock. Take a little time to soak up the buzz that swirls around the station in a blur of people, backpacks, bikes, trams, buses, vendors, pickpockets, and junkies. There should be a busker or two, maybe even a full-blown jazz or rock combo, and maybe a street organ.

Not far away, across Prins Hendrikkade at the corner of Geldersekade, is the **Schreierstoren (Tower of Tears),** from 1480, once a strong point in the city wall bristling with cannon. Its name comes from the tears allegedly shed by wives as their menfolk sailed away on voyages from which they might never return. A stone tablet on the wall shows a woman with her hand to her face. She might be weeping, but who knows what emotion that hand is really covering up?

No ambiguity surrounds the **Munttoren (Mint Tower)** on Muntplein, a busy traffic intersection at Rokin and the Singel canal. The base of the tower, from 1490, used to be part of the Reguliers Gate in the city wall. In 1620, Hendrick de Keyser topped it with an ornate, lead-covered tower, whose carillon bells sing out gaily every hour and play a 1-hour concert on Friday at noon.

A monument of a different temper is the sad remains of the **Hollandsche Schouwburg,** Plantage Middenlaan 24 (© **020/ 626-9945;** tram 9, 14), not far from the Jewish Historical Museum and the Portuguese Synagogue. All that remains of the former Yiddish Theater, which was used by the Nazis as an assembly point for Dutch Jews who were to be deported to concentration camps, is its facade, behind which is a simple memorial plaza of grass and walkways. A granite column rising out of a Star of David emblem commemorates "those deported from here 1940-45." On a marble memorial, watched over by an eternal flame, are inscribed the 6,700 family names of the 60,000 to 80,000 deportees who passed through here, few of whom survived the war. The site is open daily from 11am to 4pm. Admission is free.

Most of Golden Age Amsterdam's wealth was generated by trade, and most of that trade was organized by the Verenigde Oostindische Compagnie (V.O.C.), based at **Oost Indisch Huis (East India House)** on Oude Hoogstraat, off Kloveniersburgwal. Dating from 1606, this former headquarters of the first multinational corporation now belongs to the University of Amsterdam, but you can stroll into the courtyard.

You might also be interested in **West Indisch Huis (West India House),** at Herenmarkt, off Brouwersgracht. On the north side of this little square is a red-brick building, built as a meat-trading hall in 1615 and that in 1623, became headquarters of the Dutch West India Company, which controlled trade with the Americas. It now houses educational organizations, including the John Adams Institute, an American-oriented philosophical and literary society. In the courtyard is a statue of Peter Stuyvesant, one-legged governor of Nieuwe Amsterdam (later New York City) from 1647 until the British took over in 1664. There's a sculpture depicting the first Dutch settlement on Manhattan Island, founded in 1626.

Not far from West India House is Amsterdam's first university, the **Athenaeum Illustre,** at Oudezijds Voorburgwal 231. Founded in 1631, the Athenaeum moved here in 1632, to occupy the 15th-century Gothic Agnietenkapel (Church of St. Agnes) and convent of the Order of St. Francis, whose nuns lost their place to the Dutch Admiralty after the religious upheaval of 1578. The building is now the University of Amsterdam Museum.

OTHER MONUMENTS & SIGHTS

The **Homomonument,** on Westermarkt beside the Westerkerk church, is three granite blocks in the shape of pink triangles (the shape of the Nazi badge for homosexuals), forming a larger triangular outline. One block, a symbol of the future, points into the Keizersgracht; one, at ground level, points toward the nearby Anne Frank House; the other, a sort of plinth about 50cm (20 in.) high, points toward the offices of COC, a gay political organization). Designed by Karin Daan, the monument memorializes gays and lesbians killed during World War II and persecuted throughout the ages.

The precariously tilting **Montelbaanstoren,** the "leaning tower of Amsterdam," a fortification at the juncture of the Oude Schans and Waals-Eilandsgracht canals, dates from 1512. It is one of few surviving elements of the city's once powerful defensive works. In 1606, Hendrick de Keyser added an octagonal tower and spire.

Made of African azobe wood, the famous **Magere Brug (Skinny Bridge),** a double-drawbridge, spans the Amstel between Kerkstraat and Nieuwe Kerkstraat. This is the latest successor, dating from 1969, to the 1672 original, which legend says was built to make it easier for the two wealthy Mager sisters, who lived on opposite banks of the river, to visit each other. The footbridge, one of the city's 60 drawbridges, is itself a big draw, especially after dark, when it is illuminated by hundreds of lights. A bridge master who gets around by bike raises it to let boats through.

Though most of the **Blauwbrug (Blue Bridge)** over the Amstel at Waterlooplein looks gray to me, since a recent renovation, its lanterns are once again as blue as when Impressionist artist George Hendrik Breitner painted the scene in the 1880s. The cast-iron bridge, inspired by Paris's Pont Alexandre III and opened in 1884, is named after a 16th-century timber bridge painted Nassau blue after the 1578 Protestant takeover.

4 More Attractions

Artis ✪✪   If you're at a loss for what to do with the kids, the Artis is a safe bet. Established in 1838, the oldest zoo in the Netherlands houses more than 6,000 animals. Of course, you find the usual tigers, leopards, elephants, camels, and peacocks no self-respecting zoo can do without. Yet there's also much more, for no extra charge. There's the excellent Planetarium (closed Mon morning), and a Geological and Zoological Museum. The Aquarium, built in 1882 and renovated in the late 1990s, is superbly presented, particularly the sections on the Amazon River, coral reefs, and Amsterdam's own canals, with their fish population and burden of urban detritus. Finally, there's a children's farm, where kids help tend to the needs of resident sheep, goats, chickens, and cows. You can rest for a while and have a snack or lunch at Artis Restaurant. Artis gets 1.2 million visitors yearly.

Plantage Kerklaan 38-40. (✆) **020/523-3400.** Admission 13€ adults, 9€ children 4-11, children under 4 free. Daily 9am-5pm. Tram: 9, 14 to Plantage Middenlaan.

Heineken Experience   The experience unfolds inside the former Heineken brewing facilities, which date from 1867. Before the brewery stopped functioning in 1988, it was producing more than 100 million liters (26 million gal.) annually. The fermentation tanks, each capable of holding a million glassfuls of Heineken, are still there, along with the multistory malt silos and all manner of vintage brewing equipment and implements. You "meet" Dr. Elion, the 19th-century chemist who isolated the renowned Heineken "A" yeast, which gives the beer its taste. In one amusing attraction, you stand on a moving floor, facing a large video screen, and get to see and feel what it's like to be a Heineken beer bottle—one of a half-million every hour—careening on a conveyor belt through a modern Heineken bottling plant. Best of all, in another touchy-feely presentation, you "sit" aboard an old brewery dray-wagon, "pulled" by a pair of big Shire horses on the video screen in front of you, that shakes, rattles, and rolls on a mini-tour of Amsterdam.

It *is* fun, I have to admit. But serious types can take cold comfort from a multiscreen presentation on the evidently dire state of fresh-water resources around the world.

Stadhouderskade 78 (at Ferdinand Bolstraat). © 020/523-9666. Admission 7.50€; under 18 admitted only with parental supervision. Tues-Sun 10am-6pm. Closed Jan 1, Dec 25. Tram: 16, 24, 25 to Maria Heinekenplein.

Holland Experience   This multidimensional film and theater show takes you through the landscapes and culture of Holland at different periods of its history and today. If you've ever nervously wondered what would happen to the city if all that seawater should ever break through the defensive dikes, Holland Experience will give you a taste. In a simulated dike collapse, 80,000 liters of water pour toward you. Other exhibits include farming and fishing scenes. The show isn't as good as they could easily make it, or as the steep admission price would justify (and 80,000 liters isn't all *that* much water), but it does give you something of a nutshell picture of Holland. If you're not much into traipsing around heavy-duty cultural museums, this is a reasonably pleasant way to spend an hour or two on a rainy day. The toilets (I can vouch only for the men's) are themselves of interest; they're designed to look like the deck of a ship passing along the Dutch coast, and come complete with marine sound effects and a salt-air breeze.

Waterlooplein 17. © 020/422-2233. Admission 10€ adults, 8€ seniors, children 12 and under free. Daily 10am-10pm. Tram: 9, 14 to Waterlooplein.

Madame Tussaud's ℛ   If you like your celebrities with a waxen stare, don't miss Madame Tussaud's. The Amsterdam version of the famous London attraction has its own cast of Dutch characters (Rembrandt, Queen Beatrix, Mata Hari), among a parade of international favorites (Churchill, Kennedy, Gandhi). The Amsterdam branch reopened in March 2002, after a "facelift" that cost more than 4 million euros. During the refurbishment, all of the wax portraits were sent to Tussaud's Studio's in London for a makeover. Some, like David Bowie, have a complete new look. Among new figures that have been added are Kylie Minogue, Bono, and Bob Marley. Exhibits bring you "face to face" with the powerful and famous and let you step into the times, events, and moments that made them famous.

The popular Dutch 17th-century Golden Age exhibit received only minor changes. In the Grand Hall, styled to look like a reception room in Dutch manor around 1700, are images of world leaders, royalty, artists, writers, and religious leaders. Those portrayed are brought to life with memorabilia such as paintings, a smoking cigarette, or a picture of the most memorable moments of their lives. The Music Zone has a disco floor and a mix of video footage, music, and pictures illustrating the history of music from the 1950s to the present day. Then comes the Sport Gallery and its heroes of sport. Later, you get to "meet" TV personalities in the TV Studio Backstage, and in the Hall of Fame, both contemporary and legendary movie stars shine like it was premiere night. A video projected on a large wall-screen illustrates how wax portraits are created at Tussaud's Studio in London.

Dam 20. ℂ 020/622-9949. Admission 14€ adults, 12€ seniors, 10€ children 5-15, children under 5 free. Mid-July to Aug daily 9:30am-8:30pm; Sept to mid-July daily 10am-6:30pm. Closed Apr 30. Tram: 4, 9, 14, 16, 24, 25 to the Dam.

NEMO 🎯 NEMO, a paean of praise to science and technology, is in a strikingly modern building in the Eastern Dock, designed by Italian architect Renzo Piano, which seems to reproduce the graceful lines of an ocean-going ship. The center is a hands-on experience as much as a museum, with games, experiments, demonstrations, workshops, and theater and film shows. You learn how to steer a supertanker safely into port, boost your earnings on the floor of the New York Stock Exchange, and execute a complicated surgical procedure. One exhibit will even try to make you understand the basis of sexual attraction. Internet-linked computers on every floor help provide insights. IStudio Bits & Co is NEMO's digital world, in which you can play with images, sounds, text, websites, and your own imported material.

Oosterdok 2 (above the IJ Tunnel in the Eastern Dock). ℂ 0900/919-1100. Admission 10€ adults and children over 3, children under 4 free. July-Aug daily 10am-5pm; Sept-June Tues-Sun 10am-5pm. Bus: 22 to Kadijksplein.

MARKETS

There are more than 50 outdoor markets every week in Amsterdam, some of them permanent or semipermanent, and others just passing through. For more details, see "Markets" in chapter 6, but here are three you shouldn't miss.

The **Bloemenmarkt (Flower Market)** is one of Amsterdam's stellar spots—though you might easily think it overrated, especially since it's not easy to see that it's actually floating. Still, this is probably the most atmospheric place to buy cut flowers and bulbs. Awnings stretch to cover stall after stall of brightly colored blossoms, bulbs, and potted plants. A stroll down that fragrant line is surely one of Amsterdam's most heart-lifting experiences. Looking for a bargain-basement souvenir is made easy at the **Waterlooplein Flea Market** ☆☆☆, on Waterlooplein—naturally enough. You find all kinds of stuff here, not all of it junk, and a constant press of people with good buys on their mind. The **Albert Cuyp Markt,** on Albert Cuypstraat, is more of an everyday market for food, clothes, and other things, but is almost as colorful as the other two.

5 Green Amsterdam

Amsterdam is not a notably green city, particularly in the Old Center, where the canals are the most obvious and visible encroachment of the natural world. Still, the city as a whole has plenty of parks, including the famous **Vondelpark** ☆☆☆, a pattern of lakes, meadows, and woodland containing 120 varieties of tree that include catalpa, chestnut, cypress, oak, and poplar. Watch out for the tasty-looking "gateau" they sell there, or you may find yourself floating above the trees: Drug-laced space-cake is an acquired taste and not everyone is ready to acquire it.

Otherwise, the Vondelpark is a fairly standard park, the site of skateboarding, Frisbee-flipping, in-line skating, model-boat sailing, soccer, softball and basketball games, open-air concerts, open-air theater performances, smooching in the undergrowth, parties, picnics, arts-and-crafts markets, and, perhaps not-so-standard, topless sunbathing. Best of all, it's free, or as the Dutch say, gratis. The Vondelpark lies generally southwest of Leidseplein, with entrances all around; the most popular is adjacent to Leidseplein, on Stadhouderskade.

You can rent in-line skates from **Rent A Skate,** Damstraat 21 (© 020/664-5091), and tour the park in style. Including protective gear, it is 5€ an hour for adults, or 7.50€ for a half day and 13€ for a full day; for children 10 and under, 2.50€ an hour, 5€ for a half day, and 9.50€ for a full day.

After Vondelpark, the city's other parks are fairly tame, but the following still make pleasant escapes on a warm summer day: **Sarphati Park,** 2 blocks behind the Albert Cuyp Markt in South Amsterdam; **Beatrix Park,** adjacent to the RAI Convention and Exhibition Center; **Rembrandt Park** and **Erasmus Park** in the west of the city; **Martin Luther King Park,** beside the River Amstel; and the **Oosterpark,** in East Amsterdam.

To enjoy scenery and fresh air, you should head out to the giant **Amsterdamse Bos (Amsterdam Wood),** whose main entrance is on

Amstelveenseweg, in the southern suburb of Amstelveen. This is nature on the city's doorstep. The park was laid out during the Depression years as a public works project. By now the trees, birds, insects, and small animals are firmly established. From the entrance, follow the path to the Roeibaan, a 2km (1¼ miles) rowing course. Beyond the western end of the Roeibaan is the Bosmuseum (© 020/676-2152), where you can trace the park's history and learn about its wildlife. This free museum is open daily 10am to 5pm. Nearby is a big pond called the **Grote Vijver,** where you can rent boats (© 020/644-5119), and the Openluchttheater (Open-Air Theater), which often has performances on summer evenings. In 2000, the **Kersenbloesempark (Cherry Blossom Park)** opened in the Amsterdamse Bos, its 400 cherry trees donated by the Japan Women's Club to mark 400 years of cultural ties between the Netherlands and Japan. The best way to the Amsterdamse Bos from the city center is to take tram 6, 16, or 24 to Stadionplein and then to take any bus, except the no. 23, along Amstelveenseweg to the entrance.

Hortus Botanicus (Botanical Garden) 🐸🐸   The Botanical Garden, which was established here in 1682, is a medley of color and scent, with some 250,000 flowers and 115,000 plants and trees, from 8,000 different varieties. It owes its origins to the treasure trove of tropical plants the Dutch found in their colonies of Indonesia, Surinam, and the Antilles, and its contemporary popularity to the Dutch love affair with flowers. Among its highlights are the Semicircle, which reconstructs part of the original design from 1682; the Mexico-California Desert House; the Palm House, with one of the world's oldest palm trees; and the Tri-Climate House, which displays tropical, subtropical, and desert plants.

Plantage Middenlaan 2a (near Artis Zoo). © 020/625-9021. Admission 5€ adults, 3€ children 5-14, free to children under 5. Apr-Sept Mon-Fri 9am-5pm, Sat-Sun 11am-5pm; Oct-Mar Mon-Fri 9am-4pm, Sat-Sun 11am-4pm. Tram: 9, 14 to Plantage Middenlaan.

6 Offbeat & Alternative Amsterdam

RED LIGHT DISTRICT

This warren of streets and old canals (known as De Rosse Buurt or De Wallen in Dutch) around Oudezijds Achterburgwal and Oudezijds Voorburgwal by the Oude Kerk, a testament to the city's tolerance and pragmatism, is on most people's sightseeing agenda. However, a visit to this area is not for everyone, and if you're liable to be offended by the sex industry exposed in all its garish colors, don't go. If you do choose to go, you need to exercise some caution, because the area is a center of crime, vice, and drugs. As always in Amsterdam, there's no need to exaggerate the risks; and in fact, the nightclubs' own security helps keep the brightly lit areas quite safe. Plenty of tourists visit the Rosse Buurt and suffer nothing more serious than a come-on from one of the prostitutes.

At night especially, however, stick to the crowded streets and be wary of pickpockets at all times. There can be a sinister air to the bunches of often weird-looking men who gather on the bridges; and there is a sadder aura around the "heroin whores" who wander the darker streets. Finally, do not take photographs of the women in the windows, many of whom don't want Mom and Dad to know how they earn a living. Men are always on the lookout, and they won't hesitate to throw your camera (and maybe your person) into the canal. (George Michael seems to have had no trouble filming the video here for his risqué 1999 cover of The Police's '70s classic *Roxanne*.)

Still, it's extraordinary to view the prostitutes in leather and lace sitting in their storefronts with their radios and TVs blaring as they do their knitting or adjust their makeup, waiting patiently for customers. The district seems to reflect Dutch pragmatism; if you can't stop the oldest trade in the world, you can at least confine it to a particular area and impose health and other regulations on it. And the fact is that underneath its tacky glitter, the Red Light District contains some of Amsterdam's prettiest canals and loveliest old architecture, plus some excellent bars and restaurants, secondhand bookshops, and other specialty shops (not all of which work the erogenous zones). For more information on the Red Light District, see also chapter 7. To get there, take tram no. 4, 9, 14, 16, 24, or 25 to the Dam, then pass behind the Grand Hotel Krasnapolsky.

OFFBEAT MUSEUMS

Erotic Museum   As its name suggests, this museum presents an allegedly artistic vision of eroticism; it focuses on prints and drawings, including some by John Lennon. There is a re-creation of a Red Light alley and an extensively equipped S&M playroom, both of which are rather antiseptic and serious. The only humorous note is an X-rated cartoon depicting some of the things Snow White apparently got up to with the Seven Dwarfs that Walt never told us about.

Oudezijds Achterburgwal 54 (Red Light District). ℂ 020/624-7303. Admission 3€. Daily noon–midnight. Tram: 4, 9, 14, 16, 24, 25 to the Dam.

Hash Marihuana Hemp Museum Well, it wouldn't really be Amsterdam, would it, without its fascination with intoxicating weeds. This museum will teach you everything you ever wanted to know, and much you maybe didn't, about hash, marijuana, and related products. The museum does not promote drug use but aims to make you better informed before deciding whether to light up and, of course, whether to inhale. One way it does this is by having a cannabis garden in the joint (sorry) on the premises. Plants at various stages of development fill the air with an unmistakable, heady, resinous fragrance. And hemp, not plastic, could be the future if the exhibit on the multifarious uses of the fiber through the ages is anything to go by. Some exhibits shed light on the medicinal uses of cannabis and on hemp's past and present-day uses as a natural fiber. Among several notable artworks in the museum's collection is David Teniers the Younger's painting, *Hemp-Smoking Peasants in a Smoke House* (1660).

Oudezijds Achterburgwal 130 (Red Light District). ✆ **020/623-5961**. Admission 5.70€. Daily 10am-5:30pm. Tram: 4, 9, 14, 16, 24, 25 to the Dam.

Sexmuseum Amsterdam Behind its faux-marble facade, this museum is not as sleazy as you might expect, apart from one room covered with straight-up pornography. Otherwise the presentation tends toward the tongue-in-cheek. Exhibits include erotic prints and drawings, and trinkets like tobacco boxes decorated with naughty pictures. Teenage visitors seem to find the whole place vastly amusing, judging by the giggling fits at the showcases. Spare a thought for the models of early erotic photography—slow film speeds in those days made for uncomfortably long posing times!

Damrak 18 (near Centraal Station). ✆ **020/622-8376**. Admission 2.50€ age 16 and over only. Daily 10am-11:30pm. Tram: 1, 2, 4, 5, 9, 13, 16, 17, 24, 25 to Centraal Station.

Torture Museum You enter through an appropriately long and gloomy tunnel, and emerge with a new appreciation of why the framers of the U.S. Constitution outlawed cruel and unusual punishment. Yet one suspects the motives of the Torture Museum—and its visitors?—are not purely educational. There is a horrible fascination about devices such as the Inquisition chair, the guillotine, and assorted grotesque implements of torture, punishment, and "redemption" favored by the civil and ecclesiastic authorities in times not so far past.

Singel 449 (at the Flower market). ✆ **020/320-6642**. Admission 4€ adults, 2€ children 5-12, children under 5 free. Daily 10am-11pm. Tram: 1, 2, 5, to Koningsplein.

7 Organized Tours

CANAL TOUR BOATS

A typical canal tour boat itinerary includes Centraal Station, the Harlemmersluis floodgates (used in the nightly flushing of the canals), the Cat Boat (a houseboat with a permanent population of more than 100 wayward felines), and both the narrowest building in the city and one of the largest houses still in private hands and in use as a single-family residence. Plus, you will see the official residence of the *burgomaster* (mayor), the "Golden Bend" of the Herengracht (traditionally the best address in the city), many picturesque bridges, including the famous Magere Brug (Skinny Bridge) over the Amstel, and the harbor.

Trips last approximately an hour and depart at regular intervals from *rondvaart* (excursion) piers in key locations around town. The majority of launches are docked along Damrak and Prins Hendrikkade near Centraal Station, on Rokin near Muntplein, and at Leidseplein. Tours leave every 15 to 30 minutes during the summer season (9am–9:30pm), every 45 minutes in winter (10am–4pm). A basic 1-hour tour is 8€ for adults, 6€ for children 4 to 12, and free for children under 4.

Operators of canal-boat tours are: **Amsterdam Canal Cruises** (© 020/626-5636); **Holland International** (© 020/622-7788); **Meijers Rondvaarten** (© 020/623-4208); **Rederij Boekel** (© 020/612-9905); **Rederij Hof van Holland** (© 020/623-7122); **Rederij Lovers** (© 020/530-1090)—despite its heart-shaped logo, Lovers is not necessarily for lovers only, but is named after the man who started the company; **Rederij Noord-Zuid** (© 020/679-1370); **Rederij P. Kooij** (© 020/623-3810); and **Rederij Plas** (© 020/624-5406).

WATER BIKES

A water bike is a boat you pedal with your feet. These craft seat two or four people and can be rented daily from 10am to 10pm in summer, and to 7pm at other times, from **Canal Bike** (© **020/626-5574**). Amsterdammers look down their tolerant noses at water bikers. On the other hand, tourists love the things. No prizes for guessing who has the most fun. Your water bike comes with a detailed map. It's great fun in sunny weather, and still doable when it rains and your boat is covered with a rain shield. In summer, you can even rent a water bike for evening rambles, when the canals are illuminated and your bike is kitted out with its own Chinese lantern.

The four Canal Bikes moorings are at Leidseplein (tram: 1, 2, 5, 6, 7, 10); Westerkerk, near the Anne Frankhuis (tram: 13, 14, 17); Stadhouderskade, beside the Rijksmuseum (tram: 6, 7, 10); and Toronto Bridge on Keizersgracht, near Leidsestraat (tram: 1, 2, 5). You can rent a water bike at one mooring and leave it at another. The canals can be busy with tour boats and other small craft, so go carefully, particularly when going under bridges. Rental is 7€ per person hourly for one or two people; 6€ per person hourly for three or four people. You need to leave a deposit of 50€. A booklet containing six route descriptions is 2€.

POWERBOATS

You can be the captain of your own boat and tour the canals aboard a six-seater launch with an environmentally friendly electric outboard. **Canal Motorboats** (℧ **020/422-7007**) rents open-top launches, which can go at 3½ knots on the canals, from boat docks on Oosterdokskade (tram: 1, 2, 4, 5, 9, 13, 16, 17, 24, 25), close to Centraal Station, beside the floating Chinese restaurant Sea Palace; and on Kloveniersburgwal at the Amstel River (tram: 4, 9, 14), opposite the Hôtel de l'Europe. Between April and October, the launches are available daily from 10am to dusk, or to 10pm. The rental is 18€ for the first hour, 15€ for the second hour, 10€ for the third, and 6€ for each subsequent hour. You need to show a passport or other ID and either leave a deposit of 75€ or sign an open credit card slip.

BY BIKE

You're going to look pretty conspicuous taking one of the guided tours offered by **Yellow Bike,** Nieuwezijds Kolk 29, off Nieuwezijds Voorburgwal (℧ **020/620-6940**). Why? Because you're going to be cycling on a yellow bike along with a dozen other people also on yellow bikes, that's why. In partial compensation, you have a close encounter with Amsterdam or the nearby countryside.

BY TRAM

A **Tourist Tram,** an old-timer, does the sights on Sunday and public holidays from Easter to mid-September. It leaves from Prins Hendrikkade in front of Centraal Station; tickets are 5€ for adults, 3.75€ for seniors and children.

BY BUS

For many travelers, a quick bus tour is the best way to launch a sightseeing program in a strange city, and though Amsterdam offers its own unique alternative—a canal-boat ride—you might want to get your bearings on land as well. A 3-hour tour is 20€ to 30€; on most tours children 4 to 13 are charged half price. Major companies offering these and other motor-coach sightseeing trips are **The Best of Holland,** Damrak 34 (© **020/623-1539**); **Holland International Excursions,** Prins Hendrikkade 33A (© **020/625-3035**); **Keytours,** Dam 19 (© **020/624-7304**); and **Lindbergh Excursions,** Damrak 26 (© **020/622-2766**).

ON FOOT

Amsterdam Walking Tours (© **020/640-9072**) leads guided strolls through historic Amsterdam on Saturday and Sunday at 11am. If you'd rather guide yourself around, try **Audio Tourist,** Oude Spiegelstraat 9 (© **020/421-5580**), whose map-and-cassette packages allow you to "see Amsterdam by your ears." You can choose different tours lasting from 2 to 3 hours. Renting the cassette player, tape, and map is 8€ for adults, 4€ for children 13 and under, and seniors and holders of an Under-26 Pass get a 20% discount. Audio Tourist operates from April to September daily from 9am to 6pm; from October to March Tuesday through Sunday from 10am to 5pm.

6

Shopping

Regular shopping hours in Amsterdam are Monday from 10 or 11am to 6pm; Tuesday, Wednesday, and Friday from 9am to 6pm; Thursday from 9am to 9pm; and Saturday from 9am to 5pm. In recent years there has been something of a revolution in the previously restricted opening hours: Against the wishes of churches and other groups, many stores now stay open on Sunday as well, usually from noon to 5pm, and more and more supermarkets are staying open daily from 8am to 8pm, or even to 10pm.

1 The Shopping Scene

DUTY-FREE ITEMS   Duty-free shopping has been abolished within the European Union. This means that if you are traveling from one member country of the EU to another, you can no longer buy duty-free goods at airports, on ferries, and at border crossings. If, however, you are traveling to or from the EU from a nonmember country, such as the United States, normal duty-free shopping rules apply. Some duty-free shopping centers, like the one at Schiphol Airport, claim to have reduced prices for intra-EU travelers to a level comparable to duty-free prices for people traveling outside the EU.

BEST BUYS

ANTIQUES   Antiques lovers love Holland! And why not, when you think of all those tankards, pipes, cabinets, clocks, kettles, vases, and other bric-a-brac you see in the old Dutch paintings that still show up among the treasures of stores on Amsterdam's Nieuwe Spiegelstraat. It's the 20th century's good fortune that since the 17th century the Dutch have collected everything—from Chinese urns to silver boxes, from cookie molds to towering armoires—and should you find that while you're in Amsterdam there is a *kijkdag* (looking day) for an upcoming auction, you will realize that antiques still pour forth from the attics of the old canal houses. With 165 antiques stores in the city, there's no lack of choice.

CHEESE   Holland is the Wisconsin of Europe, well known around the world for its butter and cheese *(kaas)*. Gouda (correctly pronounced, in Dutch, *khow*-duh) and Edam (*ay*-dam) are the two Dutch cheeses most familiar to us because they have been exported from Holland for so long—since the 1700s—but once inside a Dutch cheese store, you quickly realize that there are many other interesting choices, including a nettle cheese that's a specialty of Friesland. Before you simply point to any cheese and say, "I'll take that one," you need to know that in Holland you have the choice of factory cheese, made of pasteurized milk, or *boerenkaas,* which is farm cheese that is produced in the old, careful way with fresh, unpasteurized milk straight from the cow. Boerenkaas is more expensive, of course, but it also can be expected to be more delicious. Look for the boerenkaas stamp. Another choice that you will make is between young and old cheese; it's a difference of sweetness, moistness, and a melting quality in the mouth (*jonge,* or young, cheese) and a sharper, drier taste, and a crumbly texture (*oude,* or old, cheese).

Tips Tax Return

If you live outside the European Union (EU), whatever your nationality, you're entitled to a refund of the value-added tax (VAT, or in Dutch, BTW) you pay on your purchases of 137€ or more in a store that subscribes to the refund system, in a day. On high-ticket items, the savings of 13.5% can be significant. You must export the purchases within 3 months. To obtain your VAT refund, ask for a **global refund check** from the store when you make your purchase. When you are leaving the EU, present this check, your purchases, and receipts to Customs. They will stamp the check. You can get the refund in cash or paid to your credit card at an International Cash Refund Point. At Schiphol Airport, this is the Global Refund Cash Refund Office; refunds are also available from the terminal's branch of ABN-AMRO bank. At other exit points from the EU, be sure to have Customs stamp your check and you can claim your refund later from one of 150 International Cash Refund Points worldwide. For a list of these, and for more information, contact **Europe Tax-Free Shopping,** Leidsevaartweg 99, 2106 AS, Heemstede, Netherlands (© **023/524-1909;** fax 023/524-6164; www.global refund.nl).

CHOCOLATE   Droste, Verkade, and Van Houten are three of the best Dutch brand names to look for, or you can seek out the small specialty chocolate stores that still home-make and hand-fill the boxes of bonbons. (In fact, though no Dutch person would be unhappy to receive chocolates from these manufacturers, they themselves generally prefer handmade Belgian chocolates from such makes as Wittamer, Nihoul, Neuhaus, Godiva, and Leonidas.)

CRYSTAL   Holland is not the only country that produces fine pewter ware and crystal, but the Dutch contribute both a refined sense of design and a respect for craftsmanship that combine to produce items of exceptional beauty and quality. Also, if you remember the classic Dutch still-life paintings and happy scenes of 17th-century family life, pewter objects are part of Holland's heritage. As with hand-painted earthenware, there are Dutch towns associated with each of these crafts and long-established firms whose names are well known as quality producers. Crystal, for example, has long been associated with Leerdam, south of Utrecht, and Maastricht, in Limburg, whose manufacturers have joined together to market under the names of **Royal Netherlands** in the United States and **Kristalunie** in Holland. To spot the genuine article, look for the four triangles of the **Royal Leerdam** label.

DELFTWARE & MAKKUMWARE   There are three types of delftware available in Amsterdam—Delftware, Makkumware, and junk—and since none of it is cheap, you need to know what the differences are among the three types and what to look for to determine quality. But first, a few words of historical background and explanation: delftware (with a lowercase *d*) has actually become an umbrella name for all Dutch hand-painted earthenware pottery resembling ancient Chinese porcelain, whether it is blue and white, red and white, or multicolored, and regardless of the city in which it was produced.

Delftware, or Delft Blue (with a capital *D*), on the other hand, refers to the predominantly blue-and-white products of one firm, **De Koninklijke Porceleyne Fles** of Delft. This is the only survivor of the original 30 potteries in Delft that during the 17th century worked overtime in that small city to meet the clamoring demand of the newly affluent Dutch for Chinese-style vases, urns, wall tiles, and knickknacks—real or reproduced, porcelain or pottery. Originally, pottery made at Delft was white, imitating tin-glazed products from Italy and Spain. During the 16th century, Chinese porcelain was imported to Holland—this was decorated in blue and was of superior quality. The Delftware factories refined their products, using a white tin glaze to cover the red clay and decorating it in blue. This Delft Blue became famous the world over. It was cheaper than Chinese porcelain and it was skillfully made. Polychrome decorations were also used, both on a white and on a black background.

Similarly, the term *makkumware* is becoming synonymous with multicolored—or polychrome—pottery, whereas Makkumware is, in fact, the hand-painted earthenware produced only in the town of Makkum in the northern province of Friesland and only by the 300-plus-year-old firm of **Tichelaars,** which was founded in 1660 and now is in its 10th generation of family management. Makkumware has a similar history to Delft Blue, though it exists only with polychrome decoration.

DIAMONDS   Dutch jewelers generally adhere to the standards of both the Gemological Institute of America and the U.S. Federal Trade Commission, and most will issue a certificate with a diamond they sell that spells out the carat weight, cut, color, and other pertinent identifying details, including any imperfections.

FLOWER BULBS   Nothing is more Dutch than a tulip, and no gift to yourself will bring more pleasure than to take home some bulbs to remind you of Holland all over again when they pop up every spring. You may have a problem making your choices, however, since there are more than 800 different varieties of tulip bulbs available in Holland, not to mention more than 500 kinds of daffodils and narcissi, and 60 different varieties of hyacinth and crocus. Many growers and distributors put together combination packages with various amounts of bulbs that are coordinated according to the colors of the flowers they will produce, but it's great fun—since so many bulbs are named for famous people—to put together your own garden party with Sophia Loren, President Kennedy, Queen Juliana, and Cyrano de Bergerac!

OLD-FASHIONED CLOCKS   It's true that the Swiss make the finest clocks in the world, but what they do well for the inner workings, the Dutch do well for the outside, particularly if you like a clock to be old-fashioned, handcrafted, and highly decorated with figures and mottoes or small peekaboo panels to show you the innards.

2 Shopping A to Z

ANTIQUES

A. van der Meer   For more than 30 years, A. van der Meer has been a landmark amid the fashionable stores of Pieter Cornelisz Hooftstraat and a quiet place to enjoy a beautiful collection of antique maps, prints, and engravings. And 17th- and 18th-century Dutch world maps by the early cartographers Blaeu, Hondius, and Mercator are a specialty. Also, there is a small collection of Jewish prints by Picart and 18th-century botanicals (pictures of flowers) by Baptista Morandi and 19th-century works by Jacob Jung, mostly of roses. There are also 19th-century lithographs of hunting scenes by Harris. Open Monday through Saturday from 10am to 6pm. Pieter Cornelisz Hooftstraat 112. ℂ 020/662-1936. Tram: 2, 3, 5, 12 to Van Baerlestraat.

Premsela & Hamburger   Opposite the Allard-Pierson Museum, this fine jewelry and antique silver establishment—purveyors to the Dutch court—opened in 1823. Inside their brocaded display cases and richly carved cabinets is a variety of exquisite and distinctive items. You can find decorative modern and antique silver objects and Old Dutch silver fashioned by 17th-century crafters. Feast your eyes on an 18th-century perpetual calendar, a silver plaque depicting the entrance to an Amsterdam hospital, and a variety of sterling silverware. Their workshop designs, makes, and repairs jewelry. Open Monday through Friday from 9:30am to 5:30pm. Rokin 98. ℂ 020/624-9688 or 020/627-5454. Tram: 4, 9, 14, 16, 24, 25 to Spui.

ART

Galleries abound in Amsterdam, particularly in the canal area near the Rijksmuseum, and a quick look at the listings of their exhibitions proves that Dutch painters are as prolific in the 20th century as they were in the Golden Age. The VVV Tourist Information Office publication *What's On in Amsterdam* is your best guide to who is showing and where; your own eye and sense of value will be the best guide to artistic merit and investment value.

On the other hand, posters and poster reproductions of famous artworks are an excellent item to buy in Amsterdam. The Dutch are well known for their high-quality printing and color-reproduction work, and one of their favorite subjects is Holland's rich artistic treasure trove, foreign and domestic. Choose any of the three major art museums as a starting point for a search for an artistic souvenir, but if you like modern art—say, from the Impressionists onward—you will be particularly delighted by the wide selection at the

Stedelijk Museum, Paulus Potterstraat 13 (℃ **020/573-2911**); and if you particularly like van Gogh, the **Van Gogh Museum,** Paulus Potterstraat 13 (℃ **020/570-5200**), is another good source of reproductions. And at **Museum Het Rembrandthuis,** Jodenbreestraat 4 (℃ **020/624-9486**), you can buy a Rembrandt etching for 15€ or 20€ mounted; it's not an original, of course, but it is a high-quality modern printing produced individually, by hand, in the traditional manner from a plate that was directly and photographically produced from an original print in the collection of Rembrandthuis. Or for something simpler and cheaper to remind you of the great master, Het Rembrandthuis also sells mass-printed reproductions of the etchings, or small packets of postcard-size reproductions in sepia or black and white on a thick, fine-quality paper stock (including a packet of self-portraits).

Perhaps you're more interested in an artistic, rather than photographic, view of Amsterdam or the Dutch countryside. **Mattieu Hart,** which has been in its location on the Rokin since 1878, sells color etchings of Dutch cities.

Here are just a few of Amsterdam's 140 or so galleries that hold contemporary and modern art, photography, sculpture, and African art.

Animation Art Got a favorite cartoon character? Well, Animation Art has original drawings and cel paintings of all different kinds of cartoons. A fun place for the kid in everyone. Open Tuesday through Friday from 11am to 6pm, Saturday from 11am to 5pm, and Sunday (not in Jan or Feb) from 1 to 5pm. Berenstraat 19 (between Keizersgracht and Prinsengracht). ℃ **020/627-7600**. Tram: 1, 2, 5 to Spui.

Galerie Carla Koch For ceramics and glassware, this gallery employs some of the raciest design talent in Amsterdam, meaning that their products are always different and always interesting, if inevitably not to everyone's taste. Open Monday to Saturday noon to 6pm. Prinsengracht 510. ℃ **020/639-0198**. Tram: 1, 2, 5 to Prinsengracht.

Italiaander Galleries There's a permanent exhibition of primitive art from around the world, particularly from Africa and Asia, and all sorts of ethnic jewelry. Open Wednesday to Saturday noon to 5:30pm. Prinsengracht 526. ℃ **020/625-0942**. Tram: 1, 2, 5 to Prinsengracht.

BOOKS
American Book Center You'll swear you never left the States when you see the array of best-sellers and paperbacks in the American Book Center on Kalverstraat near Muntplein, which

claims to be the biggest U.S.-style book store on the European continent. Plus, there are magazines (risqué and otherwise) and hardcover editions, hot off the presses. Prices are higher than you'd pay at home, but the selection beats any airport or hotel gift store, with categories ranging from ancient civilizations, astrology, and baby care to science, science fiction, and war. Students and teachers can get 10% off simply by showing a school ID. Open Monday through Wednesday and Friday and Saturday from 10am to 8pm, Thursday from 10am to 10pm, and Sunday from 11am to 6pm. Kalverstraat 185. ℭ **020/625-5537**. Tram: 4, 9, 14, 16, 24, 25 to Muntplein.

Athenaeum Booksellers   You can't miss this place. It's always crowded with book lovers, students, and scholars. The Athenaeum is best known for its nonfiction collection and has books in a number of different languages. There are magazine stands on the sidewalk. The store is open Monday through Wednesday and Saturday from 9:30am to 6pm; Thursday from 9:30am to 9pm; Sunday from noon to 5:30pm. Spui 14-16. ℭ **020/622-6248**. Tram: 1, 2, 5 to Spui.

Waterstone's Booksellers   Waterstone's is a British chain that has a large stock of fiction and nonfiction titles. You'll probably be able to find almost anything you're looking for on one of the three floors here. Open Monday from 11am to 6pm, Tuesday, Wednesday, and Friday from 9am to 6pm, Thursday from 9am to 9pm, Saturday from 9am to 7pm, and Sunday from 11am to 5pm. Kalverstraat 152. ℭ **020/638-3821**. Tram: 1, 2, 4, 5, 14, 16, 17, 24, 25 to Spui.

CIGARS, PIPES & SMOKING ARTICLES

Holland is one of the cigar-producing centers of the world. Serious smokers know that Dutch cigars are different, and drier, than Cuban or American smokes. It's partly because of the Indonesian tobacco and partly because of the way the cigar is made, but whatever the reason, Dutch cigars can be a pleasant change for American tobacco enthusiasts.

P G C Hajenius   This store has been Amsterdam's leading purveyor of cigars and smoking articles since 1826, first with a store on the Dam and then since 1915 in its present elegant headquarters. Cigars are the house specialty and the stock includes a room full of Havanas. Hajenius sells the long, uniquely Dutch, handmade clay pipes you see in old paintings and that are a good gift idea, and ceramic pipes, some painted in the blue-and-white Chinese-inspired patterns of Delftware. You also find lighters, cigarette holders, clippers, and flasks. Open Monday through Wednesday and Friday and

Saturday from 9:30am to 6pm, Thursday from 9:30am to 9pm, Sunday from noon to 5pm. Rokin 92-96. ✆ 020/623-7494. Tram: 4, 9, 14, 16, 24, 25 to Spui.

Smokiana & Pijpenkabinet   This place stocks a vast range of pipes from the antique, to the exotic, to the downright weird. It's where to buy that unique pipe, into which the tobacco can be tamped with an air of deliberate insouciance, and the resulting fug flaunted in the faces of nonsmokers everywhere. Open Wednesday through Saturday from noon to 6pm. Prinsengracht 488. ✆ 020/421-1179. Tram: 1, 2, 5 to Prinsengracht.

CLOCKS

Victoria Gifts   Dutch clockmakers turn out timepieces with soft-toned chimes in exquisite Old Dutch-style handcrafted cases covered with tiny figures and mottoes, insets of hand-painted porcelain, and hand-painted Dutch scenes. This small store is a happy hunting ground for these treasures. It also has a good stock of Delftware, embroidered flags, chocolates, and other quality gifts at reasonable prices. Open in summer Monday through Saturday from 9am to 8pm; in winter, Monday through Saturday from 9am to 8pm. Prins Hendrikkade 47 (opposite Centraal Station). ✆ 020/427-2051. Tram: 1, 2, 4, 5, 9, 13,16, 17, 24, 25 to Centraal Station.

CRAFTS & CURIOS

Blue Gold Fish *Finds*   "Dive into the pool of fantasy," say the owners of this colorful store and gallery. There's no real rhyme or reason to the items for sale. They cover a wide range of ceramics, jewelry, household items (including colorful lamps in the "Aladdin's Corner"), textiles, all of them running the stylistic gamut from kitsch to chic. Still, there's unity in diversity in the more-or-less fantastic design sensibility that goes into each piece. Open Monday through Saturday from 11:30am to 6:30pm. Rozengracht 17 (opposite Westerkerk). ✆ 020/623-3134. Tram: 13, 14, 17 to Westermarkt.

Cortina Papier   If you'd like the kind of personal journal that would have looked good in *The English Patient* and *Dances with Wolves,* this is the place for you. Cortina does fancy notebooks, agendas and address books, and nice lines in writing paper, envelopes, and other such products. Open Monday from 1 to 6pm, Tuesday through Friday from 11am to 6pm, and Saturday from 11am to 5pm. Reestraat 22 (between Prinsengracht and Keizersgracht). ✆ 020/623-6676. Tram: 13, 14, 17 to Westermarkt.

E Kramer Candle Shop   This place provides illumination for everything from a romantic candlelit dinner to a wake, while filling all kinds of temporary and mobile lighting requirements in between. Some of the candles are little melting works of art and some are outrageously kitschy, but all will shed some light on your activities. The store also sells scented oils and incense, and even repairs dolls. Open Monday through Friday from 10am to 6pm, Saturday from 10am to 5pm. Reestraat 20 (between Prinsengracht and Keizersgracht). ✆ 020/626-5274. Tram: 13, 14, 17 to Westermarkt.

La Savonnerie   This is the kind of clean-living store that a raff-ish place like Amsterdam can't get enough of. You can buy artisanal soap in all kinds of shapes and sizes. How about a soap chess set, soap alphabet blocks, and soap animal shapes? You can buy person-alized soap and even make your own soap. Open Tuesday through Friday from 10am to 6pm (8pm on Thurs in summer), Saturday from 10am to 5pm. Prinsengracht 294 (corner of Elandsgracht). ✆ 020/428-1139. Tram: 7, 10, 17 to Elandsgracht.

Nieuws Innovations   This store is a source for all kinds of off-beat souvenirs, such as pens in the shape of fish, lipsticks, and (per-haps too near the bone for Amsterdam) syringes; washcloths in the form of hand-glove puppets; spherical dice; finger massage sets; and many other hard-to-define but colorful little bits and pieces. Open Monday from 1:30 to 6:30pm; Tuesday, Wednesday, and Friday from 10am to 6:30pm, Thursday from 10am to 9pm, Saturday and Sunday from 11am to 6pm. Prinsengracht 297 (at Westermarkt). ✆ 020/627-9540. Tram: 13, 14, 17 to Westermarkt.

Pakhuis Amerika   All kinds of American souvenirs and antiques, imported from the United States, and just waiting to be paid for, wrapped, and brought straight back home again—and all for much more than you would have paid for them in the States! If nothing else, it's a kind of museum—your heritage (as Europeans see it) all together in one place. Open Monday through Saturday from 11am to 8pm. Prinsengracht 541 (at Runstraat). ✆ 020/639-2583. Tram: 1, 2, 5 to Prinsengracht.

't Winkeltje   This place sells knickknacks such as colored bottles and glasses; modern versions of old tin cars and other children's toys from the 1950s and earlier; big plastic butterflies; lamps shaped like bananas; and many other such useful things. A little bit of this and a little bit of that. Open Monday from 1 to 5:30pm, Tuesday through Friday from 10am to 5:30pm, and Saturday from 10am to

5pm. Prinsengracht 228 (at Leliegracht). C **020/625-1352**. Tram: 13, 14, 17 to Westermarkt.

DELFTWARE

Focke & Meltzer This main branch of a popular chain is the best one-stop store you'll find for authentic Delftware and Makkumware, Hummel figurines, Leerdam crystal, and a world of other fine china, porcelain, silver, glass, and crystal products. Open Monday through Friday from 9:30am to 5:30pm and Saturday from 9:30am to 5pm. Gelderlandplein 149, Buitenveldert. C **020/644-4429**. Tram: 5, 51 to A. J. Ernststraat.

Heinen You can save considerably on hand-painted pottery and have the fun of seeing the product made at these stores, owned by a father-and-son team who sit inside their canal-house windows, quietly painting the days away. You get quality and a good selection of useful, well-priced items. Jaap (father) and Jorrit (son) both paint in five techniques: blue and white (Delft), polychrome (Makkum), Japanese Imari, Kwartjes (a modern-looking Delft with blue, red, and gold), and Sepia (brown and red). They are official dealers of De Porcelyne Fles and Tichelaars and have a third store, in Volendam, at Haven 92. Open Monday through Saturday from 9:30am to 6pm. Prinsengracht 440 (at Leidsestraat). C **020/627-8299**. Tram: 1, 2, 5, to Prinsengracht. Spiegelgracht 13. C **020/421-8360**. Tram: 6, 7, 10 to Spiegelgracht.

DEPARTMENT STORES

De Bijenkorf De Bijenkorf is Amsterdam's best-known department store, and the one with the best variety of goods. A recent renovation changed this once-frumpy little dry-goods emporium into Amsterdam's answer to New York's Bloomingdale's. On the ground floor, you find the usual ranks of cosmetic counters in the center section, plus a men's department and odds and ends such as socks and stockings, handbags and belts, costume jewelry, and stationery. And umbrellas—plenty of umbrellas! On upper floors there's everything from ladies' fashions to *dekbedden* (down comforters), plus a bookstore, several eating spots, and even a luggage section where you can pick up an extra suitcase or tote bag to take home your purchases. Records, color TVs, shoes, clothing, personal effects, appliances—it's all here. Open Monday from 11am to 6pm; Tuesday, Wednesday, and Friday from 9:30am to 6pm; Thursday from 9:30am to 9pm; and Saturday from 9am to 6pm. Dam 1. C **020/621-8080**. Tram: 4, 9, 14, 16, 24, 25 to the Dam.

Hema Hema is the Woolworth's of Amsterdam, selling things like socks, toothbrushes, chocolate, cookies, and cheeses. If you can't figure out where to find something, your best bet is to look here. Open Monday from 11am to 6pm, Tuesday through Friday from 9:30am to 6pm, and Saturday from 9am to 6pm. Kalvertoren Shopping Center, Kalverstraat. © 020/626-8720. Tram: 4, 14, 16, 24, 25 to Muntplein.

Magna Plaza Magna Plaza is not actually a department store, but a mall, located amid the extravagant Gothic architecture of the former central Post Office. The Plaza's floors are filled with stores of all kinds and yet it's small enough to function as a kind of department store. Spuistraat 168 (behind the Dam's Royal Palace). © 020/626-9199. Tram: 1, 2, 5, 13, 14, 17 to the Dam.

Metz & Co This dramatic store, founded in 1740, is now owned by Liberty of London. It sells furniture, fabrics, kitchenware, and other traditional department-store items. The cupola and cafe are worth stopping for. Open Monday from 11am to 6pm and Tuesday through Saturday from 9:30am to 6pm. Keizersgracht 455 (at Leidsestraat). © 020/520-7020. Tram: 1, 2, 5 to Keizersgracht.

Peek and Cloppenburg Peek and Cloppenburg is a different sort of department store—or perhaps a better description is that P&C is an overgrown clothing store. Open Monday from noon to 6pm and Tuesday through Saturday from 9:30am to 6pm. Dam 20. © 020/623-2837. Tram: 4, 5, 9, 14, 16, 24, 25 to the Dam.

Vroom & Dreesman Less polished and pretentious than Metz & Co., and highly successful as a result, this is the Amsterdam branch of Vroom & Dreesman, a Dutch chain of department stores that pop up in key shopping locations all over Holland. It's a no-nonsense sort of store with a wide range of middle-of-the-road goods and prices and services to match. Open Monday through Saturday from 9am to 6pm. Kalverstraat 201-221 and 212-224 (near the Muntplein). © 020/622-0171. Tram: 4, 9, 14, 16, 24, 25 to Muntplein.

DIAMONDS

The following stores offer diamond-cutting and polishing tours, and sales of the finished product: **Amsterdam Diamond Center,** Rokin 1 (© 020/624-5787), open Friday through Wednesday from 10am to 6pm, Thursday from 10am to 6pm and 7 to 8:30pm; **Coster Diamonds,** Paulus Potterstraat 2-4 (© 020/676-2222), open daily from 9am to 5pm; **Gassan Diamonds,** Nieuwe Uilenburgerstraat 173-175 (© 020/622-5333), open daily from 9am to 5pm; **Stoeltie Diamonds,** Wagenstraat 13-17 (© 020/

623-7601), open daily from 9am to 5pm; and **Van Moppes Diamonds,** Albert Cuypstraat 2-6 (© **020/676-1242**), open daily from 9am to 5pm.

FASHIONS
WOMEN'S

Paris may set the styles, but young Dutch women—and some of their mothers—often know better than the French how to make them work. Whatever the current European fashion rage is, you can expect to see it in store windows all over Amsterdam, and in all price ranges. Some boutique faithfuls claim that they buy Paris designer fashions in Amsterdam at lower-than-Paris prices, but one quick check will tell you that designer wear is still expensive, whether you pay in guilders, francs, or hard-earned dollars.

It's more fun to ferret out the new, young crop of Dutch designers who regularly open stores in unpredictable locations all over town. Boutiques and their designers change rapidly with the tides of fashion, but the current top names and locations along the Rokin are: **Carla V., Sheila de Vries, Jan Jansen** (shoes), **Agnès B** (women's fashions), and **Puck & Hans,** whose pseudo-Japanese look catches the eye as you walk along.

Also stop by **The Madhatter,** Van der Helsplein 4 (© **020/664-7748**), for handmade hats; **Mô,** Overtoom 336 (© **020/689-4369**), for leather apparel (menswear also); and **Eva Damave,** Tweede Laurierdwarsstraat 51c (© **020/627-7325**), for knitwear.

Maison de Bonneterie   Here you find exclusive women's fashions, and Gucci bags and Fieldcrest towels and a star-studded cast of brand names on household goods and personal items. Open Monday from 1 to 5:30pm and Tuesday through Saturday from 10am to 5:30pm. Rokin 140-142. © **020/626-2162**. Tram: 4, 9, 14, 16, 24, 25 to Rokin.

MEN'S

In addition to the department stores listed above, you can find men's fashions at **Tie Rack,** Heiligeweg 7 (© **020/627-2978**), and **Guus de Winter,** Linnaeusstraat 197 (© **020/694-0252**). If you're into fancy, colorful sweaters, check out those of former cabaret performers Greg and Gary Christmas, at their boutique **Backstage,** Utrechtsedwarsstraat 67 (© **020/622-3638**).

CHILDREN'S

Children's clothing stores are everywhere. Among them are **'t Schooltje,** Overtoom 87 (© **020/683-0444**), which carries expensive but cute clothes for babies and children (well into the teen years); and the more affordable **Spetter Children's Fashion,** Van den Helstraat 53 1e (© **020/671-6249**).

FOOD & DRINK

De Waterwinkel Quality, purity, and beauty are the watchwords at the tastefully designed Water Shop. More than 100 varieties of mineral water from all over the world are on sale, ranging from ordinary, everyday water to designer water. Some of the bottles are miniature works of art in themselves. This is a store whose liquid assets are its stock-in-trade. Open Monday through Wednesday, Friday, and Saturday from 9am to 6pm, Thursday from 9am to 9pm. Roelof Hartstraat 10. © **020/675-5932**. Tram: 3, 5, 12, 24 to Roelof Hartplein.

H Keijzer H. Keijzer, which was founded in 1839, specializes in tea and coffee. It sells 90 different kinds of tea and 22 coffees. Consider taking home several 100-gram packets of teas from different parts of the tea-growing world: Ceylon Melange (or Delmar Melange), an English-style blend from Sri Lanka; Darjeeling First Flush, from India; Yunnan, from China; and Java O.P. (Orange Pekoe), from Indonesia. All of these teas are popular with the Dutch. For a nice gift, select from an assortment of tea boxes, among them a small box with a picture of the store and other buildings. Open Monday through Friday from 8:30am to 5:30pm and Saturday from 8:30am to 5pm. Prinsengracht 180. © **020/624-0823**. Tram: 13, 14, 17 to Westermarkt.

H P de Vreng en Zonen This traditional distillery creates Dutch liqueurs and gins according to the old-fashioned methods, sans additives. Try the Old Amsterdam jenever or some of the more flamboyantly colored liquids, like the bright green plum liqueur *Pruimpje prik in.* Some supposedly have aphrodisiac power. A chance to see the collection of 15,000 miniature bottles alone makes a visit worthwhile. Open Monday through Saturday from 10am to 5pm. Nieuwendijk 75. © **020/624-4581**. Tram: 1, 2, 5, 13, 17 to Martelaarsgracht.

Jacob Hooy & Co *Finds* You feel you've stepped back into history if you visit Jacob Hooy & Co. This store, opened in 1743 and operated for the past 130 years by the same family, is a wonderland of fragrant smells that offers more than 500 different herbs and spices and 30 different teas, all sold loose, by weight. Health foods, homeopathic products, and natural cosmetics are also on sale. Everything is stored in wooden drawers and wooden barrels with the names of the contents hand scripted in gold. Across the counter are fishbowl jars in racks containing 30 or more different types of *dropjes* (drops or lozenges) that range in taste from sweet to sour to salty. Open Monday from noon to 6pm, Tuesday through Friday from 8am to 6pm, and Saturday from 8am to 5pm. Kloveniersburgwal 10-12. ✆ 020/624-3041. Metro: Nieuwmarkt.

Patisserie Pompadour The counter display here is amazing. It groans under the weight of around 50 luscious pastries and tarts, complemented by endless dollops of whipped cream. You can enjoy these genuine Dutch treats in the exquisite Louis XVI tearoom or get them wrapped to go. Open Tuesday through Friday from 9:30am to 5:45pm and Saturday from 9am to 5:30pm. Huidenstraat 12. ✆ 020/623-9554. Tram: 1, 2, 5 to Spui.

GAY

Boekhandel Vrolijk The city's main bookstore for gays and lesbians stocks a wide range of books, many of them in English. It's invariably cheaper to buy here than at the gay sections of general bookstores, but still is likely to be more expensive than at home. Paleisstraat 135 (at the Dam). ✆ 020/623-5142. Tram: 1, 2, 4, 5, 9, 13, 14, 16, 17, 24, 25.

Mr B This airy store is world famous for high-quality leather goods, from basic trousers and chaps to more revealing and fetish wear. The store window's display of accessories for the S/M, leather and rubber guys, regular exhibitions of erotic art, and a great selection of piercing jewelry, ensures many a gaping tourist. Visiting tattoo and piercing artists from around the world make guest appearances for the real connoisseurs. There are cards and postcards to greet the friends you left behind. Open Monday through Friday from 10am to 6:30pm (Thurs to 9pm), Saturday from 11am to 6pm. Warmoesstraat 89 (Red Light District). ✆ 020/422-0003. Tram: 1, 2, 4, 5, 9, 13, 14, 16, 17, 24, 25 to Centraal Station.

HABERDASHERY

H J van de Kerkhof The walls of this store are lined with spools of ribbon and cord, and its notebooks are filled with examples of patches and appliqués. There are key tassels and tiebacks in all sizes, including very large "canal house" size. Open Monday through Friday from 9am to 6pm and Saturday from 10am to 5pm. Wolvenstraat 9-11. ✆ 020/623-4666. Tram: 1, 2, 5 to Spui.

Tips Floral Tributes

Should you be invited to the home of an Amsterdammer, buy flowers to take along with you. That's what the Dutch themselves do.

HOUSEHOLD

Kitsch Kitchen   The name just about says it all. You'll probably want to put on your shades before entering the world of glaringly bright colors that characterize Kitsch Kitchens' utensils and fittings in plastic, enamel, and papier-mâché. Kitsch Kitchens has extended its market by opening a second store, **Kitsch Kitchen Kids,** Rozengracht 183 (℅ **020/622-8261**), aimed at children. Open Monday through Friday from 10:30am to 6pm, Saturday from 10am to 6pm. Eerste Bloemdwarsstraat 21. ℅ **020/428-4969**. Tram: 13, 14, 17 to Westermarkt.

JEWELRY

BLGK Edelsmeden   This store is run by a group of jewelry designers who produce and sell affordable jewelry with character. Each designer has his or her own slant on things. Some of their pieces represent a new and fresh spin on classic forms, while others are more innovative and imaginative. Open Tuesday through Friday from 11am to 6pm, Saturday from 11am to 5pm. Hartenstraat 28. ℅ **020/624-8154**. Tram: 13, 14, 17 to Westermarkt.

Galerie Ra   Marvelous contemporary designs and materials turn jewelry into an art form here. Owner Paul Derrez specializes in stunning modern jewelry in gold and silver, and goes a bit further, turning feathers, rubber, foam, and other materials into pieces that he describes as "playful." Open Tuesday through Friday from 10am to 6pm, Saturday from 10am to 5pm. Vijzelstraat 90. ℅ **020/626-5100**. Tram: 16, 24, 25 to Keizersgracht.

MARKETS

The **Waterlooplein Flea Market,** Waterlooplein (tram: 9, 14), is the classic market of Amsterdam, perhaps of all Europe. It's often said that in the market's glory days before World War II, you could find amazing antiques among the junk and possibly even a proverbial dusty Rembrandt. Today your luck is more apt to run in the opposite direction. Most of the merchants now work out of tents, and some sell *patates frites met mayonnaise* (french fries, eaten Dutch style, with mayonnaise) from vans that are a long way from the pushcarts of yesteryear; but among the old CDs and leather jackets, you still find cooking pots, mariner's telescopes, coal scuttles, bargain watches, nuts and bolts, and decent prints of Dutch cities. The market is open Monday through Saturday from 10am to 5pm.

On a row of permanently moored barges, the **Bloemenmarkt (Flower Market),** Singel (tram: 4, 9, 14, 16, 24, 25), at Muntplein, sells a selection of fresh-cut flowers, bright- and healthy-looking plants, ready-to-travel packets of tulip bulbs, and all the necessary accessories for home gardening. Tulips here cost a few cents less than at the flower stands around town. Otherwise, the floating Flower Market doesn't quite live up to its billing as a prominent local tourist attraction. The market is open Monday through Saturday from 10am to 6pm.

You find just about anything and everything your imagination can conjure up at the 350 stalls of the colorful, kilometer-long **Albert Cuyp Markt,** Albert Cuypstraat (tram: 16, 24, 25). Different types of foods, clothing, flowers, plants, and textiles are all for sale. The market is open Monday through Saturday from 10am to 4pm.

Kunst- & Antiekcentrum de Looier, Elandsgracht 109 (*C* **020/ 624-9038;** tram: 7, 10, 17), is a big indoor antiques market spread through several old warehouses along the canals in the Jordaan. Individual dealers rent small stalls and corners to show their best wares. The old armoires and other pieces of heavy Dutch traditional furniture are too large to consider buying, but many dealers also offer antique jewelry, prints and engravings, and the omnipresent Dutch knickknacks. De Looier is open Saturday through Wednesday from 11am to 5pm, Thursday from 11am to 9pm.

Local artists come and show off their wares at the **Thorbecke Sunday Art Market,** Thorbeckeplein (*C* **075/670-3030;** tram: 4, 9, 14). Picking your way through the artists' tables, you find sculptures, ceramics, paintings, graphics, jewelry, and mixed-media pieces. The market runs from March to December, Sunday from 11am to 6pm.

The **Boerenmarkt (Farmer's Market)** at Noordermarkt (tram: 3, 10), also known as the Bio Market, caters to Amsterdam's infatuation with health foods and natural products. It takes place Saturday from 8am to 2pm.

MUSIC

Free Record Shop The records themselves aren't free, sadly, but the large ground floor and basement of this store hold an incredible number of cassettes, compact discs, and videos at competitive prices. Open daily from 9am to 6pm (Thurs 9am-9pm). Kalverstraat 230. ℂ 020/625-7378. Tram: 4, 9, 14, 16, 16, 24, 25 to Muntplein.

SEX

Amsterdam's free and easy—you could even say laid-back—attitude to the mysteries of the flesh has spawned a vast range of stores devoted to satisfying customers' needs, whether real or pure fantasy. Many of these stores are down-and-dirty, sleaze-ball kinds of places, but not all. Here are a couple with a sense of style.

Absolute Danny The name comes from its owner, Danny Linden, a graduate of the Fashion Academy and the Academy of Fine Arts, who brings her artistic sensibilities to bear on the erotic lifestyle her store supports. You find everything from sexy tableware (if you can imagine such a thing) to S/M clothing and accessories, with the main lines covering sexy lingerie and erotic clothing in leather and latex. Open Monday through Saturday from 11am to 9pm. Oudezijds Achterburgwal 78. ℂ 020/421-0915. Tram: 4, 9, 14, 16, 24, 25 to the Dam.

Condomerie Het Gulden Vlies The Golden Fleece condom store stocks a vast range of these items, in all shapes, sizes, and flavors, from regular brand labels to flashy designer fittings, all but guaranteeing your apparel of choice. The store claims to be the world's first specialized condom store—the start of a whole new protection racket. There is probably no significance whatsoever in the fact that the store is located on the edge of the Red Light District. Open Monday through Wednesday, Friday, and Saturday from noon to 6pm, Thursday from noon to 8pm. Warmoesstraat 141. ℂ 020/627-4174. Tram: 4, 9,14, 16, 24, 25 to the Dam.

TOYS

Some museum gift stores are good sources for toys and other children's knickknacks. Try the stores at the **Scheepvaartmuseum (Maritime Museum),** Kattenburgerplein 1 (ℂ 020/624-6601), for model ships; the **Theatermuseum,** Herengracht 168 (ℂ 020/623-5104), for masks, costumes, and minitheaters; **NEMO,** Oosterdok 2 (ℂ 020/531-3233), for all kinds of scientific toys and gadgets; and the **Tropenmuseum,** Linnaeusstraat 2 (ℂ 020/568-8215), and **Artis Zoo,** Plantage Kerklaan 38-40 (ℂ 020/523-3400), for model animals and ecological stuff.

Ever wish that your kids would take an interest in the sweet, wholesome kinds of things that children ought to like—instead of getting their kicks from zapping aliens, surfing the Web, and watching MTV? Try taking them to the stores below.

Bell Tree   Bell Tree is the place to find treasures for kids. The toys here don't blink, bleep, or run out of battery juice—many of them are actually made from wood! And they're not just modern versions of the kind of playthings that Grandma and Grandpa knew and loved, but real up-to-the-minute gear. Open Monday from 1 to 6pm, Tuesday through Saturday from 10am to 6pm. Spiegelgrscht 10-12. ✆ 020/625-8830. Tram: 6, 7, 10 to Spiegelgracht.

Kinderfeestwinkel   The name means "Children's Party Shop," and that's just what it is. Everything that a child could possibly want for celebrating the big moments in life, such as birthdays. Open Tuesday through Saturday from 10am to 6pm. Eerste van der Helststraat 15. ✆ 020/470-4791. Tram: 16, 24, 25 to Albert Cuypstraat.

7

Amsterdam After Dark

Nightlife in Amsterdam, like an Indonesian *rijsttafel,* is a bit of this and a bit of that. The cultural calendar is full, but not jammed. There's a strong jazz scene, good music clubs, and enjoyable English-language shows at the little cabarets and theaters along the canals. The club and bar scene can be entertaining if not outrageous; the dance clubs may indeed seem quiet and small to anyone used to the flash of clubs in New York City, Los Angeles, or London. However, the brown cafes—the typical Amsterdam pubs—have never been better. And there's always the movies. Amsterdam is one of the few cities on the European continent where you can see first-run blockbuster hits from the United States with their English soundtracks intact.

INFORMATION Your best source of information on nightlife and cultural events is *What's On in Amsterdam,* the VVV Tourist Office's monthly program guide in English, which costs 2€. It provides a complete cultural guide to Amsterdam, day by day, with listings for concerts and recitals, theater, cabaret, opera, dance performances, rock concerts, art films, film festivals, special museum and art gallery exhibitions, and lots more. Many hotels have copies available for guests, in some cases for free, or you can get one at the VVV offices (see chapter 2 for addresses and hours). There is also the free monthly listings magazine *Uitkrant,* in Dutch, which you can pick up at many performance venues.

MAIN NIGHTLIFE AREAS **Leidseplein,** hot and cool at the same time, is the center of Amsterdam's nightlife, with some of the city's most popular restaurants, bars, and nightspots all within dancing distance of each other. Leidseplein never really closes, so you can greet the dawn and start again. **Rembrandtplein** is a brash and brassy square that really comes alive at night, when it's awash with neon. Although it has a more downmarket reputation than Leidseplein, this area often seems even more intent on having fun, and there are enough cool and sophisticated places to go around. These two areas are connected by Reguliersdwarsstraat, which has

---

Tips   **That's the Ticket**

If you're interested in cultural events and are under age 26, go by the **Amsterdam Uit Buro (AUB)**, Kleine-Gartmanplantsoen 21 (© 0900/0191; tram: 1, 2, 5, 6, 7, 10), just off Leidseplein, and pick up a **CJP** (Cultural Youth Pass) for 11€. This pass grants you free admission to most museums and discounts on most cultural events. The AUB is open Monday through Wednesday and Saturday from 10am to 6pm, Thursday from 10am to 9pm, and Sunday from noon to 6pm.

---

some good cafes, including a few gay cafes, and also several fine clubs and restaurants. The **Rosse Buurt (Red Light District)** serves up its own unique brand of nightlife, and adjoining this is **Nieuwmarkt,** which is rapidly becoming a popular, if somewhat alternative, hangout.

TICKETS   If you want to attend any of Amsterdam's theatrical or musical events (including rock concerts), make it your first task on arrival to get tickets. Box office information is given below. **Amsterdam Uit Buro (AUB) Ticketshop,** Leidseplein 26 (© 0900/ 0191; amsterdam.aub.nl); tram 1, 2, 5, 6, 7, 10), can reserve tickets for almost every venue in town; it also handles reservations in advance from abroad. The office is open Monday through Wednesday and Saturday from 10am to 6pm, Thursday from 10am to 9pm, and Sunday from noon to 6pm. The VVV Amsterdam tourist information office (see chapter 2 for addresses and hours) can also reserve tickets, and charges 2.50€ for the service. Most upmarket and many mid-level hotels will reserve tickets as well.

1 The Performing Arts

CLASSICAL MUSIC

Amsterdam's top orchestra—indeed one of the world's top orchestras—is the famed **Royal Concertgebouw Orchestra,** which performs mainly in the Concertgebouw, but can also be found giving an occasional open-air concert in the Vondelpark. The Concertgebouw Orchestra can produce any of the great classical pieces at the tap of a baton, yet it is also willing to go out on a limb from time to time with modern and experimental works. The city's other full orchestra, the **Netherlands Philharmonic Orchestra,** fondly known as the NedPho, isn't far behind its illustrious cousin, if behind at all. It performs in the Beurs van Berlage, its main venue, and in the Concertgebouw. The NedPho has found its niche in a somewhat adventurous repertoire, which often includes opera collaborations. In addition, at either of these venues you may well catch one of Holland's other top orchestras, such as The Hague's **Residentie Orchestra** and the **Rotterdam Philharmonic,** and visiting orchestras from abroad.

When it comes to chamber music, the **Netherlands Chamber Orchestra, Amsterdam Baroque Orchestra,** and **Orchestra of the Eighteenth Century** provide plenty of possibilities, often playing with authentic period instruments and ably supported by the **Netherlands Chamber Choir.** Students of the **Sweelinck Conservatorium** fit themselves in at all possible times and places. You often hear these outfits in the Recital Hall of the Concertgebouw, the Beurs van Berlage, or in one of Amsterdam's historic churches (for information on venues, see below).

OPERA

Productions by the **Netherlands Opera** dominate the schedule at the Muziektheater. Although less well known internationally than the Royal Concertgebouw Orchestra or either of Holland's major dance companies, the Netherlands Opera has its own well-known performers and a devoted following. In recent years, under the artistic direction of Pierre Audi, it staged a successful Monteverdi trilogy before moving confidently on to Wagner's *Ring* cycle.

DANCE

The Dutch take pride in the growing international popularity and prestige of their major dance companies. The **Dutch National Ballet,** home-based at Amsterdam's Muziektheater, has a repertoire of both classical and modern works, many by choreographers George Balanchine and Hans van Manen. The **Netherlands Dance Theater,** choreographed by Czech artistic director, Jirí Kylián, is based in The Hague but frequently comes to the Muziektheater. Both companies are generally accompanied by the specialized **Netherlands Ballet Orchestra.**

MAJOR CONCERT HALLS & THEATERS

Beurs van Berlage The former home of the Amsterdam Beurs (Stock Exchange) now has the **Netherlands Philharmonic Orchestra (the NedPho)** and the **Netherlands Chamber Orchestra** under its roof. What was once the trading floor of the Exchange, built in 1903 by H. P. Berlage, has since 1988 been a concert venue with two halls—the 665-seat Yakult Zaal and the 200-seat AGA Zaal. Holland's **Concertzender** classical radio station is based here. The box office is open Tuesday through Friday 12:30 to 6pm and Saturday 12:30 to 5pm, and 1¼ hr. before performances begin. Damrak 243 (near the Dam). ✆ 020/627-0466. Tickets 7.50€-20€. Tram: 4, 9, 14, 16, 24, 25 to the Dam.

Carré   This big, plush theater on the banks of the River Amstel used to be a full-time circus, but now the clowns and animals are infrequent visitors, though spectacles such as The Flying Karamazov Brothers fill some of the gaps. In addition to opera, dance, and ballet, look out for Dutch-language productions of top Broadway and London musicals—*Les Misérables, The Phantom of the Opera, Miss Saigon, Evita, Cats,* and *42nd Street* have all been on the bill. Top names in the world of rock and pop perform here, but the biggest names now strut their stuff at Amsterdam ArenA. Get your tickets as far in advance as possible because the hottest shows sell out quickly. The box office is open Monday through Saturday from 10am to 7pm and Sunday from 1 to 7pm. Amstel 115-125. ✆ 020/622-5225. Tickets 10€-125€. Tram : 6, 7, 10 to Weesperplein.

Concertgebouw   The Concertgebouw (Concert Building) is one of the most acoustically perfect concert halls in the world and home base of the Royal Concertgebouw Orchestra. Musical performances have a distinctive richness of tone that is as much a pleasure for the performer as for the audience. During the musical season (Sept-Mar) and the annual Holland Festival, the world's greatest orchestras, ensembles, conductors, and soloists regularly perform here. Concerts and recitals are scheduled every day and often there's a choice of two programs at the same time on the same evening: one in the Grote Zaal, or Great Hall, and the other in a smaller recital hall, the Kleine Zaal, or Little Hall. Don't worry about your location—every seat in the Grote Zaal has a clear view. It's even possible to sit on the stage, behind the performers; tonal quality is slightly altered there, however, so seats are cheaper.

There are free lunchtime rehearsal concerts at 12:30pm (or thereabouts) on Wednesday in the Concertgebouw. The program may feature chamber music, symphonic performances, or abbreviated previews of a full concert to be played to paying guests that same evening. The box office is open daily from 9:30am to 7pm, and until 8pm for same-day tickets; phone orders are taken from 10am to 3pm. Concertgebouwplein 2-6. ✆ 020/671-8345. Tickets 13€-100€; summer concerts (Aug) 25€. Tram: 3, 5, 12 to Museumplein; 16 to Concertgebouwplein.

Muziektheater   In the 1980s, the construction of this superbly equipped 1,600-seat auditorium sparked street riots that sent tear gas drifting across what is now the stage. Today, it's the performances that cause a stir. The Muziektheater is one of the city's stellar performance venues and home base of the highly regarded Netherlands Opera and Dutch National Ballet. There are "musical lunches" during the concert season—free 30-minute concerts on some Tuesdays at 12:30pm (doors open at 12:15pm). The box office is open Monday through Saturday from 10am to 6pm and Sunday from 11:30am to 6pm. Waterlooplein 22 (beside the River Amstel). ℂ 020/625-5455. Tickets 20€-60€. Tram: 9, 14 to Waterlooplein.

Stadsschouwburg   Recently renovated, the plushly upholstered, 950-seat Municipal Theater is the city's main venue for mainstream Dutch theater. It also mounts Dutch, and occasionally English, productions of international plays, both classic and modern. You can also take in opera and ballet here. The baroque theater from 1894, stands on the site of earlier theaters that were destroyed by fire. Performances usually start at 8pm. Leidseplein 26. ℂ 020/624-2311. Tickets 8€-40€. Tram: 1, 2, 5, 6, 7, 10 to Leidseplein.

2 The Club & Music Scene

CONTEMPORARY MUSIC

De IJsbreker   For the latest in high-tech, electronic music, and anything else that goes out on a musical limb, this is the place. A very good cafe, with a shaded terrace overlooking the Amstel, adds to the club's appeal. Weesperzijde 23 (beside the Amstel River). ℂ 020/668-1805. Cover 7.50€-13€. Tram: 3 to Wibautstraat.

JAZZ & BLUES

Jazz, Dixieland, and blues may be American musical forms, but Europeans—and certainly the Dutch—have adopted them with gusto. July is the best month of the year for a jazz lover to travel to Europe. That's when three major festivals are scheduled almost back-to-back in France, Switzerland, and Holland, including the 3-day **North Sea Jazz Festival,** P.O. Box 87840, 2508 DE, The Hague (ℂ **070/350-1604**), held each year at the Congresgebouw in The Hague. It's a convention of the biggest names in the international jazz world, with more than 100 concerts—involving more than 600 artists—scheduled in 10 halls in 3 days.

Described below are a few of the jazz hangouts that dot Amsterdam's cityscape.

Alto Jazz Café   A regular quartet plays jazz nightly to a diverse crowd in this small, comfortable cafe. There are also guest combos and occasionally blues as well—the music is always top-notch. On Wednesday evening, the noted saxophonist Hans Dulfer plays, sometimes accompanied by his equally noted daughter Candy. Korte Leidsedwarsstraat 115 (off Leidseplein). ℂ 020/626-3249. Tram: 1, 2, 5, 6, 7, 10 to Leidseplein.

Bimhuis   This has been the city's premier jazz and improvisational spot for the past 20 years. "Bim," as locals affectionately call it, regularly features top European and American artists in a relaxed but serious atmosphere. You won't feel that you can't have a conversation, but you won't have to struggle to hear the music either. Tuesday night is workshop night; Sunday, Monday, and Wednesday concerts are rare. Oudeschans 73-77 (near the Rembrandthuis). ℂ 020/623-3373. Tickets 10€-18€. Tram: 9, 14 to Waterlooplein.

Bourbon Street   Bourbon Street, a wonderful little club for jazz, blues, and funk, hosts local talent and guests from the States and elsewhere. There's a cover charge for well-known jazz groups or musicians. The music, which tends toward Dixieland and mainstream jazz, plays well into the night. Leidsekruisstraat 6-8 (off Leidseplein). ℂ 020/623-3440. Tram: 1, 2, 5, 6, 7, 10 to Leidseplein.

Joseph Lam Jazz Club   This jazz nook beside the harbor offers Dixieland and bebop performed by local and little-known touring ensembles. The crowds tend to be mixed, consisting of couples on dates, hard-core jazz cats in berets, musicians, and younger jazz fans. The free jazz jam sessions on Sunday, which feature more experimental fare and acid jazz, are especially popular. Van Diemenstraat 8 (west of Centraal Station). ℂ 020/622-8086. Cover 5€ Sat only. Bus: 35 to Van Diemenstraat.

Maloe Melo   This small club isn't the Mississippi Delta, but Amsterdam's "home of the blues" features live blues every night and is generally packed. The music's quality varies but a pleasantly intimate setting and an eager audience make for a good time. Lijnbaansgracht 163. ℂ 020/420-4592. Cover 3€. Tram: 7, 10, 17 to Elandsgracht.

DANCE CLUBS

For local residents, the club scene in Amsterdam is generally a "members only" situation. But as a tourist, you can simply show up and, as long as your attire and behavior suit the sensibilities of the management, you shouldn't have any problems getting past the bouncer. Drinks can be expensive—a beer or Coke averages 5€, and a whiskey or cocktail, 8€—but you can nurse one drink while you dance your feet off, or down a quick beer and move on if the crowd or the music mix is not your style.

The places listed below are some of the most popular at press time, and in Amsterdam, these things don't change very quickly. But don't hesitate to ask around for new places once you get here. Of course, you can always consult the trusty *What's On in Amsterdam* for listings.

Akhnaton Jazz, African bands, and salsa are featured regularly at a spot that caters to a youthful, multiethnic, hash-smoking crowd of joyful dancers. Nieuwezijds Kolk 25 (near Centraal Station). ℂ 020/624-3396. Cover 3€-5€. Tram: 1, 2, 5, 13, 17 to Martelaarsgracht.

Amnesia Trance-house and hard-core may be part of the history of dancing by the time you read this, but if they aren't yet, this is the place to come to grips with them. This determinedly youth-oriented disco is in the Red Light District. Oudezijds Voorburgwal 3 (near Nieuwmarkt). ℂ 020/638-1461. Cover 5€-8€. Metro: Nieuwmarkt.

Back Door Enter here for some of the best musical soul food around for an over-25 crowd with a limitless appetite for hip-shaking funk and soul. Along with soul you can hoof it to '60s and '70s music. This place is best approached late, *very* late, because the action doesn't really heat up until after 3am. Amstelstraat 32 (off Rembrandtplein), ℂ 020/620-2333. Cover 5€-8€. Tram: 4, 9, 14 to Rembrandtplein.

Club Arena A former orphanage chapel with frescoed walls is the atmospheric if unlikely setting for one of the city's hottest clubs. Deejays rustle up music from the '60s to the '90s that draws a surprisingly youthful crowd to the Timezone club nights, where funk, soul, and New York disco reign. 's Gravesandestraat 51 (near the Tropenmuseum). ℂ 020/850-2400. Cover 6€-7.50€. Tram 7, 10 to Korte 's Gravesandestraat.

De Duivel Other nightclubs in Amsterdam play some hip-hop, but De Duivel is the only one to serve up rap classics and contemporary hip-hop tunes to the baggy-jeans set nightly. Reguliersdwarsstraat 87. ℂ 020/626-6184. Tram: 16, 24, 25 to Keizersgracht.

Escape Large and popular, and with a choice of several dance floors, all with flashing lights and a great sound system. On Saturday, the Chemistry club night, helmed by local deejays and an occasional big international name, takes over. Rembrandtplein 11 (ℂ 020/622-1111) Cover 7€-17€, free for students on Thursday. Tram: 4, 9, 14.

3 The Bar Scene

BROWN CAFES

Anyone who's sipped a frothy Heineken knows the Dutch can brew beer. But you haven't really tasted Dutch beer until you've tasted it in Holland, served Dutch style in a real *bruine kroeg*, or brown cafe. These traditional Dutch bars are unpretentious, unpolished institutions, filled with camaraderie, somewhat like pubs in London or neighborhood bars in the United States.

Café Chris   Café Chris opened in 1624 and has been going strong ever since. It's said to be the place where the builders of Westerkerk were paid every week or two. There are a lot of curious old features to this bar that keep drawing people year after year, including the quirky toilet in the bathroom, which, oddly, flushes from outside the door. On Sunday night loud opera music engulfs the bar, attracting a cultured bohemian crowd. Bloemstraat 42 (near Westermarkt). ℂ 020/624-5942. Tram: 13, 14, 17 to Westermarkt.

Café 't Smalle   Café 't Smalle is a wonderfully cozy spot where you're highly unlikely to get a seat, or even see one. It was opened by Pieter Hoppe in 1786 as a liquor distillery and *proeflokaal* (tasting house). If you really want an authentic brown cafe experience, you should at least try to stop by. 't Smalle has expanded its area of operations to the water's edge, with a fine terrace on the Egelantiersgracht, and to the water itself, on a boat moored alongside. Egelantiersgracht 12 (at Prinsengracht). ℂ 020/623-9617. Tram: 13, 14, 17 to Westermarkt.

De Druif   This is one of those places that not too many people know about. De Druif (The Grape) is located on the waterfront and is mainly frequented by a friendly local crowd. The bar's mythology has it that the Dutch naval hero, Piet Heyn, was a frequent patron (he lived nearby); however, as happens so often when good beer is at hand, this seems to be a tall tale come of wishful thinking—the bar opened in 1631 and Heyn died in 1629. Rapenburg 83 (behind the Eastern Dock). ℂ 020/624-4530. Bus: 22 to Prins Hendrikkade.

De Karpershoek   Opened in 1629, this bar was once a favorite hangout of sailors and seamen. The floor is covered with sand, as it was in the 17th century. Martelaarsgracht 2 (facing Centraal Station). ℂ 020/624-7886. Tram: 1, 2, 5, 13, 17 to Martelaarsgracht.

De Vergulde Gaper   This place is a double delight. In bad weather you can retreat into the warm, cozy brown cafe atmosphere indoors, and in good weather you can sit on a terrace beside the

Prinsengracht—if you can get a seat. There's an unseemly dash whenever a table becomes free. Prinsenstraat 30 (at Prinsengracht). ℂ 020/624-8975. Tram: 1, 2, 5, 13, 17 to Martelaarsgracht.

Gollem   More than 200 different beers are on sale in this ever-popular brown cafe near Spui. Many of them are international, and in particular, Belgian favorites, but look for some weird-and-wonderful brews from around the world. Raamsteeg 4 (off Spui). ℂ 020/626-6645. Tram: 1, 2, 5 to Spui.

Hoppe   Standing room only is often the space situation here and the crowds sometimes even overflow onto the sidewalk. It seems that, quite by accident, Hoppe has become a tourist attraction. Locals love this spot, which dates from 1670, and often pass through for a drink on their way home. A convivial atmosphere and authentic decor make it a great place to while away an afternoon. It's worth stopping by just to see it. Spui 18-20. ℂ 020/420-4420. Tram: 1, 2, 5 to Spui.

In de Wildeman   Tucked away in a medieval alley, this wood-paneled *bier-proeflokaal* (beer-tasting house) dates from 1690. The tile floor and rows of bottles and jars behind the counters are remnants of its earlier days, when it functioned as a distillery. Today it serves 17 draught and 200 bottled beers from around the world. There is a separate room for nonsmokers. Kolksteeg 3 (off Nieuwezijds Voorburgwal). ℂ 020/638-2348. Tram: 1, 2, 5, 13, 17 to Nieuwezijds Kolk.

Reijnders   It would be hard for a cafe in this prime location not to be something of a tourist trap—but Reijnders has succumbed only a little to this temptation and can perhaps be forgiven. This is a brown cafe with a long and noble tradition, outstanding looks, and a glassed-in front porch that offers a great vantage point for viewing the comings and goings of Leidseplein. Leidseplein 6. ℂ 020/623-4419. Tram: 1, 2, 5, 6, 7, 10 to Leidseplein.

't Loosje   This is a friendly place in the up-and-coming Nieuwmarkt area, popular with students, artists—and guidebook writers. It was built around 1900 and was originally used as a waiting room for the horse-drawn tram. The walls are still ornamented with tiles from that period and a painting of the South Holland Beer Brewery. There are lots of beers on tap. Nieuwmarkt 32-34. ℂ 020/627-2635. Metro: Nieuwmarkt.

TASTING HOUSES

There are only three major differences between a brown cafe and a *proeflokaal,* or tasting house: what you customarily drink, how you drink it, and who owns the place. The decor will still be basically brown and typically Old Dutch—and the age of the establishment may be even more impressive than that of its beer-swilling neighbors—but in a tasting house you traditionally order jenever (Dutch gin, taken "neat," without ice) or another product of the distillery that owns the place. Then, to drink your choice of libation, custom and ritual decree that you lean over the bar, with your hands behind your back, to take the first sip from your well-filled *borreltje* (small drinking glass).

Brouwerij 't IJ   In addition to the usual features, this proeflokaal has a fascinating location—it's situated in an unused windmill in the city's old harbor area—and a small brewery. You can take guided tours of the beer-making facilities (Fri at 4pm), and then taste the brewery's Pilzen (5% alcohol by volume), Mug Bitter (5%), Pasij (7%), or Zatte (8%) brews. One popular new Brouwerij 't IJ concoction is Columbus, a hearty wheat beer that's reddish, flavorful, strong (almost 10% alcohol by volume), and the new brew of choice among many Amsterdam barflies. Funenkade 7 (at Zeeburgerstraat). ℂ 020/684-0552. Tram: 6, 10 to Mauritskade.

D'Admiraal   This tasting house has a small and pleasant outdoor cafe patio. There are also sofas and big comfortable armchairs inside—oh yes, and 15 different *jenevers* and 55 liqueurs, plus a fair Dutch dinner and snacks menu. Herengracht 319 (along the canal near Oude Spiegelstraat). ℂ 020/625-4334. Tram: 1, 2, 5 to Spui.

De Drie Fleschjes   Not much has changed in this tidy and charming tasting house since "The Three Little Bottles" opened in 1650, except that in 1816 Heindrik Bootz liqueurs took over and have been tasted here ever since. There are 52 wooden casks along the wall facing the bar. Open Monday through Saturday from noon to 8:30pm, Sunday from 3 to 8pm. Gravenstraat 18 (off the Dam, behind the Nieuwe Kerk). ℂ 020/624-8443. Tram: 1, 2, 4, 5, 9, 14, 16, 24, 25 to the Dam.

De Ooievaar   This tiny place, the smallest proeflokaal in Holland, sells jenevers and Oudhollandse liqueurs. It's a pleasant place, with a bright bar area to offset the brown walls and wooden casks. Sint Olofspoort 1 (at the Zeedijk). ℂ 020/625-7360. Tram: 1, 2, 4, 5, 9, 13, 16, 17, 24, 25 to Centraal Station.

't Doktertje   This antiques-filled tasting house is near Spui, the main square of the Student Quarter. Ask to sample the homemade *boeren jongen* and *boeren meisjes,* the brandied fruits—raisins and apricots—that are traditional introductions to "spirits" for Dutch

Great Dutch Drinks

The Dutch are famous for their gin, or *jenever,* and their beer. The former is a fiery, colorless liquid served ice cold to be drunk "neat"—it's not a mixer. You can get flavored jenever—from berry to lemon—and just as with cheese, you can get *oude* or *jonge* (old or young) jenever, and every bar has a wide selection of most or all of the above on its shelves. Jonge is less sweet and creamy than the oude variety, but both are known for their delayed-action effectiveness.

jongen and *meisjes,* boys and girls. Rozenboomsteeg 4 (off Spui). © 020/ 626-4427. Tram: 1, 2, 4, 5, 9, 14, 16, 24, 25 to Spui.

Wynand Fockink *(Finds* Don't waste your breath—regulars here know all about the little English pronunciation bomb hidden in the Dutch name. This popular *proeflokaal* dates from 1679. Aficionados of the 50 varieties of Dutch jenever and 70 traditional liqueurs on display often have to maneuver for elbowroom to raise their glasses One of the attractions here that wows visitors is the collection of liqueur bottles on which are painted portraits of every mayor of Amsterdam since 1591. That ought to set your pulse racing. Open daily from 3 to 9pm. The attached *lunchlokaal* is, as its name implies, open for lunch. Pijlsteeg 31 (off the Dam). © 020/639-2695. Tram: 4, 9, 14, 16, 24, 25 to the Dam.

MODERN CAFES

Amsterdam has many contemporary cafes that are neither brown cafes nor your friendly neighborhood watering holes (many examples of both categories are acceptably trendy in themselves). You may hear some contemporary cafes described as "white cafes," as distinct from brown cafes. You may also hear talk of the "coke-trail circuit," though that's a bit passé nowadays.

Bayside Beach Club "Life's a beach," they say, at the Beach Parties in this Florida-style bar-restaurant-dance place. The waitresses here in minimalist Stars-and-Stripes bikinis seem to have been specially chosen for, shall we say, aesthetic purposes; but lest the establishment be accused of sexism, let me hasten to add that the male staff also seems to have been selected from an International

Male catalog. There's live music and deejays on two different levels. Sunday is ladies night (free cocktails and an all-male revue). Halve Maansteeg 4-6 (near Rembrandtplein). ℂ 020/620-3769. Tram: 4, 9, 14 to Rembrandtplein.

Café Dante This is art gallery chic. The owners cover the walls with a different exhibition of modern art every month. Feel free to wander in and around. Spuistrat 320 (at Spui). ℂ 020/638-8839. Tram: 1, 2, 5 to Spui.

Café Schiller It may be a little unfair to include Schiller in this designation, with its implication of trendiness. Schiller's style seems timeless. A bright glassed-in terrace on the square and a finely carved Art Deco interior make a good setting for the friendly, laid-back atmosphere, good food, and lively crowd of artistic and literary types. Rembrandtplein 36. ℂ 020/624-9864. Tram: 4, 9, 14 to Rembrandtplein.

Frascati Frascati belongs to a category similar to Schiller's, except that in this case its own good looks are complemented by a theatrical bent. The surrounding neighborhood is rife with alternative theater, and Frascati is a major player in this minor league. Nes 59 (behind Rokin). ℂ 020/624-1324. Tram: 4, 9, 14, 16, 24, 25 to Spui.

Kanis en Mailand On a redeveloped island named KNSM Eiland in the old Eastern Docks Area, the cafe takes its moniker from a clever Dutch play on words—or more accurately on sounds. Equally inventive is a time-warp design that lets you step from 1990s functional urban architecture on the outside into a "traditional" brown cafe interior. The illusion is genuine enough that K&M has become a near classic on the city's cafe roster and a legend in its own lunchtime for freshly made snacks. Levantkade 127. ℂ 020/418-2439. Bus: 32 to Levantkade.

Seymour Likely Woe unto you if you enter here wearing out-of-date duds. And it's no use wailing that they were the latest and hippest thing only yesterday—that's the whole point. The lips of all those beautiful young things inside that aren't curled around a glass, or each other, will be curled into a sneer. Cruel it may be, but you can always withdraw and try your luck across the road at Seymour Likely's offspring, Seymour Likely 2, which attracts a slightly older crowd. Nieuwezijds Voorburgwal 250 (near Amsterdam Historical Museum). ℂ 020/627-1427. Tram: 1, 2, 5, 13, 17 to Nieuwezijds Voorburgwal.

GAY & LESBIAN BARS

The gay scene in Amsterdam is strong, and there is no lack of gay bars and nightspots in town. Below are listings of some of the most

Smoking Coffeeshops

Tourists often get confused about the city's smoking "coffeeshops." Well, it's simple, if controversial: You go to a coffeeshop to buy and smoke cannabis. Though technically illegal, the practice is tolerated. For coffee and a snack you go to a *cafe* or an *eetcafé*—usually, though, the coffee sold in a "coffeeshop" is surprisingly good, considering it's only an excuse for selling something else.

Licensed and controlled, coffeeshops not only sell hashish and marijuana, but also provide a place where patrons can sit and smoke it all day if they so choose—they're one reason why most of Amsterdam's drug aficionados are laid-back and gooey-eyed, as opposed to scary-dangerous and wild-eyed.

Each coffeeshop has a menu listing the different types of hashish and marijuana it sells, and the tetrahydrocannabinol (THC) content of each. Hashish comes in two varieties: white and black. The black hash is usually more powerful, but both are pretty strong. Local producers, who are tolerated so long as they don't go in for in large-scale production (some of their wares are used in pain relief), have developed a Super Skunk hash that is said to be better than imported stuff from Lebanon and Morocco. Connoisseurs say the best has a strong smell and is soft and sticky. A 5-gram bag costs

popular spots for gay men. For lesbians, the scene is a little more difficult to uncover. Places that are hot now might not be later, so you might want to call or visit **COC,** Rozenstraat 14 (© **020/623-4079**), the office/cafe headquarters of the Organization of Homosexuals in the Netherlands. The office and telephone lines are open daily from 10am to 5pm. More information should be available from the **Gay and Lesbian Switchboard** (© **020/623-6565**).

Amstel Taveerne   One of the city's oldest and most traditional gay bars, this is the kind of place where about an hour after happy hour everyone starts singing popular songs. Although the songs are in Dutch, the crowd welcomes visitors from other countries, so don't be afraid to sing along. Amstel 54 (off Rembrandtplein). © **020/623-4254.** Tram: 4, 9, 14 to Rembrandtplein.

from 3€ to 8€, depending on the quality. Coffeeshops also have hashish joints *(stickie)* for sale, rolled with tobacco.

Coffeeshops are not allowed to sell alcohol, so they sell coffee, tea, and fruit juices. You won't be able to get any food, so don't expect to grab a quick breakfast, lunch, or dessert. You're usually allowed to smoke your own stuff, so long as you buy a drink.

Some of the most popular smoking coffeeshops are **The Rookies,** Korte Leidsedwarsstraat 145-147 (© 020/694-2353); **Borderline,** Amstelstraat 37 (© 020/622-0540); and the shops of **Bulldog** chain, which has branches around the city (the **Bulldog Palace** is at Leidseplein 15; © 020/627-1908). Like the John Travolta character Vincent Vega in *Pulp Fiction,* you'll find it's mostly fellow high-seeking tourists you'll be gazing at through the fug of bitter-smelling smoke that passes for an atmosphere in these places.

Toker's tip: Don't buy on the street. You stand a fair chance of being ripped off, the quality will be questionable, and there may be unpleasant additives. For more details, including coffeeshop reviews, pick up a copy of the English-language *Mellow Pages* for 3€ from "good" bookstores.

Café April   It's said that every gay visitor to Amsterdam goes here at least once, so you're likely to make friends that hail from around the world. A light menu is served. **April's Exit,** an affiliated dance club at Reguliersdwarsstraat 42 (© 020/625-8788), is close by, and many people from the Café April head over after happy hour. Reguliersdwarsstraat 37 (near the Flower Market). © 020/625-9572. Tram: 1, 2, 5 to Koningsplein.

Cockring   The most popular gay disco in town generally lays down no-nonsense, hard-core, high-decibel dance and techno music on the dance floor. More relaxed beats in the sociable upstairs bar make a welcome break. Warmoesstraat 96 (Red Light District). © 020/623-9604. Tram: 4, 9, 14, 16, 24, 25 to the Dam.

Saarein   Once a female-only enclave with a feisty atmosphere, the bar is now open to both genders and has livened up a bit.

Attractions include pool, darts, and pinball. The recent change in atmosphere has included the addition of food, with a well-priced dinner menu of Continental fare from 6pm to 9:30pm. Open Sunday through Thursday from 5pm to 1am, Friday and Saturday from 5pm to 2am. Elandstraat 119 (Jordaan). ☎ 020/623-4901. Tram 7, 10, 17 to Marnixstraat.

Vive-la-Vie This lesbian bar celebrated its 20th anniversary in 2000. The place attracts a young, lively crowd before club-hopping time, and lipstick isn't forbidden. The sidewalk terrace offers excellent summertime relaxation and a fine view of the flocks of tourists in neighboring Rembrandtplein. Open Sunday through Thursday from 2:30pm to 1am, Friday and Saturday from 3pm to 3am. Amstelstraat 7 (off Rembrandtplein). ☎ 020/624-0114. Tram: 4, 9, 14 to Rembrandtplein.

4 The Red Light District

Prostitution is legal in Holland, and in Amsterdam most of it is concentrated in the Red Light District. Even if you don't want to play, this is a place you may want to see at night, when the red lights reflect from the inky surface of the canals. Lots of visitors come here out of curiosity or just for fun. There's no problem with wandering around, and you don't need to worry much about crime as long as you stick to the busier streets and keep an eye out for pickpockets. While you can josh with the hookers behind the windows, taking pictures of them is a no-no; large and observant men are always on the lookout and will have no qualms about throwing your camera (and maybe you) into the canal. Visiting women going around in groups of two or more won't be noticed any more than anyone else, but a single female might be subject to misrepresentation.

The Red Light District, known in Dutch as the *Rosse Buurt,* isn't very big. The easiest way in is on Damstraat, beside the Krasnapolsky Hotel on the Dam. Then stick to the main drag on Oudezijds Voorburgwal, as far north as the Oude Kerk, the venerable Old Church, which stands watch over this passable representation of Sodom and Gomorrah. If you don't mind the weird-looking, sad-sack males and the "heroin whores" hanging around on the bridges, you can go further in, to the parallel canal, Oudezijds Achterburgwal, and the cluster of good bars and restaurants, many of the latter Chinese, at Nieuwmarkt.

You pass lots of red-fringed window parlors populated by women, few of them Dutch, who favor a minimalist dress style, and who tap (or pound) on the windows as likely looking customers go by. Then, there are peep-show joints with private cabins; dark and noisy bars; theaters offering a popular form of performance art; bookshops filled with the illustrated works of specialists in a wide range of interpersonal relationships; video libraries; and dedicated apparel and appliance stores.

Without going into detail about the services on offer in the Red Light District, here are a couple of places that have shown an enduring popularity with visitors.

Bananenbar   Bananas are an essential prop in the nightly drama here, and audience participation is encouraged. Needless to say, the show is mainly of interest to males on temporary vegetarian diets. Let your sense of taste be your guide. Oudezijds Achterburgwal 37. ℭ 020/ 622-4670. Tram: 1, 2, 4, 5, 9, 13, 16, 17, 24, 25 to Centraal Station.

Casa Rosso   In its own words, Casa Rosso puts on "one of the most superior erotic shows in the world, with a tremendous choreography and a high-level cast." Not everyone would describe it in those exact words, perhaps, but this is the local market leader in live shows. Oudezijds Achterburgwal 106-108. ℭ 020/627-8943. Tram: 4, 9, 13, 14, 16, 24, 25 to the Dam.

Index

See also Accommodations and Restaurants indexes below.

RESTAURANTS

Wickedly honest guides for sophisticated travelers—and those who want to be.

FROMMER'S® COMPLETE TRAVEL GUIDES

Alaska
Alaska Cruises & Ports of Call
Amsterdam
Argentina & Chile
Arizona
Atlanta
Australia
Austria
Bahamas
Barcelona, Madrid & Seville
Beijing
Belgium, Holland & Luxembourg
Bermuda
Boston
Brazil
British Columbia & the Canadian
  Rockies
Budapest & the Best of Hungary
California
Canada
Cancún, Cozumel & the Yucatán
Cape Cod, Nantucket & Martha's
  Vineyard
Caribbean
Caribbean Cruises & Ports of Call
Caribbean Ports of Call
Carolinas & Georgia
Chicago
China
Colorado
Costa Rica
Denmark
Denver, Boulder & Colorado
  Springs
England
Europe
European Cruises & Ports of Call
Florida

France
Germany
Great Britain
Greece
Greek Islands
Hawaii
Hong Kong
Honolulu, Waikiki & Oahu
Ireland
Israel
Italy
Jamaica
Japan
Las Vegas
London
Los Angeles
Maryland & Delaware
Maui
Mexico
Montana & Wyoming
Montréal & Québec City
Munich & the Bavarian Alps
Nashville & Memphis
Nepal
New England
New Mexico
New Orleans
New York City
New Zealand
Northern Italy
Nova Scotia, New Brunswick &
  Prince Edward Island
Oregon
Paris
Philadelphia & the Amish Country
Portugal
Prague & the Best of the Czech
  Republic

Provence & the Riviera
Puerto Rico
Rome
San Antonio & Austin
San Diego
San Francisco
Santa Fe, Taos & Albuquerque
Scandinavia
Scotland
Seattle & Portland
Shanghai
Singapore & Malaysia
South Africa
South America
South Florida
South Pacific
Southeast Asia
Spain
Sweden
Switzerland
Texas
Thailand
Tokyo
Toronto
Tuscany & Umbria
USA
Utah
Vancouver & Victoria
Vermont, New Hampshire &
  Maine
Vienna & the Danube Valley
Virgin Islands
Virginia
Walt Disney World® & Orlando
Washington, D.C.
Washington State

FROMMER'S® DOLLAR-A-DAY GUIDES

Australia from $50 a Day
California from $70 a Day
Caribbean from $70 a Day
England from $75 a Day
Europe from $70 a Day

Florida from $70 a Day
Hawaii from $80 a Day
Ireland from $60 a Day
Italy from $70 a Day
London from $85 a Day

New York from $90 a Day
Paris from $80 a Day
San Francisco from $70 a Day
Washington, D.C. from $80 a Day

FROMMER'S® PORTABLE GUIDES

Acapulco, Ixtapa & Zihuatanejo
Amsterdam
Aruba
Australia's Great Barrier Reef
Bahamas
Berlin
Big Island of Hawaii
Boston
California Wine Country
Cancún
Charleston & Savannah
Chicago
Disneyland®
Dublin
Florence

Frankfurt
Hong Kong
Houston
Las Vegas
London
Los Angeles
Los Cabos & Baja
Maine Coast
Maui
Miami
New Orleans
New York City
Paris
Phoenix & Scottsdale

Portland
Puerto Rico
Puerto Vallarta, Manzanillo &
  Guadalajara
Rio de Janeiro
San Diego
San Francisco
Seattle
Sydney
Tampa & St. Petersburg
Vancouver
Venice
Virgin Islands
Washington, D.C.

FROMMER'S® NATIONAL PARK GUIDES

Banff & Jasper
Family Vacations in the National
  Parks
Grand Canyon

National Parks of the American
  West
Rocky Mountain

Yellowstone & Grand Teton
Yosemite & Sequoia/ Kings Canyon
Zion & Bryce Canyon

America Online Keyword: Travel
Booked seat 6A, open return.
Rented red 4-wheel drive.
Reserved cabin, no running water.
Discovered space.

You Need A Vacation.

700 Airlines, 50,000 Hotels, 50 Rental Car Companies, And A Million Ways To Save Money.

Travelocity.com
A Sabre Company
Go Virtually Anywhere.